CATALOGUE

OF THE

STEARNS COLLECTION

OF

MUSICAL INSTRUMENTS

BY

ALBERT A. STANLEY

THE UNIVERSITY OF MICHIGAN
ANN ARBOR, MICHIGAN
1918

Paperback ISBN: 978-0-472-75197-6

PREFACE

This Catalogue is neither a treatise on the phenomena of sound, nor a disquisition on the origin and evolution of musical instruments.

It is obvious, however, that the scientific principles on which the various processes of tone-production are based must be stated; it is equally evident that some theory as to the priority of type must be accepted as a starting point in the evolution of instruments, and, also, that no classification is possible that does not rest on a definite evolutionary sequence. Therefore, the ultimate foundation for the facts noted in these pages must rest on those phases of the subject the full exploitation of which is specifically disavowed as its end.

In the attempt to make this publication of real assistance to those who wish to view the collection intelligently, particular stress is laid on the musical possibilities of specific groups, not neglecting to bring to notice the frequently strongly marked individual note of single representatives of these families. Again, those instances in which humanity makes the appeal are accentuated. Possibly a realization of all the personal and communal implications inhering in the uses of certain instruments may give even to those who look upon a collection as furnishing the means for satiating curiosity while killing time, worthier and more inspiring points of view. That the restrictions of space forbid an extended consideration of these implications is regretted, but it is hoped that the limited references to them will encourage further investigation.

Great collections are, in the main, reflections of the personality and individual bias of their founders. Historical, or personal associations; decorative beauty and grace of form; a *penchant* for a certain class of instruments may be guiding factors in selection. Collections thus influenced reveal personality, and frequently are of greater interest than the larger collections assembled under the ægis of some government. It is interesting to note that most of our private collections are domiciled on some university campus. The "Steinert" (Yale); the "Frismuth" (Pennsylvania), and "Stearns" (Michigan) Collections, support this interesting statement. The largest American collection, the "Crosby Brown" (Metropolitan Museum, New York) is not remote from Columbia University, and may therefore be utilized for purposes of general instruction and specific research. For such purposes the Stearns Collection is peculiarly adapted, as it is pre-eminently a collection of types.

It may be questioned whether any gift to the University has added more, if as much, to its resources for original work than this. The Collection itself is supplemented by a comprehensive selection of the special literature pertaining to instruments and their uses, the extent of which will be realized by reference to the Bibliography at the end of this Catalogue. The scope of the Collection will be revealed in the following pages and need not be detailed at this point.

The quarters assigned it in the Museum proved to be so conspicuously inadequate that, on the completion of the Hill Auditorium, the instruments—including those secured by the Beal-Steere Expedition (1870-75)—were removed to their present location (April, 1914).

The installation has proceeded uninterruptedly from the date of its removal up to the present, relieved only by the arduous, but delightful, task of organizing the material forming the basis of the Catalogue. In the placing of the instruments, the reconciliation of such conflicting factors, as scientific sequence, geographical distribution, ethnological considerations, and artistic grouping, presented many problems the solution of which was exceedingly difficult. Occasional lapses in classification, or infelicities in grouping, have been unavoidable; for, while the space appears to be ample, in reality it is somewhat restricted. There are a few gaps in certain classes, for the filling of which the generosity of those who are interested in the subject is confidently relied upon. This confidence is predicated on the fact that while the present installation was in progress, several important accessions were received, and valuable contributions are constantly being made.

In this connection it is significant that, of the thirty-eight important collections cited by Sachs in his encyclopedic work on musical instruments, five are listed as private, while several of the most comprehensive civic collections are gifts from public-spirited citizens. Again, many of the collections resulting from governmental aid owe their origin to the initiative of some musical scientist, by whose name they are generally known, if not to the general public, at least to cognoscenti.

One of the choicest private collections, that of the Rev. F. W. Galpin, of Harlow, England, has been transferred from its former home in his fifteenth-century manse, in the historic Hatfield Parish, to our shores. While this process has robbed it of the distinct charm lent by such appropriate surroundings, this country has gained an invaluable musical asset.

Sachs' list could be extended considerably by the inclusion of American collections not referred to by him. This is largely due to the fact that many of them have no catalogues, a remark equally applicable to certain minor European collections. To remove this fatal objection, which has applied to the Stearns Collection, is the purpose of this publication. At this point it is of distinct advantage to note certain guiding principles of procedure, which have been consistently followed.

Detailed marginal references to the general literature of the subject, and specific acknowledgements of the ordinary available sources will be omitted; only distinctly important contributions will be thus noted.

Of authoritative publications on the subject none have been of greater assistance, than the works of the Rev. Francis W. Galpin, M.A., F.L.S.,

Victor C. Mahillon, and Dr. Curt Sachs; while in our own country, Mr. E. H. Hawley, and Miss Frances Morris have rendered distinct service, especially in all that pertains to native, i. e., Indian instruments.

In cases of disputed orthography, etymology, or classification, the authority of Curt Sachs, or Mahillon, will, in most cases, be considered final.

In the transliteration of many Oriental and native names errors have arisen, a condition which makes reference to some standard authority imperative. For example, in certain names, the French *ch* and the German *sch* have been used instead of *sh*, which is more nearly correct, for English-speaking peoples at least. Frequently the etymology of a word is definitive, but in the past many errors of this sort have been carelessly passed on. Again, an instrument may appear to occupy a zone either between two classes, or inclining towards one or the other according to the point of view of the investigator. The attempt has been made to remove some of these misconceptions, but occasionally to do so is either to invite disaster, or to establish the superiority of the interrogation point over the period.

Whenever possible, the names given, both of European and Extra-European instruments, are those by which they are known in the countries from which they come, the question of origin not being involved. As the introductions to each special type, or prominent representative thereof, give designations in English, French, Italian, and German, this plan need not cause any confusion. In cases where this procedure would obtrude itself unnecessarily it will be followed with discretion, and in Cases I, II, and III, only exceptionally will European instruments be so indicated.

It is impossible to fully acknowledge the importance of the preparatory investigations made by the Rev. Philip G. Schenk, A.M., while the valuable assistance rendered by Professor Francis W. Kelsey in the make-up of this publication, and of Mr. George R. Swain, in solving the difficult problem of securing adequate photographs for the illustrations, must be gratefully mentioned.

The generous financial assistance given by Mr. Frederick K. Stearns also imposes a great obligation, as does the cheerful aid in proof reading given by Dr. Burton G. Grim and Asst. Professor Earl Vincent Moore.

Finally, the sympathetic attitude of the Honorable Board of Regents, and their unquestioning liberality must be gratefully acknowledged, for had it not been for their support the present housing of the Collection would have been impossible.

ALBERT A. STANLEY.

Ann Arbor, 1918.

ERRATA

Page 50, *terra-cotta* instead of terra cotta.

Pages 53, 65, *cowrie-shell* instead of cowrie shell.

Page 54, under No. 336: the caption—Section B.—Drums with Two Vibrating Membranes, was omitted.

Page 69: the dimensions under No. 429 are those of No. 431.

Page 76, No. 484: *28.3 cm.* instead of 8.3 cm.

Page 101, No. 694: "the latter with keys" should be deleted.

Page 127, No. 890: *Georg* instead of George.

Pages 138, 140, *Tribe* instead of tribe in titles of Nos. 968 and 982.

Page 148, *resonator* instead of resonators.

Page 185, No. 1258, *superimposed* instead of super-imposed.

Facing page 188: in title of Plate XIII, *Case VIII* instead of Case IX.

Page 198, under Sec. B, lines 6 and 9: *harpsichord* instead of harpischord.

Page 208, No. 1363: *896* instead of 886.

Page 220, *a'''* instead of A'''.

Page 220, Foot-note 3: *76* instead of 85.

Page 235: M. R. Harrington omitted.

Page 241, after India, insert—Italy, 22, 23, 24, 25, 27, 28, 29, 30, 31, 32, 38, 41, 65, 68, 69, 72, 75, 83, 84, 88, 96, 97, 98, 99, 101, 104, 113, 117, 118, 119, 120, 121, 125, 128, 129, 130, 131, 141, 146, 152, 153, 157, 160, 161, 162, 163, 164, 165, 173, 189, 191, 192, 193, 199, 200, 201, 203, 207, 208, 209, 210, 211, 221.

Page 257: *Tambourin de Gascogne* instead of Tambourine de Gascogne.

CONTENTS

ILLUSTRATIONS

THE DONOR

Frederick Stearns

Frederick Stearns was born in Lockport, New York, April 8, 1831, and died in Savannah, Georgia, January 13, 1907. Of sturdy Puritan stock he displayed in his long and useful life the sterling qualities of his ancestry.

At fifteen years of age he was apprenticed to a firm of druggists in Buffalo, where, through close application to duty and consistent improvement of every opportunity for strengthening his scientific equipment, he developed into a chemist of unusual attainments. Following the lead of his ambition, he came to Detroit in 1855, where he established a drug store. This was soon merged into a manufacturing pharmaceutical laboratory, prophetic of the present great establishment (incorporated in 1882).

Mr. Stearns was, however, more than a successful business man. He was an idealist, a lover of beauty and a born collector. Indeed, after having traveled extensively for years in the interests of what had become the absorbing pursuit of his life, he retired (1887) from active participation in the enterprise which owed its existence to his far-sighted initiative, that he might indulge his passion unhampered.

With characteristic generosity, he made his friends, and the public, "partners of his artistic joy," and enriched the Art Museum of his adopted city by the gift of several important collections. It is with no disparagement of their value that it must be stated, with no qualification, that the most valuable of the collections made by him is the unique assemblage of musical instruments known by his name. Representing seventeen years (1881-1897) of tireless and energetic labor, it stands as his most fitting monument. With keen appreciation of the fitness of things, he determined to donate the collection to the University of Michigan. It was tendered to the Board of Regents late in 1898, and accepted at the first meeting thereafter, January 17, 1899. In 1901 Mr. Stearns' services to his home community, and to the University, were recognized by conferring on him the degree of Master of Arts, an act alike honorable to the University of Michigan and the recipient. After the formal transfer of the collection his interest did not cease, and he added instruments, at intervals, well-nigh up to his death. Realizing the scope of the work of identification and organization of the literature, in 1902 he established a Fellowship in Music, which was held for two years by Philip G. Schenck. It is to be hoped that the example of Mr. Stearns will inspire an increasing number of successful business men to realize that the pursuit of the ideal may carry with it joys denied to those the records of whose lives are to be found only in ledgers and bank-books.

CLASSIFICATION

Introductory Remarks

Vibrating bodies are of two types. In the first, the substance is possessed of sufficient elasticity to respond to an inciting cause and vibrate with the rapidity and regularity necessary to the production of a musical tone (Metal Plates). In the second, the substance must be brought into a state of tension, or action, in order that it may so respond as to attain the same result. (Membranes, Strings, or Air.) The inciting cause may be Friction (rubbing, bowing); Impact (blow of stick, hammer, or shaking); Plucking (forcibly drawing the body from a quiescent position and allowing it to return—Guitar type); Sympathetic Vibration (influence of an external vibrating agent); or, in the case of wind instruments, directing air under pressure into a tube containing air in a quiescent state.

To attain the requisite sonority, the tone produced by the vibrating substance must be reinforced by a Resonator. The Resonator takes on many forms, and, in the case of a hollow rattle, the body itself is a resonator. Every known process of tone production and all types of musical instruments may be included in these generalizations.

Through the operations of the principles underlying tone-production, and the action of the various tone-producing media, just enumerated, we have Tone, as such. Tone, however, is not an end in itself but a means, and it is only through the operation of some external agency that it can be directed to a conscious end. This external agency is a Musical Instrument.

The obvious queries as to the genesis, definition, and evolution of this puissant agency must be considered at this point, as they are fundamental.

A musical instrument gives expression to aesthetic impulse and is concrete evidence of an emotional demand. Consequently its nature and range are determined by emotional necessity, be that necessity never so primitive.

Undoubtedly, primitive man first responded to the call of rhythm; therefore his first instruments must have been of the rhythmical type. Before he had developed sufficient initiative, observation, and power of coördination to create such instruments, Nature furnished them in great abundance, and the desire for the accentuation of rhythmical movement and the expression of pent up emotion prompted their use. This clearly indicates the starting point from which the evolution from the simplest to the most complex types must have proceeded.

A definition of a musical instrument broad enough to include natural sonorous bodies, as well as those constructed by primitive man in imitation of Nature's handiwork, would run somewhat as follows:

"A musical instrument is anything outside of the members of the body that can be used to establish or emphasize any element of music." While this definition is sufficiently elastic to include all types, even the most modern, the following rather extended definition is more in accord with modern notions. "A musical instrument is a structure through which the means of producing a series of coördinated tones of determinate pitch, dynamic possibilities, and varied *timbre* are so brought under control and made responsive to the will, that a conscious artistic end may be realized."

Following these observations regarding the genesis and definition of a Musical Instrument, it may be said that the answer to the third query will be found in the Collection itself.

GENERAL SCHEME OF CLASSIFICATION

CLASS I. Instruments with Vibrating Body.
CLASS II. Instruments with Vibrating Membrane.
CLASS III. Instruments with Vibrating Column of Air.
CLASS IV. Instruments with Vibrating String, or Strings.
CLASS V. Instruments with Vibrating Strings, Reeds, or Columns of Air, Controlled by a Key-board.

DETAILED SCHEME OF CLASSIFICATION

CLASS I—INSTRUMENTS WITH VIBRATING BODIES

Section A. Vibrating Bodies, Serrated, and Plane Surfaces.
Section B. Vibrating Plates, and Hollow Bodies of Metal.
Section C. (a) Vibrating Bars of Wood, with Resonator.
(b) Vibrating Segments of Resonator Body (Wood).
Section D. Vibrating Tongues of Wood or Metal.
Section E. Vibrating Bars, or Rods, of Metal.
Section F. Vibrating Tongues, or Bars, of Metal, Actuated by Mechanism, or Bowed.

CLASS II—INSTRUMENTS WITH VIBRATING MEMBRANE, OR MEMBRANES

Section A. One Vibrating Membrane with Resonator.
Section B. Two Vibrating Membranes with Resonator.
Section C. One Vibrating Membrane with Shallow Resonator (Rim) in which are Metal Discs.
Section D. Sympathetically Vibrating Membrane with Resonator.

Novel Treatments of Vibrating Bodies.

Sub-Section I. Vibration induced by Friction.
Sub-Section II. Vibration induced by the Singing Voice.

Unique Processes of Tone Production.

Class III—Instruments with Vibrating Column of Air.

Section A. Vibrating Column of Air enclosed in a Vertical Cylindrical Tube, with no lateral Openings.

Section B. Vibrating Column of Air in a Vertical Cylindrical Tube, with lateral Openings.

Section C. Vibrating Column of Air in a Vertical Cylindrical Tube, with lateral Openings and Mouth-piece.

Section D. Vibrating Column of Air in a Horizontal (Transverse) Cylindrical Tube, with lateral Openings and Mouth-hole.

Section E. Vibrating Column of Air in a Vertical, Cylindrical Tube, with lateral Openings, and Modified by the Action of a Single Beating-Reed.

Section F. Vibrating Column of Air in a Vertical Conical Tube, with lateral Openings, Modified by the Action of Double Beating-Reeds.

Section G. Vibrating Column of Air in a Cylindrical, or Conical, Vertical Tube, Modified by the Action of Single and Double Beating-Reeds, with an Air Reservoir, or Bellows.

Section H. Vibrating Column of Air in a Vertical Cylindrical Tube, Modified by the Action of a Free Reed.

Section I. Vibrating Free Reeds Actuated by Bellows and Controlled by Keys, or Pistons.

Sub-Section I. Vibrating Free Reeds Actuated by the Breath, (with or without keys).

Sub-Section II. Free Reeds, with Air Reservoir Operated Mechanically; Reeds Controlled by Pistons, or Keys.

Sub-Section III. (a) Vibrating Column of Air in an Organ Pipe (Cylindrical or Conical); (b) Vibration Modified by the Action of a Beating or Free Reed.

Section J. Vibrating Column of Air enclosed in an Animal Tusk, Horn, Gourd, or Wooden Tube, with Mouth-hole in Body, and no lateral Openings.

Section K. Vibrating Column of Air enclosed in a Metal or Wooden Tube, ending in a Bell, with Cup-Mouthpiece and no lateral Openings.

Section L. Vibrating Column of Air enclosed in a Metal or Wooden Tube, ending in a Bell, (a) with lateral openings, opened and closed by the fingers or keys; (b) with additional lengths of tubing incorporated in the structure, and controlled by valves, operated by pistons or keys; (c) with a movable tube (Slide) operated by the hand.

CLASS IV—INSTRUMENTS WITH VIBRATING STRING, OR STRINGS.

Section A. One Vibrating Plucked String. (Strings may be plucked either by the Fingers or by Plectra.)

Section B. Vibrating Plucked Strings running free. (Free strings are such as are accessible from both sides.)

Section C. Vibrating Plucked Strings running free, whose Pitches may be changed (a) by Hooks, (b) by Mechanism.

Section D. Vibrating Plucked Strings running close to Resonator.

Section E. Vibrating Plucked Strings running over Frets and Bridges. The Zither is an exception, as it has no Bridge.

Section F. Vibrating Strings actuated by Impact.

Section G. Vibrating Strings running over Bridge and "True" Finger-Board, Actuated by the Friction of a Bow. In primitive and certain Oriental types the Finger-Board is missing.

Section H. Vibrating Strings Actuated by the Friction of a Resined Wheel, and Controlled by Sliders, operated by Keys.

CLASS V—INSTRUMENTS WITH VIBRATING STRINGS, COLUMNS OF AIR, OR REEDS, CONTROLLED BY A KEY-BOARD MECHANISM.

Section A. Vibrating Strings Actuated by Impact, through a directly-acting Key-board Mechanism.

Section B. Vibrating Strings Actuated by Plucking, through an indirectly-acting Key-board Mechanism.

Section C. Vibrating Strings Actuated by Impact, through an indirectly-acting Key-board Mechanism.

Section D. Vibrating Columns of Air inclosed in Organ pipes, Actuated by Mechanically operated Bellows, and Controlled by an indirectly acting Key-board.

Section E. Vibrating Free Reeds, with mechanically operated Bellows and Key-board Mechanism.

The *Violon-avec-clavier* (No. 1330 Case XIV) falls in Classes IV and V.

ACCESSORIES

Mutes, Violin and Guitar Cases, Crooks, Batons, Engravings, Manuscripts, Models, etc., are not included in the Classification but are given numbers in the Catalogue.

GENERAL INFORMATION

The numerical succession of Cases follows the evolution of the instruments therein displayed. With the exception of a few instances in which, for physical reasons, it has been found impossible to retain an exact scientific sequence, the arrangement in each case follows the evolution of the type it contains. This evolution runs from *Right* to *Left* and from the *Top* to the *Bottom* of the Case. The names of donors appear in parentheses. The instruments from the Beal-Steere Collection are indicated by (B-S). New accessions (since May 1, 1916) are indicated by a red star, at left of number.

To indicate an important distinction, in the following lists the technical term "Compass" is used to define the limits within which a reasonably extended and coherent tone-series may be so displayed as to establish a tonality. In certain instruments the range is very restricted or, as is the case in many primitive instruments, the tones are unrelated. In such cases the term "Pitches" will be employed.

The tones constituting the compass of an instrument are defined, as to their actual pitch, by their inclusion in given octaves, i. e., *chromatic series extending from a given C to the b above.* The pitch of these octaves will be designated, for series above middle C, by accent marks placed at the right of the letter, and by small letters, or one or more capital letters, for those below that tone. These octaves are named as follows:

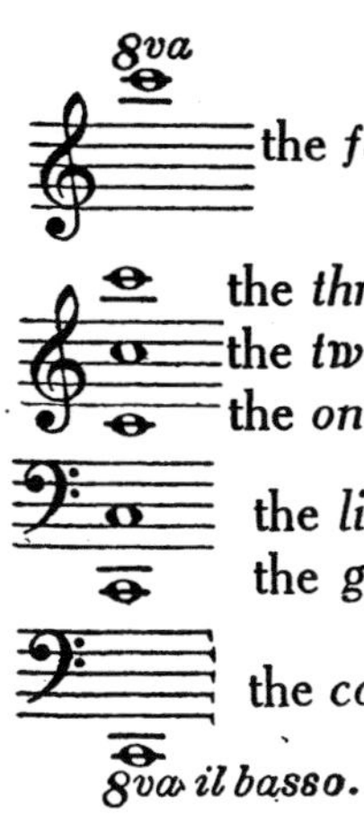

From — the *four-marked octave*—viz. c''''.

From — the *three-marked octave*—viz. c'''.
From — the *two-marked octave*—viz. c''.
From — the *one-marked octave*—viz. c'.

From — the *little octave*—viz. c
From — the *great octave*—viz. C.

From — the *contra octave*—viz., CC.

From the C below CC the *double-contra octave*—viz. CCC.

The same system will be employed in indicating the pitches of the tones included in a restricted or unrelated series.

In attaching the numbers no fixed rule could be followed, but wherever possible, they are placed at the *left of the instrument.*

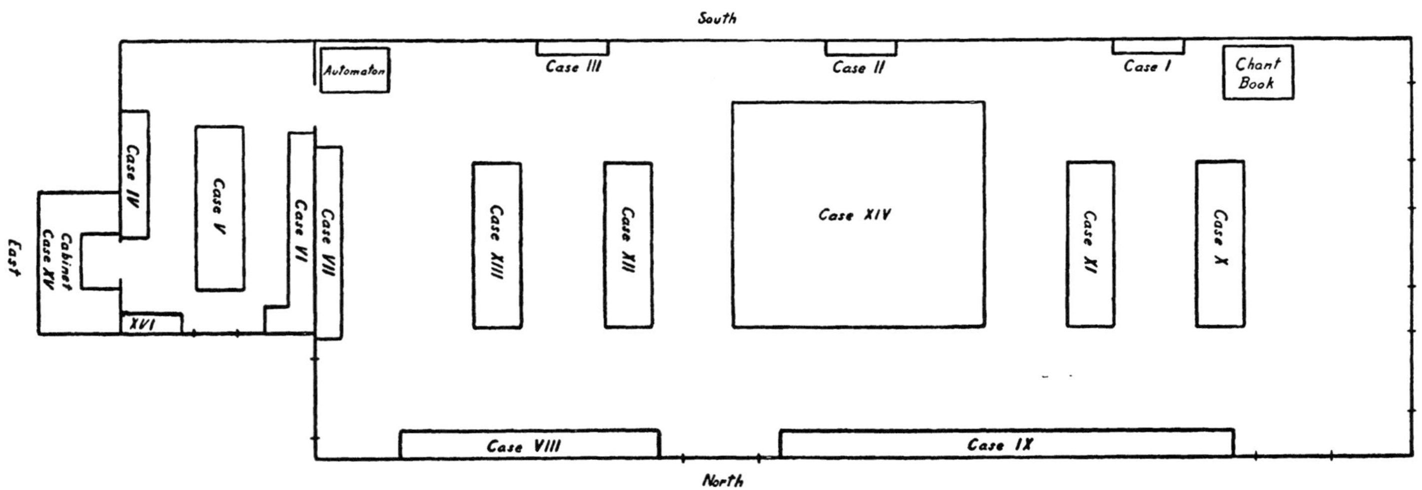

FLOOR PLAN OF STEARNS' COLLECTION

THE SUCCESSION OF CASES

CASE I.

CLASS I. INSTRUMENTS WITH VIBRATING BODIES.

Section A. Vibrating Bodies, Serrated, and Plane Surfaces.
Rattles, Clappers, Castanets.

Section B. Vibrating Plates, and Hollow Bodies of Metal.
Gongs, Cymbals, Bells.

Rattles (Fr. *Hochet;* Ger. *Rassel*) are shaken, whereby the solids they contain are brought into violent contact with the body of the instrument and induce vibration. Clappers (Ger. *Klapper*)* and Castanets (Fr. *Castagnettes;* Ital *Castagnette;* Ger. *Kastagnetten*) consist of two or more plane, or slightly hollowed surfaces which are brought into contact with each other when the instrument is shaken. Serrated surfaces are rasped. Cymbals are generally struck together. Gongs are struck on the outside. Bells are set in vibration by the blow of a "clapper," which, swinging loosely inside, strikes the inside surface of the mass at a point of contact known as the "sound bow." The sleighbell type—which is allied to the rattle, being shaken—is an exception. In Chimes rung by hand, the bells swing through the smallest arc of a circle within which the clapper can act. When operated mechanically, or automatically, the bells are generally struck on the outer rim. The term "Chime" (Fr. *Carillons;* Ital. *Soneria di campane accordate;* Ger. *Glockenspiel*) is also used to designate a number of small bells, or gongs, arranged on a handle, ring, or belt, by means of which they may be shaken.

1. NE-GAH-NE-GA-AH GUS-TAH-WE-SEH. Medicine-man's Rattle. Gourd. . Seneca Indians, Cattaraugus Reservation, Erie County, N. Y. Length, 38 cm.; of body, 15 cm. Diameter, 11 cm.

2. MARACA, or MARRAGA. Gourd, decorated with feathers. . . . Brazil Length, 26 cm.; of body, 17 cm.; diameter, 11 cm.

The Amazon Indians look upon this rattle as a species of tutelary god. In personal or communal crises it is consulted, always with the assistance of the medicine man, who generally interprets its speech in terms coinciding with his desires. *Maraka* is an alternative spelling, and *maruga* is the name of a similar rattle used in the West Indies in the *tango*, in connection with the *guiro*.

---

* *Klapper* (Ger.) is not the only foreign equivalent for "clapper," but *Sonnaille* (Fr.), and *Sonaglio* (Ital.), do not represent the type exhibited in Case I.

3. NOTCHED-STICK RATTLE.[1] Wood. Rasped.....Nassau, Bahamas
Known in its home as the "Hog-fiddle."
Length, 67.5 cm. Width, 2.2 cm. Thickness, 1.5 cm.

4. NE-GAH-NE-GO-AH GUS-TAH-WE-SEH. In material and source similar to No. 1, with the exception of the handle, which is of hard wood.
Length, 38 cm.; of body, 19 cm.; diameter, 17 cm.

Wherever the gourd (*cucurbitaceae*), specifically the calabash (*Lagenaria vulgaris*) is found, its adaptability to serve as a rattle by itself, or as material for its manufacture, has been recognized. Therefore its geographical distribution determines the range of this particular type.

Wm. Strachey, Gent, writing in 1610-1612, and speaking of the music of the Virginian Indians, says: "Their chief instruments are rattles made of small gourdes or pompion shells, of these they have base, tenor, counter tenor, meane and treble; these myngled with their voyces, sometymes twenty or thirty togither, make such a terrible howling as would affright rather than give pleasure to any man."[2]

5. BASKET DANCE RATTLE. Woven rattan....Cameroon, W. Africa
This rattle resembles the *gadza* of Zanzibar.
Length, 15 cm. Width, 8 cm. Depth, 6 cm.

6. GAH-NO-WA GUS-TAH-WE-SEH.[3] Turtle Rattle....Seneca Indians
Length, 50.5 cm.; of body, 28 cm. Width, 22 cm. Depth, 7.5 cm.

7. KNEE RATTLE. Iron ....Nubia, Africa

An iron pod, enclosing three iron balls, is attached to a leather strap, a section of which (25 cm.) is covered with cowrie-shells (*Cypraea moneta*). In this, as in all cases where they are used for decoration, the shells are so hung as to display the ventral side.

Length, 62 cm.; of iron pod, 17 cm.

8. RATTLE. Turtle shell and toes of sheep...................
..........Moqui Indians, Arizona, and Zuni Indians, New Mexico
Length, 12.5 cm. Width, 9.5 cm. Thickness, 4 cm.
The Hopi Indians call a similar rattle *yung-uh-sho-na*.[4]

9. RATTLE. Nutshells (68), attached to bands of cloth.......Brazil
Length of bands, 125 cm.; width, 1.5 cm. Average size of nut, 2 by 1 cm.

---

[1] For facts regarding the distribution of this type see Frances Morris, "Catalogue of the Crosby Brown Collection," N. S., Vol. II, pp. 134, 180, 184, 189, 203. This catalogue is replete with information; future reference to it will give the name of the author only.

[2] "The Historie of Travaile into Virginia Brittania." Hak. Soc., 1849, p. 79.

[3] Morris, p. 155.

[4] Morris, p. 101.

10. RATTLE .... East Africa
A band of braided cocoanut sinnet from which hang 67 small wooden rods.
Length of band, 30 cm. Length of each rod, 10.5 cm.; diameter, 8 mm.

The natives of the western coast of the W. Torres Straits have a rattle called the *padatrong* in which rods are used, but not as in this type.[5]

An interesting rattle of this type found among the Patagonian Indians is described by Sir Francis Drake as follows: "Theire men being delighted much with danceing, make instruments of musick, which being made of barkes of trees, and sewed together with thredds of gutts of ostriges, like lute strings, and little stones put in them and painted over, are like our children's rattles in England, these they hang by strings at their girdles, when they are disposed to sport themselves; which no sooner begin to make a noise but they beginn to dance, and the more they stirr their stumps the greater noyse or sound they give and the more their spirits are ravished with mellodye; inso much that they dance like maddmen and cannot stay themselves unto death if som friend pluck not away the bables, which being taken away, they stand as not knowing what has become of themselves for a long tyme."[6]

11. RATTLE. Two cords, on which 49 cocoons are strung .... Africa
Length, 132 cm. Average length of cocoons, 2 cm.

12. RATTLE. Globular bells of nut shells (65), strung on a cord. Mexico
Length, 76 cm. Average diameter of bells, 2.5 cm.

13. RATTLE. Seed-pods (38), strung on cords .. Yaqui Inds., N. Mexico
Length, 36 cm. Average length of pods, 4 cm.

14. RATTLE. Seed-pods (13), on handle. Mendicino Indians, California
Length, 25 cm.; of handle, 10 cm.; of pods, 5 cm.

15. RATTLE. Nut-shells (31), on cord of cocoanut sinnet ...... Africa
Length, 32 cm. Average width of nuts, 6 cm.

16. RATTLE. Cedar, in form of a bivalve-shell. Haidah Inds., B. Columbia
Length, 16 cm.; of shell, 8 cm. Width, 6.5 cm.

17. RATTLE. Cedar, painted red and black .... Alaska
Length, 16.2 cm. Width, 7 cm. Thickness, 2.5 cm.
(Israel G. Russell.)

18. RATTLE. Shells of Brazil-nuts (53), on hoop of braided withes. Peru
This unique specimen was secured in the native village of Chanuci. Frequently they are decorated with feathers.
Diameter of hoop, 23 cm. Average width of nuts, 6 cm.
(B-S.)*

---

[5] A. C. Haddon, "The Ethnography of the Western Tribes of Torres Straits." Jour. Anth. Inst., XIX, p. 375, Pl. IX, Fig. 7.

[6] "Voyages of Sir Francis Drake about the World," Hak. Soc., 1854, p. 50.

* The Beal-Steere Expedition was financed by the Honorable Rice A. Beal, and conducted by Professor James B. Steere. The instruments designated (B-S), were collected by Professor Steere.

19. RATTLE. Ten wooden rods, 12 cm. long, strung on a leather thong. This rattle is of very doubtful antecedents.
Length of each rod, 15 cm.

20. RATTLE .... Lake Tanganyika, C. Africa
Forty-eight small bivalve-shells attached by cords to an armlet of canvas, 27 cm. long and 2.3 cm. wide.

21. RATTLE. Iron, in form of a pod .... Cape Palmas, Africa
Length of pod, 12 cm.
(Miss M. Scott.)

22. GHUNGHURU. Anklet Rattle. White metal.............. India
Interlacing rings of white metal, to each of which—and also to the clasps at the end—a group of three small globular bells is attached. These rattles are worn by the Nautch girls. Similar bells are worn on the ankles of post-runners.
Length of anklet, 22 cm. Diameter of each bell, 8 mm.

23. RATTLE. Braided rattan........................ British Guiana
Length, 16 cm. Width at base, 4.5 cm.

24. RATTLE. Braided grass........... Cape Prince of Wales, Alaska
Diameter, 6 cm. Thickness, 3.5 cm.

25. RATTLE. Woven rattan............ Upper Congo, Central Africa
Length, 20.5 cm. Diameter, 7.5 cm.

26. RATTLE. Cedar .... Tsimshian Indians, British Columbia
Decorated with head of *Hoorts*, "the bear," on face.
Length, 22.5 cm. Width, 11.5 cm. Thickness, 8 cm.

27. RATTLE. Gourd...................... Moqui Indians, Arizona
Length, 13 cm. Width, 7.5 cm. Thickness, 10 cm.
The Karaja Indians, Brazil, call a similar rattle *uälu*.

28. ULI ULI. Gourd, decorated with feathers*.............. Hawaii
The *uli uli* is used to mark the time in the *hula*.
Diameter of face, 30 cm. Length of gourd, 18 cm. Diameter, 11 cm.

29. CLAPPER. Bone. Used with drum 340 (Case V) .. Dahomey, Africa
The handle, a bone slightly curved at the end, is 30 cm. long. On either side of a flat bone fastened to this handle, a thin, spade-shaped bone is loosely fastened by leather thongs. These bones are 7.5 cm. long and their greatest width is 6 cm.

---

* The name assigned this rattle by Edge-Partington and Heape—"Ethnographical Album of the Pacific Islands," Series I, plates 49 and 52, fig. 2—is *hulili-hula*, while Mahillon *Catalogue du Musée Instrumental du Conservatoire Royal de Musique de Bruxelles*, Vol. III, p. 249, gives *uliuli*.

30. SHAK-SHAK. Wood and membrane. . . . . St. Thomas Island
Length, 41 cm. Diameter of body, 9.5 cm. Depth, 4 cm.

31. GA-NON-GAH GASDA-WE-SA.[7] Horn. . . . Seneca Indians, New York
Length, 22.5 cm. Diameter, 7.5 cm.
(Nos. 1, 4, 6, and 31 were collected and presented by Mr. M. R. Harrington.)

32. RATTLE. Three semi-spherical seed-shells, on a handle. . . . . . Africa
Length, 28 cm. Diameter of shells, 5 to 7 cm.

33. RATTLE. Decorated gourd. . . . . Porto Rico
Length, 25.5 cm. Diameter of gourd, 7.5 cm.

34. BRACELET RATTLE. Chank-shell (*Turbinella pyrum*). . East Africa
Diameter of ring, 10 cm.

35. AYACACHTLI. Bell-rattle. Pottery. . . . . Ancient Mexico
The surface is decorated with incised geometric designs.
Diameter, 5 cm.

36. HOOP RATTLE . . . . Alaska
Two concentric rings of withes, and dew horns of deer
Diameter of larger hoop, 23.5 cm.; of smaller, 18 cm.

37. RAVEN RATTLE. Wood . . . . Haidah Indians, British Columbia
Decorated with a carving of *Hooyeh*, "the raven."
Length, 30 cm. Width, 9 cm.

38. WILD-DUCK RATTLE. Wood . . . . Alaska
Length, 28.5 cm. Width, 7 cm.
(Israel G. Russell.)

39. RATTLE. Wood. . . . . Auk Indians, Alaska
Length, 27.5 cm. Thickness, 4.5 cm.

40. CLAPPER. Wood . . . . . . Tlingit Indians, N. W. Coast, N. America
This clapper represents the killer whale.
Length, 34 cm. Diameter, 6 cm. Thickness, 6 cm.

41-42. PUILI. Time-markers. Bamboo . . . . Hawaii
Two joints of bamboo are split about two-thirds of their full length into tongues 4 mm. wide. Every alternate splint is removed. The larger joint is struck with the shorter.
Lengths, 62, and 51 cm.; diameter, 5.5; 24, and 22 splints.

43. GUIRO, or WIS GUIRRA. Gourd. Rasped. . . . . Porto Rico
Length, 45 cm. Diameter, 12 cm.
(Mrs. Frederick G. Novy.)
Evidently the negro name *wisharow* is a corruption of *wis guirra*.

---

[7] Morris, p. 159.

44. GUIRO. Serrated surface. Rasped . . . . St. Thomas
Length, 32 cm. Diameter, 8 cm.

The Chinese *yü** (Jap. *gyo*), a wooden tiger with metal, or wooden teeth inserted in its back in lieu of vertebrae, is the most typical "serrated surface" instrument. Savages affect a jaw-bone, with teeth.

In an account of the "Dance in Square Congo" (New Orleans), George W. Cable bears witness to the inspiration drawn from such an instrument, of exactly the same structure as those which the negroes of Central Africa use in their merry-makings.[8]

45-46-47. SHAKUJO. Sistrum type. Bronze, on wooden staff. . . . Japan
Lengths, 24.3—159, and 27 cm., respectively.

The Sistrum was used in the worship of Isis and was found in all the countries in which this special cult was introduced. It consists of a metal frame in which are transverse bars carrying rings (also of metal), which are sounded by shaking the instrument.

48-9-50-1-2-3-4. PAI PAN, or P'E PAN. Wood . . . . China
Two slabs are struck by a third which is very thin (7 mm.).*
Length of each slab, 26 cm.; width, 5.2 to 6.4 cm.; thickness, 1 cm. (B-S.)

According to Moule (pp. 18 and 19) there are various sizes of the *p'ai pan*. "They are used in the theater, being held in the left hand by the man who beats the *pang kou*" (Case IV., No. 301). "One piece is held firmly in his hand so that a slight turn of his wrist brings it against the other two pieces which hang loosely over his thumb." *Pan yen* is one of the Chinese names for musical time, *pan* standing for bar, or the accented beat, and *yen* for the unaccented member—as, one *pan*, one *yen*—two-membered; 'one *pan*, two *yen*'—three-membered time. *Chin pan* stands for a rapid, and *man pan* for a slow movement.

55. EKIREI. Metal gong-rattle . . . . Japan
Two concave ring-like shells of metal are brought together face to face, and the hollow space thus formed contains several small metal balls.
Diameter, 4.5 cm.

56. RATTLE. Wood, and metal discs. . . . . Italy
Used with No. 81 as a fiddle and bow.
Length, 63 cm. Width, 4 cm. Thickness, 1.3 cm. 12 discs.

---

* Moule, the latest authority on the subject, in "Chinese Music," Jour. N. China Branch Roy. As. Soc., states that the *yü* is made of *ch'u* wood (*Catalpa kaempferi*); that the stick should be of the same wood; that from the time of the T'ang dynasty (618-907) bamboo has also been used; and, finally, that the tiger should not be hit on the head.

[8] "Century Magazine," Vol. XXXI, pp. 519-22.

* In placing the slabs it was found necessary to assign each slab a number. A like procedure obtains in Case II, Nos. 141-151, 167-182, and 185 to 202, and in Case III, Nos. 211-12-13. In the final tabulation the proper deductions are made.

57. TIME-MARKER. Wood, incised ....Source unknown
Length, 31 cm.; of incision, 24 cm. Width, 2.3 cm.

58. GUIRO, or WIERO. Gourd, serrated ....St. Thomas Island
Length, 43 cm. Diameter (widest), 7 cm.

59. TIME-MARKER, or LIME-SPOON ....New Guinea
Wood, with lime-filled etching.
Length, 39 cm.

60. CLAPPER. Wood ....N. W. Coast of Alaska
Length, 38 cm. Greatest diameter, 6 cm.

61-62. KARABIB. Castanets of iron ....Soudan, Africa
In each pair, two flat iron discs are joined by a bar of the same material, which serves as a handle. Cowrie-shell decoration.
Length, 28.5 cm. Diameter of discs, 9 cm.

63. CLAPPER. Wood ....Alaska
Length, 19.5 cm.

64. CASTANETS. Copper ....Patagonian Indians, Argentina
Length, 7.5, and 5.5 cm. Diameter, 5.6, and 4.8 cm.

65. DABBOUS. Dervish whirling-rattle, and dagger. Iron. Aintab, Turkey
Length, 34 cm.; of chains, 12 cm. Diameter of head, 9 cm.

66. KHATTALA, or KHATTALI. Iron castanets ....India
Held loosely in the hand and shaken.
Length, 14.6 cm. Thickness, 1.5 cm.

67. TIME-BEATER. Wood, with two longitudinal incisions........Italy
This idiophonic device, when struck violently against a hard surface, yields a sharp incisive tone. It is of the same class as the *hyoshigi*, of Japan;[9] two sticks which serve to attract the attention of an audience to the beginning of an athletic performance, as in the Parisian theaters the rise of the curtain is announced by three blows of a stick, *Les trois coups*, on the stage floor.
A similar contrivance was used by the Franciscan monks to rouse the sleepers. Bonanni, *Gab. arm.*, p. 154, Pl. CXXIX.
Length, 48 cm.; of incisions (3) 33 cm. Width, 4.5 cm.

68. TRICCA-BALLACCA. Clapper. Boxwood ....Italy
Three hammers are so arranged on a frame, that when it is swung, the two outer hammers, which hang loosely, strike the middle one, which is firmly fixed in the frame. The outer hammers may be manipulated by the hands.
Listed as a rattle by Curt Sachs.[10] Length, 33 cm.

---

[9] J. S. Piggott, "The Music and Musical Instruments of Japan," p. 210. Future references to this work will give the name of the author only.

[10] Curt Sachs, *Reallexikon der musikinstrumente*, p. 392. This work will be referred to under the name of the author.

69. TRICH VARLACH. Similar to No. 68. Black walnut.........Italy
Length, 42 cm.

70. CASTANETS. Ebony ....England
Length, 11 cm. Diameter, 4.1 cm.

71. CASTANETS. Boxwood ....England
Length, 28 cm.; of handle, 19 cm.; of body, 9 cm. Width, 5 cm.

72. CASTANETS. Boxwood ....Uruguay
Length, 7 cm. Diameter, 4.5 cm.

73-74. FINGER MASKS. Wood and wool...Esquimaux, North America
These grotesque objects are worn on the fingers of dancers.
Diameter, 5.2 cm.

75. BOATSWAIN'S RATTLE. Wood ....United States Navy
Length, 34 cm.

76. BOATSWAIN'S RATTLE. Wood ....United States Navy
Length, 33.5 cm.

77. WATCHMAN'S RATTLE. (Toy.) Wood..............England
Length, 19.5 cm.

78. WATCHMAN'S RATTLE. (Fr. *Crécelle;* Ital. *Raganella;* Ger. *Ratsche.*) Wood. Length, 25 cm..................England
In this type a tongue of wood is set in vibration by contact with a cog-wheel, secured to a handle which serves as a pivot on which the structure is rotated.

79. ANKLANG. Bamboo tubes in frame......................Java
Height, 77.5 cm. Width, 28 cm. Length of tubes, 31, 41 cm. Diameter, 3, 4.5 cm.

80. ANKLANG. Similar to the preceding example...............Java
Height, 93 cm. Width, 34 cm. Length of tubes, 16.5, 30, and 44 cm. Diameter, 2.8, 3.5 and 5.5 cm.

The *anklang* plays a very important part in the Javanese orchestra. The two specimens shown in this case give but a faint idea of its range. In the western, mountainous sections of Java, bands of forty or fifty natives, each with an *anklang* decorated with feathers,[11] accompany their wild dances with its sonorous music, which has more to commend it than would seem possible. *Anklung* is an alternative spelling.

Length, 12.3 cm. Width, 4 cm. Thickness, 2.5 cm.

81. RATTLE. Wood, and metal discs. Used with No. 56........Italy

[11] Sir Thomas Stafford Raffles, "A History of Java," p. 334.

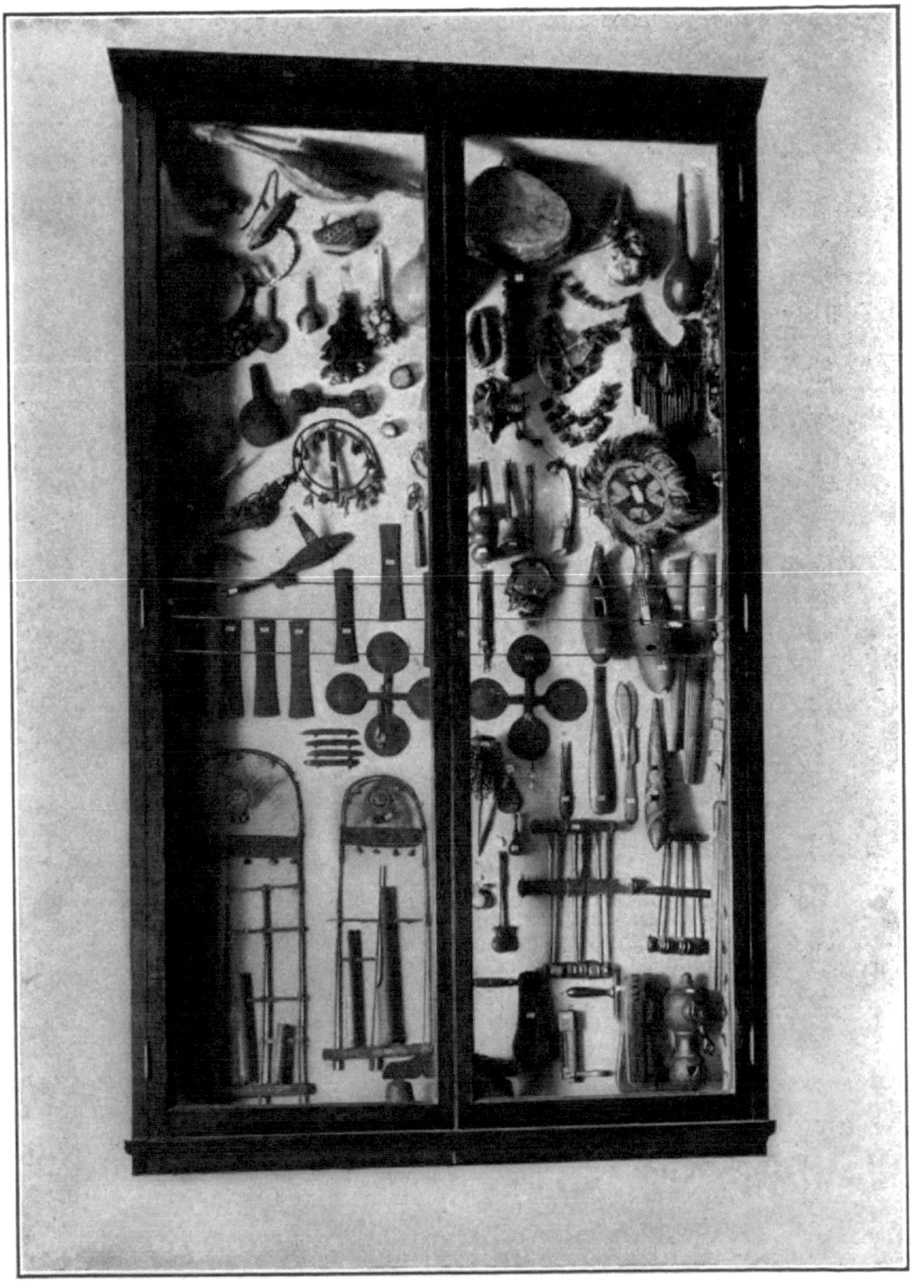

PLATE I.

CASE I. NOS. 1 TO 108 (RIGHT TO LEFT)

(No. 3 transferred to Case V., No. 55 changed to No. 3. New No. 55, not shown)

82. DOUBLE BELL. Wood . . . . Upper Congo, Africa
Length, 25.5 cm. Each bell is 9.5 cm. long, 7 cm. wide, and 5.5 cm. thick.
Collected by the Belgian explorer, M. Casman.
A double-bell called *n'goma na shuma* is found in this region, but, as it is of iron, the name cannot be applied to this unless, as frequently happens in indigenous instruments, the material used is incidental rather than typical.

83. BELL AND WHISTLE. Wood. . . . . Upper Congo, Africa
The egg-shaped bell (4.5 cm. long and 3.7 cm. in diameter) has three wooden tongues. The whistle (15 cm. long) is made to sound by blowing across the top.

84. DOUBLE BELL. Wood . . . . Mayumba, Africa
Each bell (7 x 6.6 cm.) has three wooden tongues and is painted white with black stripes. The connecting handle is 6.7 cm. long and 2.5 cm. in diameter.

85. DEVIL BELL. A section of nut. . . . . West Central Africa
Length, 9.7 cm. Width, 9 cm. Thickness, 5 cm.

86. BELL. Terra-cotta . . . . Ancient Egypt
Height, 6 cm. Diameter at base, 6.5 cm.

87-88-89. BELLS. Bronze . . . . Ancient Egypt
Heights, 13.7-10-7 cm. Diameters, 8-6-4.8 cm.

90. BELL. Bronze . . . . Etruria, Ancient Italy
Height, 13 cm. Diameter, 8 cm.

91-92-93. BELLS. Bronze . . . . Ancient Egypt
Heights, 3-5-7.5 cm. Diameters, 3.5-4.7-3.8 cm.

94. BELL. Bronze . . . . Etruria, Ancient Italy
Height, 5 cm. Diameter at base, 3.5 cm.

95-96. BELLS. Bronze . . . . Ancient Egypt
Heights, 4-6 cm. Diameters, 4-4.7 cm.

97-98. CYMBALS. Bronze, heavily patinated. . . . . Italy
Diameter of each, 9 cm. Depth, 3.5 cm.
The patination (*aerugo*) on these reproductions of the originals in the Naples Museum, represents a modern use of chemicals rather than the passage of the centuries. On Nos. 87 to 96 incl. the patina is genuine.
Cymbala and *acetabula* are Greek and Roman cymbals of a rather deeper basin-type than those here listed.

99. Fetish Bell. Iron .... Liberia, Africa
Among the African natives iron bells exist in many unique forms.
Height, 18.6 cm. Width, 8.4 cm. Thickness, 5.5 cm.

100. Bell. Iron, with carrying-strap........ Lake Tanganyika, Africa
Length, with strap, 99 cm.; of bell, 15.4 cm. Diameter, 3.5 cm.

101. Bell. Iron .... Angoni, Central Africa
Height, 5 cm. Width, 5.5 cm. Thickness at base, 3.7 cm.

102. Herd Bell. Brass .... Sparta, Greece
Height, 10 cm. Diameter, 10 and 4 cm.
(Francis W. Kelsey.)

103-104-105-106-107. Cowbells. Brass .... Switzerland
Varying sizes from 6 to 10 cm. high, and 5 to 7 cm. in diameter.

108. Chime. Bell metal. Pitches, f, e flat, g................. France
Height, 10 cm. Diameter of bells, 11.8-12-11.6 cm.

CASE II.

CLASS I. Section B. Vibrating Plates, and Hollow Bodies of Metal.

The Bell (Fr. *Cloche;* Ital. *Campana;* Ger. *Glocke*) is made of various alloys, but generally of "bell-metal" (Fr.*Aloi;* Ital. *Metallo da campane;* Ger. *Glockenspeise*), copper and tin in the proportion of three to one. Brass and bronze are occasionally used. Copper is seldom employed as it produces a dull tone. Oriental alloys are in some cases quite unusual in their composition but are very effective. Gongs (onomatopoeic) are made of various alloys, generally of copper and tin. Cymbals (Fr. *Cymbale;* Ital. *Piatti;* Ger. *Becken*) are almost invariably made of brass, although this practice does not always obtain in the Orient.

109. GONG. Copper alloy .... Borneo
Largest of the series of ten, known as the *koulintaugau.*
Diameter, 47 cm. Depth, 21.5 cm.

110. CHIME .... Italy
Twelve brass bells, arranged on an oval hoop with handle. The larger bells are fastened to the inside of the hoop, the smaller to a cord running cross-wise.
Diameter of hoop 35.3 and 40 cm. Diameter of larger bells, 8.5 cm.; of smaller, 4 cm. Handle 37 cm. long.

111. CAI CHUONG, or CAI CHUONG CHUA. Temple bell. Bronze. . Anam
Height, 40 cm. Diameter at base, 22.2 cm.

112. TUBULAR BELLS. Nickel-plated bronze. (f and a flat) ...... Italy
Length of longer tube, 123.5 cm.; of shorter, 113 cm. Diameter, 2.9 cm.

A new type of bell has been developed in England, which is nothing more nor less than a cylindrical bar of steel. The dissonant over-tones are eliminated, and the "hum" note is evolved as soon as the bar is struck. By means of an ingenious mechanism, devised by Dr. T. Lea Southgate, the bells when combined in a Chime, can be "dampened," or softened, making them more responsive to artistic demands.

113. MUSICAL SLEIGH-BELLS. Nickel-plated bronze............. Italy
Diameters of bells, from 2.5 to 3.2 cm.

114. ELEPHANT BELL. Brass .... India
Height, 17 cm. Diameter at base, 13.5 cm.
These bells are hung on the trappings of the sacred elephants at Delhi.

115. ZANG-I-JAMI'. "Bell of the Mosque." Iron . . . . Persia
Zang is the ordinary Persian word for bell. Sachs (p. 430) gives *Zeng*. dim. *zengil*. *Jami'* refers to a large mosque as opposed to *masjid*—a small place of prayer. Following the vowel *i* it takes the genitive case. This is given on the authority of a leading American Orientalist.
Height, 17 cm. Diameter, 17 cm.

116. MASS BELL. Low, open-work body of iron . . . . Germany
Three small bronze bells serve as clappers.
Height, 14.5 cm. Diameter at base, 10.2 cm.

117. FURIN, "Wind-bell." Brass . . . . Japan
Three streamers, consisting of small brass plates and discs terminating in small bells in the shape of a flower calyx, hang from the clapper.
Height, 7.5 cm. Diameter at base, 7.3 cm. Length of streamers, 44 cm.

118. MASS BELL. Middle Ages . . . . Germany
Of brass, with open-work sides. Decorated with arabesques, and four figures in relief, emblematic of the four evangelists, whose names appear on outer surface.
Height, 15 cm. Diameter at base, 11.5 cm.

119. ZANG-I-JAMI'. A replica of No. 115 . . . . Persia

120. TEMPLE BELL. Bronze . . . . Japan
Height, 20.3 cm. Diameter at base, 12.3 cm.

121. FURIN, "Wind-bell" . . . . Japan
Similar to No. 117 excepting that the streamers end in globular bells.
Length of streamers, 23 cm.
The *furin* are suspended from the eaves of temples, and other buildings. The *feng-ling* (Chin.) and *pang-ḳiang* (Cor.) are variants.

122. MUSICAL SLEIGH-BELLS. Similar to No. 113 . . . . Italy

123. TUBULAR BELLS. Nickel-plated bronze (f, e flat, g) . . . . Italy
Lengths of tubes, 100, 109, and 81.5 cm.

124-125. SONOG-TOHOCE-WA-FARAH. Brass cymbals . . . . Egypt
As the name indicates, these cymbals are used at the ceremony of circumcision.
Shallow bosses, and flat rims. Diameter, 26.8 cm. Depth, 3 cm.

126. GOAT BELL. Brass . . . . Italy
Semi-conical body of brass with rough surface. Smooth flat bands serve as decoration.
Height, 12 cm. Diameter at base, 6 to 5.2 cm.

127. COWBELL. Brass . . . . Italy
Height, 13 cm. Diameter at base, 7.5 to 7 cm.

PLATE II.

CASE II. PERSIAN GONG, NO. 177

128. LO. Gong. Brass alloy .... China
The comparatively shallow body is decorated with six circular stripes in black.
Diameter, 67 cm. Depth, 3 cm.
(B-S.)

129. DRILBU. Temple hand-bell. Bronze.................. Thibet
The handle, of brass, represents the thunder-bolt-*dorje*.
Height, 16 cm. Diameter at base, 6.5 cm.

130. BELL. Bronze. Decorated in relief............ Benin, W. Africa
Height, 10.3 cm. Diameter at base, 6 cm.

131. BELL. Bronze .... Italy
Decorated with the coat of arms of the de Medici Family. The bust of a Bishop with his mitre and robes forms the handle.
Height, 25.5 cm. Diameter at base, 4.6 cm.

132. BELL. Brass, elaborately decorated.................... France
Height, 10.2 cm. Diameter at base, 5.7 cm.

133. BELL. Bronze. In form it resembles the ancient *hiuen-chung*... China
Height, 10.5 cm. Diameter at base, 15 to 3.8 cm.

134. BELL. Bronze .... Burmah
Height, 10.5 cm. Diameter at base, 8.6 cm.

135. BELL. Brass alloy .... Burmah
The fantastic handle is supported by two grotesque monsters.
Height, 21.8 cm.; of bell 9.5 cm. Diameter at base, 12.8 cm.

136. DONKEY BELL. Bronze. A second bell serves as a clapper... Persia
Height of larger bell, 9.8 cm.; of smaller, 4.5 cm. Diameter of larger bell, 6.2 by 5.1 cm.; of smaller, 3.6 by 3 cm.

137. CAI CHIENG. Gong. Alloy .... Anam
The exterior surface is elaborately decorated in black and gold; the interior is painted a dull red. Incurved rim and large boss.
Diameter, 52 cm. Depth of rim (*thanh*), 8 cm.; of boss (*vu*), 3 cm. Width of boss, 7 cm.

138. BELL. Bronze .... Italy
A statuette of Venus bathing forms the handle.
Height, 21 cm. Diameter at base, 9 cm.

139. CHIME. Sixteen small diamond-shaped brass bells.......... India
Length of each bell, 4 cm. Diameter, 3 cm.

140. SHOKO. Gong, of lacquered brass, elaborately decorated.... Japan
Height, 41 cm. Width, 30.5 cm. Depth, 3 cm.
On the face, lacquered brown, is a representation of the Shinto god of of wealth and good fortune, standing on bags of rice.

141. Po, or Seau-po. Cymbal. Used with No. 151 . . . . China
Diameter, 28.8 cm. Depth, 3 cm.
(B-S.)

142. Kagura-sudsu. Chime . . . . Japan
Thirteen globular brass bells hanging from metal rings, which are fastened to a handle.
Length, 40 cm. Diameter of bells, 3 cm.; of rings, 6 and 4 cm.

143. Library Bell. Brass . . . . Italy
The handle, which unscrews, contains a box for sand and a case for quills. Height, 15.5 cm. Diameter at base, 7.5 cm.

144. E-sudsu. Temple hand-bell. Bronze. Incised decorations . . . Japan
Length, 17.5 cm. Diameter, 6.5 to 5.5 cm.

145. Tanta. Gong. Bronze . . . . China
Diameter, 23.7 cm.

146. Nihoihagi. Brass cymbal, used with No. 162 . . . . Japan
Diameter, 34 cm. Depth, at boss, 3 cm.

147. Bell. Pottery, enamelled in colors . . . . Switzerland
Height, 9.5 cm. Diameter, 8.5 to 4.5 cm.

148. Lo. Gong of brass . . . . China
Diameter, 50 cm. Depth, 4 cm.

149. Sagat, or Saggat. Finger-cymbals. Brass, scalloped edges . . Egypt
Diameter of each cymbal, 5 cm. Depth, 4.2 cm.

150. Finger Cymbals. Similar to No. 149.

151. Po, or Seau-po. Brass cymbal, used with No. 141 . . . . China

152-153-154-155. (Right side of Case.) Gongs . . . . Borneo

156-157-158-159-160. (Left side of Case.) Gongs . . . . Borneo
Nos. 152-160, inclusive, belong to same set as No. 109.
The copper alloy is very friable, and in its constituent parts seemingly unlike most Oriental mixtures.
Average diameter of gongs, 18.7 cm.; depth, 4.2 cm.

161. Chinchichi. Circular brass gong used by mendicant priests . . . Japan
It generally rests on a brass panel.
Diameter at top, 7.3 cm.; at rim, 9.5 cm. Depth, 3.2 cm.

162. Nihoihagi. Used with No. 146 . . . . Japan

163. Shoko. A bronze gong generally hung in a frame . . . . Japan
Diameter, 13.5 cm. Depth, 3.8 cm.

164. ANIMAL BELL. Brass . . . . Italy
Diameter, 4.5 cm.

165. SHOKO. Similar to No. 113 . . . . Japan
Diameter, 11.8 cm. Depth, 3.5 cm.

166. ANIMAL BELL. Brass, nickel-plated . . . . Italy
Diameter, 5.5 cm.

167. CYMBAL. Brass. Modern. Used with No. 182 . . . . Italy
Diameter, 35.7 cm. Depth, 3 cm.

168. DOBACHI. Gong. Bell metal . . . . Japan
The cup-shaped gong rests on a cushion which is placed on a carved and gilded frame. Its tone is very clear and of beautiful quality. The *dobachi* is called *keisu* by certain Chinese sects.
Diameter, 13 cm. Height, 6.5 cm.; of stand, 9.5 cm.

169. DORA, or COREAN GONG. Brass . . . . Japan
Diameter, 35 cm. Depth of rim, 3.2 cm.

(B-S).

170. GOAT BELL. Of the sleigh-bell type. Brass . . . . Egypt
Diameter, 10 cm.

171. DOBYOSHI. Copper cymbals used by dancers to mark the time. . Japan
Diameter, 10.5 cm.

172. CARILLONS. Harness bells. Brass, nickel-plated . . . . Italy
Three bells, each 5.6 cm. in diameter, carried on a pillar.

173. "SISTRUM." 25 small bell-metal gongs—giving the chromatic scale from b flat′ to b flat‴ . . . . France
Diameter of gongs, 15 to 4 cm.

174. "CLOCHETTE DE TIMON." Brass, nickel-plated . . . . Italy
Two gongs of different pitches placed edge to edge.
Diameter of larger gong, 7.8 cm.; of smaller, 7.5 cm.

175. TALA. Cymbals. Brass alloy . . . . India
Diameter, 6.4 cm. Depth, 2.7 cm.

176. CARILLONS. In material and use, similar to No. 172 . . . . Italy
Diameter of each small bell, 4.1 cm.; of larger bell, 5.6 cm.

177. GONG. Of white metal, in the form of a keystone . . . . Persia
The upper corners are elongated and bent forward at right angles. The face is elaborately etched with arabesques, figures of men and animals, and inscriptions, the latter often being "puzzles to native scholars unless the content is known beforehand or can be guessed."
Length, 39.5 cm. Width, 18.5 to 25 cm. Thickness, 8 to 7 mm.

178. DORA. Gong. Brass . . . . Japan
Diameter, 23.3 cm. Thickness, 8 mm.

179. WANIGUCHI, or "Shark's-mouth gong" .... Japan
This gong is hung at the entrance to a temple, and struck with a thick rope suspended before it for that purpose.
Diameter, 28 cm. Depth, 11 cm.

180. KAJIREI, or ZICHIREI. Chime .... Japan
Three ring-like bells, or gongs, of bronze are strung upon a wire bent to a circle, which is fastened to a handle (missing). Each bell is made of two sections, joined at the inner edges, leaving the outer edges slightly apart. Which of the names given is applicable rests upon one's definition of bell and gong. There appears to be no more reason for calling this a rattle (Sachs, pp. 200, 430), than the *kagura-sudsu.*
Diameter of bells, 10.2 to 5 cm.; of ring, 16 cm.

181. MASS BELL. A frame of brass, in the form of a Greek cross. Germany
Each arm bears a shallow gong-shaped bell surmounted by a Latin cross.

182. CYMBAL. Brass. Modern. Used with No. 167............ Italy

183. DIAPASON. Bell metal. Pitch:—a′..................... Italy
Diameter of gong, 9.2 cm. Depth, 3 cm.

184. CHIME .... Egypt
Four globular bells of brass, attached to a bottle-shaped standard, resting on four legs.
Height, 10.3 cm. Diameter of each bell, 1.7 cm.

185 to 202. HAND BELLS. Bell metal.................... England

The bells have straps for handles. On one side of the clapper a leathern damper is attached. When cleverly manipulated they produce a pleasing effect, and the music of "bell ringers"—like the Peak Family—at one time was much in vogue.

Diameter of bells, from 14.2 cm. (the largest), to 7.5 cm (the smallest). Height, from 7.3 to 16.5 cm.

Compass: the diatonic scale of B flat major from f to d″, with b natural, b natural′, and f sharp′ interpolated, b and e′ duplicated.

Omitting mention of the many significant facts regarding the relations bells have sustained to personal and communal life, a very interesting excerpt from the diary of Christopher Columbus is herewith given. It is dated Punta Santa, Dec. 25, 1492. "While the Admiral was talking to him (the King) another canoe arrived from a different place bringing some pieces of gold, which the people in the canoe wanted to exchange for a hawk's bell; for there was nothing they desired more than these bells."[1]

[1] "Journal of Columbus," Hak. Soc., 1893, p. 135.

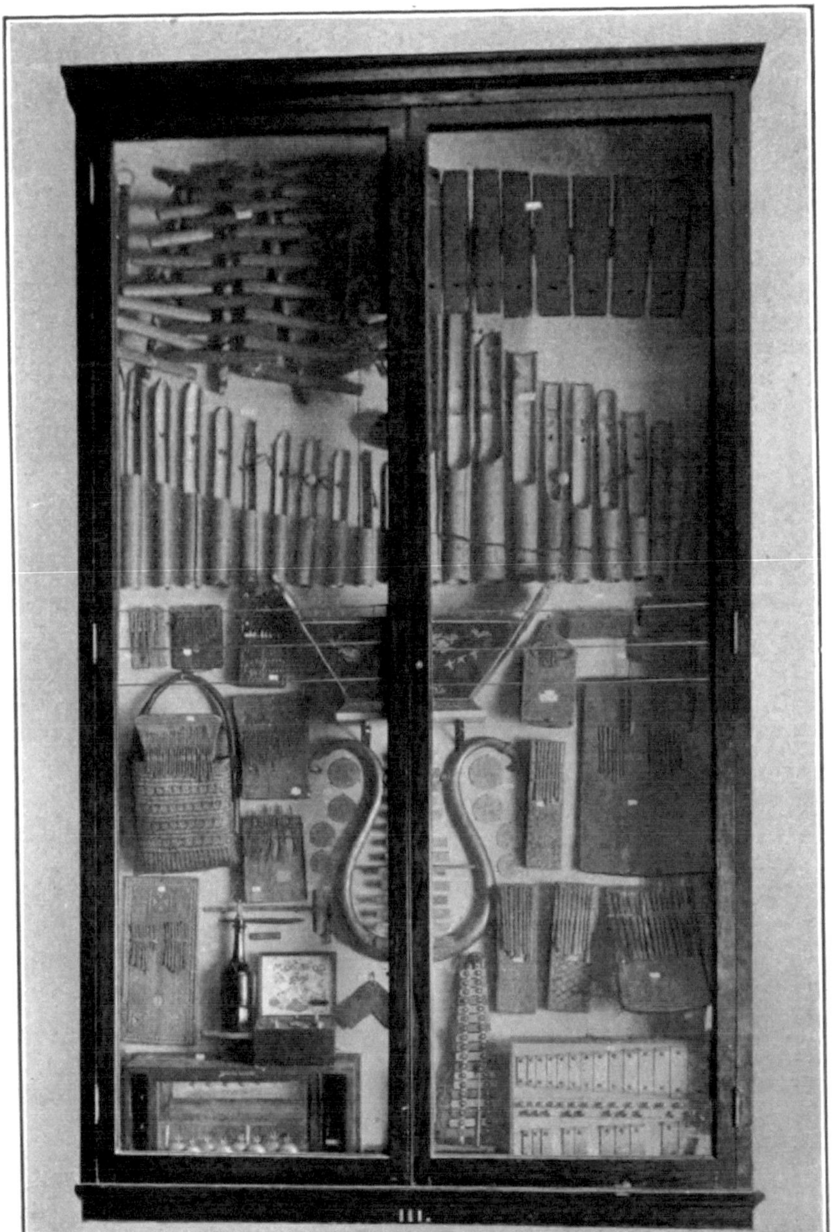

PLATE III.

CASE III. NOS. 203 TO 260 (RIGHT TO LEFT)

CASE III.

Section C. (a) Vibrating Bars of Wood, with Resonator. Xylophones.
(b) Vibrating Segments of Resonator Body (Wood). Harmonicons.

Section D. Vibrating Tongues of Wood or Metal. Sanzas.

Section E. Vibrating Bars, or Rods, of Metal. Carillons.

Section F. Vibrating Tongues, or Bars, of Metal with Mechanism. Music-boxes, Partition Mustel.

The instruments in Sections C and E are struck. Those in Section D are plucked, in Section F are plucked or struck.

203. RANAT-EK. Xylophone. Wood .... Siam

Twenty-one graduated bars of hard red wood, united by lacings of heavy cord, are laid along the edges of a curved boat-like structure —in this example decorated with ivory inlay. This resonator rests on a square base. The bars are tuned, either by hollowing out the ends, or by affixing lumps of gum, cement, or lead, to the under surface.

Length of frame, 93.5 cm. Height, 43 cm. Length of bars, from 26 to 31 cm.; width, 3.4 to 4 cm.; thickness, 1.4 cm.

204. RONEAT-EK. Xylophone. Wood. (Over Case VI) .... Cambodia

Length of frame, 118 cm. Height, 5.2 cm. Length of bars, 39 to 30 cm.; width, 5.2 to 4.5 cm.; thickness, 1.3 cm.

205. PATTALA. Xylophone. Wood. (Over Case VI) .... Burmah

A reproduction. Elaborately decorated with inlay of light-colored wood.

The *pattala* is the Burmese *ranat*, with bars (16 to 18) of the *Bambus gigantee*. In Siam it is known as the *takkag*.

Length of frame, 125 cm. Height, 50 cm. Length of bars, 24 to 28 cm.; width, 5.2 to 4.5 cm.; thickness, 1 to 2 cm.

The *ranat* (Camb. *roneat*) exhibits four forms:—*ranat-ek*, the highest pitched, usually with 21 bars; *ranat-lek*, low pitch, 17 bars; *ranat t'hum*, an octave lower in pitch than the *ranat-ek;* and the *ranat thong*, in which the bars are of bronze. The Siamese have four types of orchestra; *mahoree*, *bhimbat*, *kling khek* and *lao phan*. The *ranats* are used in the first two.

The Javanese *gambang* (not in Collection) is of the *ranat* type. In its two forms, the *gambang gangsa* (6 to 18 metal bars), and the *gambang kaju* (variable number of bars) it is almost invariably found in their *gamelang* (orchestra).

206. IZAMBILO. Wooden bars with resonators. . . . . . . Zulu-land, Africa
The ten bars of *intgan* wood—of graduated width—are fastened by thongs into a frame of bent wood, which is suspended from the shoulders of the performer by carrying-cords. Each bar is fitted with a resonator of the shell of the *Strychnos McKenii.*

Length of frame, 89 cm. Width, 44 cm. Length of bars 32.5 cm., width, 8.5 to 4.5 cm. Diameter of resonators, 7 to 10 cm.

Pitches—f, f sharp, b, c sharp′, d sharp′, f′, f sharp′, g sharp′, a′, and b′.

The *marimba,* of which this is a typical specimen, is also widely distributed throughout Latin America. While, like many other importations from Africa, it displays variations, in essentials they are identical with the original type.

207. STROHFIEDEL. Xylophone. Wood and straw . . . . Germany
Thirty-two wooden bars of varying lengths (three duplicates), laid in four parallel columns on slender fasces of straw, give, when struck, the chromatic scale from f sharp to b flat″.

Length, 60 cm. Width, 90 to 40 cm. Length of bars, 11.4 to 25.3 cm.

The foregoing instruments are of the xylophone type. The dividing line between this and a kindred type in which the process of tone-production is similar has never been distinctly drawn; therefore the use of the term "harmonicon" to define such an instrument as the *teponatzli* (Case IV, No. 269) is suggested. This is proposed with full appreciation of the danger involved in running counter to established precedents, the etymological implications of the term, and its definitions by lexicographers. To justify this differentiation the following important distinction is submitted: in the harmonicon the vibrating tongue, or elastic section, is of the same body as the resonance chamber, or surface; in the xylophone, independent vibrating bodies rest on a resonator, which is *not* of the same body. The first type may also be reckoned in the gong class, for a wooden gong, or bell, embodies the principle on which the distinction rests. While the differentiation suggested may appear arbitrary, it would prevent such confusion of terms as is found in Engel's "Catalogue of Musical Instruments in the South Kensington Museum," in which he lists the *ḳo ḳ'ing*—which he calls *ḳing* (p. 46)—and the *ranat-eḳ* (p. 316)—a typical xylophone—as harmonicons, although they are quite unlike. American and English lexicographers apply the term "harmonicon" to the mouth-harmonica —a free-reed instrument—also to the orchestration—a mechanical instrument —and include in their definitions two types of harmonika, one of glass hemispheres (rubbed) and one of metal or glass bars (struck with hammers).

208. TJALANG. Harmonicon. Bamboo tubes. . . . . Java
Ten tubes of bamboo, strung on two cords. The eleventh tube (middle) is missing. The instrument is suspended from a branch of a

tree, and the tubes are struck with sticks. Listed as a xylophone by Sachs (p. 388), it might, not illogically, be called a chime- harmonicon.

Length, 74.5 to 23.3 cm. Diameter, 7 to 4.2 cm.

This type of instrument is called "idiophonic" by Curt Sachs, and "autophonic" by Mahillon.

209. RESONATOR. Of the type used to reinforce the tone in No. 206.

210. "BAMBOO BELLS." Ten attuned bamboo tubes......United States

In this instrument, and in the *tjalang*, each tone-producing tube is also a resonator.

The ten tubes, when struck with rubber-tipped sticks, give the diatonic scale from c to d′, with b flat added.

Length, 59 to 31 cm. Diameter, 5 to 4 cm.

211-12-13. DOLI-DOLI. Xylophone ....Nias Island

Three slabs, half-round cross-section, placed over a hole in the ground and struck with two sticks. Pitches: f′, g′, a′.

Lengths, 36 to 49 cm. Widths, 5.3 to 4.2 cm. Thickness, 3 cm.

214. STEEL-HARMONICA ....United States

Twenty-two steel bars of graduated length, resting upon a deep trapezoidal wooden frame.

Length of frame, 66 cm. Width, 8 to 5 cm. Length of bars, 14.5 to 4.6 cm.; width, 2.5 cm. Compass, the diatonic scale from c′ to c′′′′.

215. PAN. Harmonicon type. Wood ....China

The *pan* is an oblong, rectangular block of *shitan* wood, in which a slit 11.5 cm. long, is cut. Beaten with a brass-headed stick, of the same wood, 13 cm. long.

Length, 15.4 cm. Width, 5.5 cm. Thickness, 3 cm.

(B-S.)

The *pan* is generally a part of a mendicant's outfit, but is also used in the orchestra, when it is fastened to the tripod of the *pang kou* by cords passing through two holes in one end of the block.

216. TIME-BEATER. Native name uncertain..................Anam

Similar to the preceding, excepting that it has two resonance cavities—each 12.6 cm. long, 4.5 cm. wide, and 5 cm. deep—cut in opposite sides of the block. The whole is elaborately decorated with inlaid scroll designs. This variant is also found in China.

Length, 16.6 cm. Width, 6.1 cm. Thickness, 5.4 cm.

217. PAN. Similar in structure, size and source to No. 215.

(B-S.)

218. KINANDA. Sanza. Wood. Iron tongues......Congo River, Africa
A hollow, rectangular resonance body of one piece slightly upturned at one end, carries 5 iron tongues (originally 8), which rest upon an iron bridge and wooden block secured by an iron cross-bar and staples.
Length of tongues, 10.3 to 9.4 cm.
Kinanda appears to be a generic name for almost any African musical instrument. In this specific instance it is applied in that sense. The persistent migrations of instruments, and the bewildering confusion in nomenclature, practically precludes absolute accuracy in naming indigenous instruments.

219. MOKKIN. .... Japan
Sixteen bars of *shitan* wood rest on a wooden boat-shaped frame, artistically decorated in black and gold lacquer. The two beaters are also of *shitan* wood.
Length of frame, 71 cm. Height, 36 cm. Length of bars, 29.5 to 18.1 cm.; width, 2.5 cm.; thickness, 1.3 cm.

220. EKENDE. Sanza. Wood. Iron tongues.....Bateke, Congo, Africa
The resonance box carries 9 iron tongues—fastened as in No. 215. On each tongue, between the bridge and block, one or two glass beads are strung, which, when the tongues vibrate, produce a buzzing sound. There are two sound-holes in the body, which is decorated with brass tacks.
Length of body, 22.7 cm. Width, 11 cm. Thickness, 4.5 cm. The tongues are from 1.8 to 12 cm. long.

221. KISANGHI. Sanza. Wood. Iron tongues............West Africa
The body is decorated in a series of small incised circles. In addition to the twanging of the 14 iron tongues, fastened in the usual manner, loose iron rings, running along a wire at the bottom, contribute the buzzing effect so much admired by the natives.
Length of body, 16.2 cm. Width, 12.7 cm. Thickness, 1 cm. Length of tongues, 3.5 to 6.2 cm.

222. IBEKA. Sanza. Wooden body and tongues..........West Africa
This very primitive specimen of a widely distributed type combines a body of flat pithy stalks, held together by cross-bars of wood, and nine wooden tongues.
Length, 15.5 cm. Width, 8.7 cm. Length of tongues, 14.8 to 12 cm.

223. MBIRA. Sanza. Two groups of rattan tongues........South Africa
A rectangular board, stained black, and decorated with incised lines following its outline forms the body. On it two groups of bamboo tongues are fastened by straps of braided rattan. The pitches of the groups (of 8 tongues each) are practically identical.
Length, 49 cm. Width, 27 cm. Tongues, from 13.2 to 10.3 long.

224. BUNDUMA. Sanza. Wooden body and tongues..........Soudan
The rectangular resonance box is artistically decorated with poker-work. Eight smoothly finished rattan tongues are fastened to the body with vegetable fibre. Under these tongues is a small triangular sound-hole.
Length, 32 cm. Width, 10.5 cm. Thickness, 3.8 cm. Length of tongues, 15.3 cm.; width, 2.6 cm.

225. KISANGHI. Wood. Iron tongues ....Angola, W. Africa
This consists of an approximately square resonance-box, from one piece of soft wood stained black and carrying incised decorations. The upper surface bears 24 iron tongues, grouped by fives and sevens. Ring rattle inside of lower end.
Length, 22 cm. Width, 20 to 16.5 cm. Thickness, 8 to 3 cm. Longest tongue, 11.2 cm.; shortest, 6 cm.

226. KISANGHI. Sanza, with case. Iron tongues..Angola, ...W. Africa
The body—29 cm. long, and 21.5 to 17.8 cm. wide—is supplied with an artistically woven case of rattan splints. The 23 iron tongues, arranged in a haphazard fashion and each carrying an iron collar in addition to those at the base, constitute the tone-producing media.

227. NSIMBI. Sanza. Iron tongues ....Upper Zambesi, Africa
Nineteen iron tongues are arranged unsystematically on a hollowed block, 21.5 cm. long, 16 to 15 cm. wide, and 4 to 1.5 cm. thick. The instrument is held by the sides with both hands, the tongues being plucked with the thumbs. This is the usual manner of performance.

228. KANKOBELE. pl. *tunkobele*. Sanza. Bamboo tongues...W. Africa
A rough board—33.3 to 34.5 cm. long, and 19.3 cm. wide, to which half of a large calabash shell (18 cm. in diameter) is attached by rattan withes—forms the resonator. To this, fifteen bamboo tongues, from 20.2 to 17.8 cm. long, and 1 cm. wide, are fastened in the usual manner. Lumps of black gum, affixed to the upper or under side of the tongue illustrate the usual tuning process.
(G. Schwab.)

229-230. BANT'YOU. Sanzas, elaborately decorated...Benin, W. Africa
Somewhat larger, and with longer tongues than No. 224.

231. MBIRA. Sanza. Two groups of rattan tongues.......South Africa
A flat board, darkened by burning and carrying carved geometrical designs in which the chief figure (thrice repeated) resembles a Maltese cross, serves as a resonating surface. To this surface two groups, each of 8 bamboo tongues resting on wooden bridges, are fastened by a braided cord of rattan strips.
Length, 42.5 cm. Width, 1.2 cm. Thickness, 1.2 cm.

While the tone-series produced by plucking the elastic strips of cane or metal in the Sanza does not appeal to the Western ear, it possesses for the unsophisticated native a potent charm. It would be impossible to give any but approximate pitches to the tones produced, but it is significant that there is a rude system governing their various groupings. In primitive songs we find interval relationships that necessitate a special notation—resembling the "curves" employed in defining relations remote from music—and only through the use of such a method could the exact pitches of many primitive instruments be given.

232-233. "MUSICAL COINS." Steel discs. Scale of C. . . . United States
Diameter from 8.3 to 5.7 cm.

234. CARILLONS, "a lameo d' acer." Steel bars. . . . . France
A lyre-shaped frame of beaten brass, supported on a long wooden handle, carries 14 attuned steel bars. With the additional bars listed as Nos. 252-3, the chromatic scale from c′ to g″ is made possible. The bars may be so adjusted as to establish any desired tonality. Formerly very much in vogue in military bands.
Length of frame, 109 cm. Length of bars, 18 to 16.8 cm.; width, 2.3 cm.; thickness, 8 mm.

235. MUSICAL BAR. Iron. Pitch:—F sharp. . . . . Italy
Length, 151 cm. Diameter, 1 to 3 cm.

236. TRIANGLE. Steel . . . . India
Entire length, 71 cm.

237. MOKURI, or MUKKURI. Jewsharp. Bamboo. . . . . Ainus, Japan
In a flat strip of bamboo, 10 cm. long, and 1.4 cm. wide, a flat tongue, 8.4 cm. long and 4mm. wide, is cut. This tongue is thinned at the lower end, and is set in vibration by the fingers or the pin attached to one end by a fine cord.

The Jewsharp (Fr. *Guimbarde;* Ital. *Scacciapensieri;* Ger. *Maultrommel, Brumeisen*), possibly a corruption from Jawsharp, is widely distributed and occasionally is given names which seem to have no relation to its character, as *ḳutsi-biwa* (Jap.) and *ḳ'ou chin* (Chin.).

238. JEWSHARP. (With case—a node of bamboo) . . . . Borneo
Body of bamboo with half-round cross-section. Native name unknown.
Length, 10.1 cm. Width, 1.3 cm. Length of tongue, 7.7 cm.
(B-S.)

239. KULANG. Jewsharp . . . . Moro Tribe, Philippine Islands
Body, of rattan, 31.3 cm. long and 1.2 cm. wide, with a short tongue, 7.2 cm. In many respects it resembles the earlier *darubi* of the West Torres Straits, between Australia and New Guinea.

240. DARUBIRI. Jewsharp . . . . New Guinea
Of rattan, rounded at one end and gradually tapering to a point at the other. The tongue runs nearly the whole length. The whole is stained black.
Length, 13.8 cm. Widest diameter, 1 cm.

241. MUKKURI. Jewsharp . . . . Formosa
Usual structure. Length, 6.5 cm. Width, 2.3 cm.
(B-S.)

242-243-244. JEWSHARPS. Metal. Modern . . . . United States

245. STEEL-HARMONICA. "Schoenhut's Patent" . . . . United States
The body, straight on one side and with incurving outline on the other, carries 18 steel bars, which, when struck with hammers, give the diatonic scale from c to f‴.
Length, 49 cm. Width, 16 to 5 cm. Length of bars, 14 to 6 cm.; width, 1 to 9 cm.

246. KEI, or HOKYO. Gong. Bronze . . . . Japan
A flat plate in the form of a carpenter's square. Inscriptions on both sides of surface. Struck with a peculiar Y-shaped mallet, tipped with bone.
Length of each arm, 13 cm.; width, 6 cm.; thickness, 4 mm.

247. MUSIC-BOX, "Monopol" . . . . Germany
Thirty-nine tongues of varying lengths, cut in a thin plate of steel, thus forming a comb, are made to sound by plectra, operated by a perforated disc which is rotated by clock-work.
Length of case, 19.6 cm. Width, 16.6 cm. Height, 11.7 cm.

248. MUSICAL BOTTLE . . . . Germany
A small music-box driven by clock-work is concealed in the base of the decanter. When the bottle is tipped it plays an air, but is silent when the upright position is resumed.
Height, 33 cm. Diameter, 9.2 cm.

249. PARTITION MUSTEL. Metal bars . . . . France
A set of 24 attuned rectangular bronze plates of graduated length and width are arranged in chromatic sequence from c′ to b″. The plates are struck by a mechanism operated by "touches," arranged in the pianoforte key-board order. It was invented in 1888 by Victor Mustel (Paris) to serve as a standard of pitch. It is housed in a walnut case.
Length of case, 48.5 cm. Height, 12 cm. Width, 33 cm. Length of bars 7 to 14 cm.; width, 2 to 4 cm.; thickness, 2 mm.

250. TUNING FORK. (König.) Steel. Pitch: c′ . . . . France
The fork which is 15.7 cm. long, and 3 cm. wide, stands on a rectangular box, containing a drawer in which it may be placed. A tuning fork gives a pure tone, relatively free from harmonics. Attempts have been made at various times to utilize a series of such forks in a key-board instrument, but they are curiosities rather than real contributions.

251. MUSIC-BOX. Steel tongues with mechanism. Modern. . . . Switzerland
The repertoire is as follows:

1. "Pinafore"—"He is an Englishman."
2. "Mabel"—Valse.
3. "Trial by Jury"—"Lancer No. 1."
4. "Le Petit Duc"—"La Lecon de chant."
5. "Madame Favart"—"The artless Thing."
6. "My Lost Dream."
7. "La Juive"—"Guard du Siegneur."
8. "Les Cloches de Corneville"—Valse.

The mechanism, inclosed in a walnut case, inlaid with ivory, consists of a brass cylinder in which small pins are set, and which is made to revolve by a powerful spring. As the cylinder revolves these pins engage slender steel teeth, and, in this example, a set of nine bell-gongs. By shifting the cylinder longitudinally different groups of teeth are plucked, and a more or less extended repertoire is established. The music-box is a civilized *sanza*, raised to the *n*th power.

Length, 56 cm. Width, 15.4 cm. Height, 26.4 cm. Length of teeth, 75 in number, from 6.2 to 4.7 cm.

Signed—"Musique de Genève."

252. STEEL BARS. Supplementary to No. 234. . . . . France
By substituting these for certain ones in No. 234 new tonalities are made possible.

253. STEEL BARS. Evidently these belong to a chime . . . . France

OVER CASE VII.

254. CAMEL BELLS. Brass. Arranged on a frame . . . . Egypt
An upright, rectangular frame of turned posts—68 cm. high, 38 cm. wide, and 37 cm. deep—carries a board—70 cm. high and 35 cm. wide—the top of which is of ornamental scroll work, inlaid with mother-of-pearl. The front is covered with sheet iron, fastened with large flat-headed iron nails. Against this, 24 brass bells, of flattened conical form, are hung. This formidable structure, placed vertically on the back of a camel, figures in public processions, especially in marriage trains.

The bells are 5.5 cm. wide, 8.5 to 7 cm. high, and 3 to 4 cm. thick.

255. Camel Bell. Copper . . . . Egypt
Height, 13.3 cm. Diameter at base, 6.5 cm.

256. Chinese Pavilion, (Fr. *Chapeau chinois*) . . . . Italy
A steel rod—47 cm. long—set in a wooden handle, and decorated with a brass ball near the top, carries a brass crescent—23 cm. long —and, just above, a bell 10 cm. in diameter and 6.5 cm. in height. Four very small bells hang from the crescent and three from the bell.

257. Chapeau chinois (Ger. *Schellenbaum*) . . . . Italy
A wooden handle, 152 cm. long, bears a brass rod on which are loosely fastened, so as to turn freely, a brass crescent, a piece of sheet brass in the form of a lyre, and a scalloped cone of the same metal. To the crescent 18 small brass bells, alternately conical and spherical in shape, are attached; to the lyre 14, and to the cone 16 similar bells are fastened. The cone, by its resemblance to a Chinese hat, is responsible for the French designation.

258. Kre-wain . . . . Siam and Burmah
Sixteen attuned gongs of brass alloy are arranged on a frame. The performer squats on the ground in the middle of this frame (which lies flat) and strikes the gongs with a mallet.
Pitches:—a flat'', g flat'', f'', e flat'', d'', d flat'', a', b flat', a flat', g flat', e', e flat', c flat', b flat', d flat', and e flat'.
Inner diameter of frame 54.5 cm.; outer 90.2 cm.; of gongs 6.2 to 4.7 cm. Depth of gongs, 6.5 cm.

259. Schellenbaum. Similar to No. 256 . . . . Germany
Length of rod, 58 cm. Other dimensions similar to No. 256.

260. Cowbell. Bronze. Sixteenth century . . . . Switzerland
The heart-shaped body is fashioned from thin bronze, and is supplied with an iron tongue. Two long iron buckles serve to adjust the broad leather strap about the neck of the animal.
Height, 35 cm. Width, 46 cm. Thickness, 30 cm.

The instruments in Cases II and III are full of suggestion. Memories of the worship of Cybele are invoked by the cymbals, whose lure is still potent in orgiastic music; in the modern orchestra the gong incites to action, inspires terror, or presages death; the castanet and triangle give the characteristic atmosphere of the dance under Southern skies, while the xylophone gives more reality to the "Dance of Death" than Holbein's illustrations; in short, in principle the modern treatment of these instruments lies along the same lines as their ancient uses.

CASE IV.

Class I. Sections B and C.

261. Gong, "Pompeian door-bell." Iron . . . . Ancient Italy
This reproduction was made from a genuine gong in the Naples Museum. The present plate was cast from one which was undoubtedly ancient. It was in so many fragments that it could not be hung, and no modern process could unite the parts. The iron frame is frankly modern.
The fragments of the original plate are placed on floor before No. 264.
Diameter of disc, 26 cm. Thickness, 4 mm.

262. Mo-kug-yo (Chin. *Mu-yü;** Anam. *Cai mo*) . . . . Japan
This rare specimen dates from the eleventh century. It was taken from an old Buddhist temple at Nara, and presented to Mr. Stearns by Senator Kanda, Governor of Hiogo. The body of this gong, or bell, is carved in conventional designs, and the handle represents two billing Ho-birds.
Length, 42 cm. Extreme height, 37 cm. Diameter, 35.5 cm. Length of slit, 57 cm.; width, 1.4 to 2.7 cm.

263. Dobachi. "The copper cup." Metal gong . . . . Japan
On the outer rim an inscription runs—"Dedicated on the third of this seventh month of Tempo (July, 1832), by Oka-i-uji, for the use of all his ancestors." The tone, produced by an upward, oblique stroke of a leather-padded stick, is of a beautiful quality and of remarkable duration. Although the *dobachi* generally rests on a cushion, placed on a low lacquered stand, it is occasionally suspended in a frame.
Height, 27 cm. Diameter at rim, 35.5 cm.

264. Kei, or Hokyo. Gong. Alloy . . . . Japan
The plate, cast in the form of a truncated half-lozenge, hangs in a frame of hard, polished wood, and is struck with a beater of hard wood. It is decorated on both sides with rosettes and representations of the Ho-Ho bird in low relief.
Length, 21.3 to 17 cm. Average width, 8.5 cm. Height of frame, 61 cm.

---

* The lidless eyes on the *mu yü* (fish) are symbolical of wakefulness. (Moule., p. 22.)

265. SHOKO. Gong. Some rare alloy . . . . Japan
This type was the first metal instrument introduced into Japan. Used in the *bugaku* orchestra with the *tsuri-daiko*. It consists of a flat, broad ring of metal, with a slightly convex surface, surmounted by the *kwa-yen*, or flame ornament.
Diameter of ring, 21.5 cm. Height of frame, 90 cm.

266. KYSE-ZEE. Metal gong . . . . Burmah
A flat, triangular plate, with the lower corners rounded, resembling the *kre-tsi* of Burmah—the Siamese *lan-kan*—is suspended in a frame of dark red wood, 46 cm. in height. The tone is of a rich flute-like quality, and the vibrations continue for 60 seconds. The pharisaical Buddhist instead of making long prayers "to be heard of men," draws attention to himself by striking this gong.
Length, 24 cm. Greatest width, 15.3 cm. Thickness, 1 cm.
Exhibited at the International Exhibition, Calcutta, 1884.

267. KEI, or HOKYO. Gong . . . . Japan
The plate, of alloy, is cast in a conventionalized leaf form. It bears traces of gilding and inscriptions in archaic characters. In form it resembles the Chinese *ko-ch'ing*, and is of great antiquity.
Height, 22.5 cm. Greatest width, 23 cm. Height of frame, 60 cm.

268. DRUM. Wood . . . . Upper Congo, Africa
The body—oval cross-section, and slightly swelling at the middle—is of a dark-red wood. In a ridge, running along the top, an incision 27 cm. long and 2.5 cm. wide is cut. On either side of this slit and opposite each other, two blocks, 5.3 cm. long, project, reducing the width of the slit at that point to 5 mm., and dividing the larger opening into two equal parts, through which the interior is hollowed out, forming a resonator. The projections are sufficiently elastic to vibrate with great rapidity when struck, and, being of different thickness, produce two tones of different pitch. This type of drum is used in the dance, and for signalling.
Length, 39 cm. Diameter at ends, 14.5 by 11 cm.

269. TEPONATZLI. Drum, or harmonicon, of wood. . . . . Ancient Mexico
The body of this facsimile of a pre-Columbian type consists of a slightly flattened cylinder of wood, decorated in conventional Aztec designs in low relief. In the top, a cut, resembling an elongated letter H, leaves two vibrating tongues, 18 cm. long, 1.5 cm. wide, and 8 mm. thick, with the free ends opposite each other.
Length, 50.5 cm. Diameter, 14 to 18 cm.

270. TEPONATZLI. Wood. Facsimile . . . . Ancient Mexico
The body, of stained wood, is of rectangular form, with carvings of cords and tassels on the sides. A grotesquely carved human head, resting on two hands, forms the termination of one end. The tone-producing media are two tongues, each 57 cm. long, and 6.4 cm. wide, running parallel to each other.
Length, 85 cm. Width, 18.5 cm. Height, 14.5 cm.

271-272. M'KUL, or NKU . . . . French Congo, Africa
In principle and means of tone-production these drums are identical with No. 268. The bodies are of light-colored wood in the form of a hollow cylinder, somewhat flattened, and are decorated with poker-work and rude carvings.
Length, of No. 271, 56.5 cm.; of No. 272, 64.5 cm. Diameter of No. 271, 27.5 by 22.5 cm.; of No. 272, 29 by 24.5 cm.
The *atupani*—signal-drums of the Ewe Tribe—are used in pairs, the *atupani-atsu*—masculine—and the *atupani-asi*—feminine.[1]
Nos. 268-271-272 are used by the natives in a species of telegraphy for which reason they are sometimes called "talking drums." Nos. 269-270 illustrate the same principle although they have a technical relationship to the harmonicon type.

The "talking drums"—the African negro's "wireless"—under the manipulation of an expert native, convey information with accuracy and inconceivable rapidity. A traveller, journeying from the Upper Congo to its mouth may be certain that his characteristics will be known to the natives along the entire course of the river in a few hours after he sets out, and he will be hampered or assisted according to the information given. If generous in his dealings, he will be cordially welcomed, if penurious in his bestowal of gifts his lot will be a hard one. Drums of the same type serve the Samoa islander as guides in thick weather, for each island has a drum of specific pitch.[2]

CLASS II. VIBRATING MEMBRANE, OR MEMBRANES, WITH RESONATOR.

Section A. Drums with One Vibrating Membrane (Head).

The three important constructive features of a drum are (1) the Barrel, (2) the Head, (3) the method of securing the tension of the Membrane, or Head. In the following descriptions the material of the barrel, and the kind of membrane used will be noted, but the devices through which tension is secured are so numerous that they cannot be given in connection with individual instruments. The following is a summary of these processes.

---

[1] Sachs, p. 22.

[2] Those who would know the wider significance of these early types are referred to the scholarly and illuminating article, "Music of Primitive Peoples," by Willy Pastor—*Zeitschrift für Ethnologie*, 1910, pp. 654-675, a translation of which is given in the Report of the Smithsonian Institution, 1912, pp. 678-700.

While not infrequently the skin, or head, is directly attached to the barrel by cement (Case V, No. 324), or some resinous gum (No. 276), it is generally fastened to a hoop. This is pressed down the barrel by the hands (No. 281), by wedges (No. 294), or by thongs which have previously been soaked in water (No. 239). In No. 303, the whole head was soaked in water. In some types of East Indian drums, the thongs are tightened by wooden rollers (Case V, No. 370). The method shown in No. 353 is always indicative of European influence. In primitive forms, withes of some sapling, or cords of vegetable fibre are employed (Case V, No. 343). The heads of all Chinese drums are fastened by rude wrought-iron nails (No. 297). Pegs are occasionally used (No. 310). Lumps of resinous gum are sometimes attached to the head for tuning purposes (No. 281). In noting the material used for the head, "hide" means an untanned skin. "Skin" indicates that the hide has been tanned. The terms "raw" and "rough," applied to parchment, refer to the relative fineness of the treatment it has undergone.

It must be noted that, as a rule, these methods are so persistent that most of them are definitive of type and source.

273. KETOBONG. Wood. Lizard-skin . . . . Borneo
The head is drawn taut over the upper end of the vase-shaped body by rattan braces attached to a hoop which is forced down the barrel by wedges. Tuned with a lump of resinous gum fastened to the head. This drum is used by priests and priestesses in the "noise treatment" of sickness. The barrel contains a rattan snare.
Length, 44 cm. Diameter at head, 13 cm.

274. ARPA. Wood. Lizard-skin . . . . New Guinea
Long cylindrical body of hard, dark-red wood expanding towards either end. In the middle section rises a handle, carved from the body. The head is held in place by a hoop wound with rattan. The *arpa* is held in the left hand, while the right strikes or rubs the head.
Length, 65 cm. Diameter of head, 13 cm.

275. ARPA. Same type and source as No. 274 but smaller.
Length, 42 cm. Diameter of head, 8.5 cm.

276. KABA. Slightly curved body of wood. Skin. . . . . New Guinea
Along one side of the cylindrical body runs a carved ridge in the middle of which a handle is cut. The surface is carved in low relief with the background filled in with lime. The head is of the skin of some aquatic bird, fastened to the body with cement.
Length, 27.5 cm. Diameter at head, 6 cm.

277. ARPA. Wood. Lizard-skin . . . . New Guinea
The handle represents an animal.
Length, 58.5 cm. Diameter of head, 13 cm.

278-9-80. DRUMS. Arpa type. Usual materials..........New Guinea
These drums display only minor variations in size and decoration from the preceding examples.

(B-S.)

281. ARPA. Wood. Snake-skin ....Fly River, New Guinea
The surface of this typical body is carved in geometrical patterns, with background colored in white and brown. The open end carries a large pendant tuft of black hair. The head is secured by a double band of rattan. Drums of this type are widely distributed.
Length, 105.3 cm. Diameter of head, 18 cm.

282. I NGOMBA. Wood. Rawhide ....Lower Guinea
The body is of stained wood, slightly swelling in the middle section, and, from a point 30 cm. from one end gradually decreasing in diameter. Two heads of thin rawhide—the larger 15 cm. and the smaller 8.5 cm. in diameter—are drawn taut by twisted thongs (also of rawhide) which run through holes in the edge of the heads. It is probable that the smaller head is not struck but forms the end of the drum.
Length, 157.8 cm. Greatest diameter, 17 cm.

283. TAM-TAM. Wood. Rawhide........Bolobo, Congo River, Africa
Over one end of a jar-shaped body of wood the head is drawn taut by rawhide thongs knotted together and drawn under the smaller end. It is carried under the left arm and beaten with the palm of the right hand.
Height, 50.8 cm. Diameter, 7 to 19.2 cm.
This very primitive drum is suggestive of either the *bate* or *fanke*, both of Sierra Leone; it has the wooden body of the one, and the tension of the other.

284. DRUM. Wood. Parchment ....Sierra Leone, Africa
This is an evolution from No. 283. By extending and elaborating the waist—the section between the pedestal and body of the drum—many unique variants are formed. A widely distributed form, found in Africa and among nearly all primitive peoples.
Height, 45 cm. Diameter at head, 18 cm.

285. DRUM. Gourd. Parchment ....Uganda, Africa
The kettle-shaped body is elaborately decorated with incised lines. The head is secured by numerous gut cords fastened to wooden pegs, and also wound about the body. This is a typical form.
Depth, 25.6 cm. Diameter, 26.5 cm.

286. DRUM. Gourd. Parchment . . . . Uschachi, Africa
Over the larger end of the funnel-shaped body the head is fastened by a cord of twisted rawhide, from which hang long narrow strips of the same material.
Length, 26 cm. Diameter, 4 to 17 cm.

287. DRUM. Gourd, decorated with cowrie-shells. Parchment. . . Africa
The long, conical body is decorated with four longitudinal rows of cowrie-shells, two of which are fastened to a strap, which, running over the head, forms a handle.
Length, 42.5 cm. Diameter, 6.7 to 13.7 cm.

288. DRUM. Section of elephant tusk. Zebra-hide . . . . . . Soudan, Africa
Decorated with rows of cowrie-shells and glass beads.
Length, 23 cm. Diameter, 12 by 14 cm.

289. DRUM. Section of cow's-horn. Parchment . . . . Soudan, Africa
Length, 15 cm. Diameter, 4 to 8 cm.

290. DRUM. Calabash shell. Parchment . . . . Soudan, Africa
The shallow bowl-shaped body is decorated with burnt lines, and carries a cord of braided leather. The parchment head is stretched over iron pegs, and is decorated with emblematic figures in colors.
Depth, 14.5 cm. Diameter of head, 25.5 by 29 cm.

291. DRUM. Calabash shell. Parchment . . . . Soudan, Africa
Similar to the preceding, but with plain head.
Depth, 11.5 cm. Diameter of head, 12.5 by 18.5 cm.

292. ARPA. Wood. Lizard, or fish-skin . . . . New Guinea
The long body, stained black, is constricted at the middle and terminates in a representation of the open jaws of the Orca, or "whale-killer." The head is fastened by cords and a resinous gum, lumps of which are affixed to the head.
Length, 95 cm. Diameter of head, 17.5 cm.

293. DRUM. Wood. Parchment . . . . New Caledonia
The body, stained black, is in the form of an elongated goblet, and is decorated with five bands of red paint. The head is fastened by closely placed braces of leather, passing under a hoop of twisted rattan at the base of the bowl. It is practically identical with the Burmese *ozee*.
Length, 88.5 cm. Diameter of head, 21 cm.

294. DRUM. Section of bamboo. Parchment . . . . Java
The head, attached by narrow bands of bamboo to a hoop of the same material, is tightened by wedges.
Length, 68 cm. Diameter, 12 cm.

295. ARPA. Wood. Lizard-skin .... New Guinea
The long body bears a handle at the middle, and is decorated with carved bands. The open end is a representation of the open jaws of a crocodile. It resembles the *warup* of the West Torres Straits so closely that it might be so designated.[3]
Length, 76 cm. Diameter at head, 14.8 cm.

In Africa the drum is regnant and exhibits not only many types, but also a great number of variants, for each native is his own drum-maker. Such variants are products of primitive industry in all quarters of the globe. Specimens of such may be seen in Nos. 284 and 292. Many of these drums are wonderfully decorated. In the Völkerkunde Museum, Berlin, are drums the construction of which must have engaged at least two generations.

296. PA-IPU, or HOKEO. Gourd .... Hawaii
Two gourds of unequal size are so fastened together as to form a constriction at the middle. Made to sound by dropping on the ground.
Lengths of gourds, 23.5 and 35 cm. Diameters, 26.2 and 30 cm.

297. KOU. Wood. Hogskin .... China
The body, of light-colored wood, is in the shape of a deep bowl, with a dome-like top in which is a circular opening, 11 cm. in diameter. The entire top is covered with hogskin fastened by flat-headed iron nails. Two bands of twisted rattan pass around the body.
Kou is the Chinese generic name for drum.
Height, 26.5 cm. Greatest diameter, 30 cm.
(B-S.)

298. DRUM. Pottery. Parchment .... Source unknown
Height, 27 cm. Diameter of body, 13 cm.; of head, 10 cm.

299. PANG KOU. Wood. Hogskin .... China
The round body, in the form of a shallow inverted basin, is made from sections of hard wood, held together by an iron band. The inside surface slopes to the middle leaving on opening 4 cm. in diameter. To the outer surface a head is fastened by iron nails.
Depth, 7.9 cm. Diameter, 19.4 cm.

300. PANG KOU. A replica of No. 299 .... China

301. PANG KOU, or MAN T'OU KOU (Loaf drum) .... China
Wood. Hogskin. Similar in structure and size to the preceding, but mounted on a tripod. A *pan* (Case III. No. 215) is attached to the tripod and played at the same time.
Height of tripod, 71 cm.

[3] A. C. Haddon, "Ethn. of Western Tribes of Torres Straits," p. 375.

302. PUNIU. Gourd. Skin of the Kala-fish . . . . Hawaii
The bowl-shaped body bears a head tightened by cords of flax running to a cloth-covered hoop at the base. A tassel of twisted cords hangs from this hoop. The *puniu* is beaten with a flexible whip made from twisted *hau-hala* cords. Used in the *hula-hula* dance.
Depth, 12 cm. Diameter of head, 14 cm.

303. GA-NO-GO-O.[4] Water-drum. Wood. Hide. Seneca Indians, New York
The lower part of a paint keg serves as a body. To secure the proper tension, the head, which is of a dark, thick and flexible leather, is soaked in water and drawn taut by a tightly fitting hoop of wood, covered with cloth. The size of the resonance cavity is regulated by pouring water into the barrel through a small hole, which is afterwards stopped with a plug. This drum figures in the social and religious activities of many American Indian tribes, but its vogue is not restricted to this side of the ocean.
Depth of body, 8.5 cm. Diameter of head, 24 cm.
(M. R. Harrington.)
The Crosby Brown Collection (Metropolitan Museum of Art, New York) has a fine display of Indian instruments.

304. CAI TRONG BOC. Wood. Parchment . . . . Anam
The body—inverted basin type—is lacquered black, with a gilded band of metal at the bottom. The head bears the symbol of Eternity, in red, against a circular green background.
Diameter, 17.3 to 13 cm. Depth, 7.4 cm.

305. KOU. Wood. Hogskin . . . . China
A round hollow body of wood 15 cm. in length maintains the diameter of the upper end (15 cm.) to a point 11 cm. below, when it slopes inward to a diameter of 8 cm. with an opening 6.5 cm. wide. The upper section, which bears the head, is painted red, and the lower blue.

306-307. TABLA ARRAKEB . . . . Arabia
The bodies of these kettle-drums are of copper, and the heads of parchment.
Depth, 7 cm. Diameter of heads, 12.6 cm.

308. NAQQAREH. Slate. Rawhide . . . . Africa
The drum shown—a shallow bowl of slate, with head—is one of a pair, connected by a short bar (3 cm.) of the same material, which bore the carved figure of an alligator. The handle and one drum are missing.
Diameter, 9.5 cm. Depth, 4 cm.

---

[4] Morris, p. 141.

309. NAQQAREH, or TABL . . . . Egypt

This hand-drum has a body of terra cotta, with head of translucent membrane, secured by flaxen cords.

Depth, 9 cm. Diameter, 13 cm.

310. TABLA EL-DARAUSHA. Metal. Parchment . . . . Egypt

The body, in the shape of a flattened bell, bears a head held in place by heavy spikes projecting from the edge of the body. It is held in the left hand and beaten with a leather strap. It is used during *Ramadan* to waken the sleepers (at 2:00 A. M.) that they may eat.

Depth, 12 cm. Diameter, 17 cm.

The *tabla el-musaher* is similar, and is beaten with a stick by the reciter *musaher*—who, during *Ramadan*, nightly recites before the houses of the wealthy.

311. NAGARA. Pottery. Parchment . . . . India

The deep bowl-shaped body is of black pottery, to which a head is fastened by a hoop, from which run cotton braces to a heavy hempen band at the base. The head is weighted with a circular patch of resinous gum, placed somewhat to the side of the center.

Depth, 20 cm. Diameter of head, 22 cm.

312. THONG. Lacquered earthenware. Snake-skin . . . . Anam

The body resembles a long-necked and very slender vase, with head at the upper end. The head is fastened by strips of leather running from the hoop to a pad of the same material at the bottom, and the tension is secured by three bands of cloth—white, red, and green—which are drawn tightly around the strips.

Length, 34.5 cm. Diameter of head, 9 cm.

313. TIKARA. Pottery. Parchment . . . . India

Practically identical with No. 311, excepting that the color of the pottery is red and the tension secured by rings.

Depth, 18 cm. Diameter of head, 22 cm.

Pottery is frequently used as material for the barrels of Oriental drums. As this substance is non-vibratory this practice has little to commend it.

314. KETTLE-DRUM. Copper. Parchment . . . . France

This small drum has the typical body of the kettle-drum, and the head is fastened by hand-screws.

Depth, 17.2 cm. Diameter of head, 19.5 cm.

314A. KETTLE-DRUMS. Copper. Parchment . . . . .United States

The cauldron-shaped bodies are mounted on iron standards on which they turn freely, thus operating an inside mechanism by means of which they are tuned, by increasing or decreasing the tension of the heads. This is generally done by hand-screws placed at intervals around the upper circumference of the body.

Height of larger (F to c) drum, 42.9 cm.; of smaller (B flat to f), 36.9 cm. Diameters, 37.9 cm.; and 32.9 cm.

(University Musical Society.)

The Kettle-drum (Fr. *Timbale;* Ital. *Timpano;* Ger. *Pauke*) is the most artistic member of the drum family. Formerly a pair sufficed, but three, and even more, drums, with freer tunings and frequent extensions of the former normal compass, are now used. The necessity for rapid changes of pitch in modern scores has also led to the introduction of mechanically tuned drums. First constructed by Pfundt of Leipzig (1806-1871), they have been greatly improved by Vocka, of Dresden, who is now the leading maker. By the use of light metal tubing, and hollow mechanical parts, the former excessive weight has been reduced to a minimum. The tuning mechanism is operated by a foot pedal, and the pitches are registered on a scale.

The mediaeval designation "Naker" (Kettle-drum), is a corruption of the Arabic *nacareh, or noqqaryeh,* from which the modern name "Naqqareh" for Turkish, Syrian and Arabian drums of this type is derived. *Nacaire, naguarre* (old Fr.); *nacara* (old Span.) and *nagara* (Beng.) have the same origin, while *taballo* (Ital.); *atabal* (Span.); *atabor* (Prov.); *tabla* (E. Ind.), and the African *a-tabule,* are drawn from the Arabic *tabl* (pl. *atbal*).[5]

---

[5] Sachs, pp. 266, 268, 267, 372, 21, 22, 372, 22, 372.

CASE V.

CLASS II. Section A.

315. KETTLE-DRUM. Wood. Antelope-skin .... Sierra Leone
The body is stained black and carries two rawhide handles at rim. The head is secured by rawhide braces which run to a ring, under which wedges are driven to increase the tension. The heads of the two drum-sticks are of wood covered with rawhide, while the flexible handles are made of twisted thongs.
Depth, 30 cm. Diameter of head, 46 cm.

316. NAQQAREH. Hammered copper. Antelope-hide........... Egypt
The head of this kettle-drum is secured to the upper rim of the body by heavy copper spikes set closely together and by interlacing rawhide thongs running to a ring at the base. Beaten with wooden drumsticks—*ḳa'ddabah*. A pair of such drums is hung over the backs of camels and used in religious and festal processions.
Depth, 31 cm. Diameter of head, 45 cm.

317. DAMAMA. Coarse terra-cotta. Parchment................ India
The semi-conical body bears one head secured by rawhide braces, and at one side a leather loop serves as a handle.
This drum, said to have been a favorite of the Mogul Akbar (1542-1605), and to date from the Moslum immigration, is used in the *nahabat*, or marriage festivities.
Depth, 40 cm. Diameter of head, 36 cm.

318. NAQQAREH. Brass. Antelope-hide .... Egypt
The base of the broad, shallow body—with greatest diameter in the middle section—is covered with elaborate arabesques and Arabic inscriptions. Thong tension.
Depth, 21 cm. Diameter at middle, 54 cm.; at head, 46 cm.

319. KETTLE-DRUM. Red palm-wood. Antelope-hide... Uganda, Africa
The deep, bowl-shaped body carries two heads, the larger of which is beaten with two sticks, while the smaller serves as the bottom of the drum. Closely placed cords of twisted rawhide, running from head to head, secure the proper tension.
Depth, 38.5 cm. Diameter of larger head, 41 cm.; of smaller, 19 cm.

320. TABL SHAMEE. Wood. Antelope-skin .... Egypt
This unusually large specimen of its type has a shallow basin-shaped body, stained black. The head is secured by wooden spikes. To an iron ring, at the rim, a strap may be fastened.
Depth, 15.2 cm. Diameter of head, 38.2 cm.

321. GENDANG REBANA. Wood. Thick parchment. . . . . Celebes
The body is of the same general shape as the preceding, but the wood is of light color. In the base is a semicircular opening 28 cm. in diameter. Tension is secured by two narrow strips of rattan which are led through holes in the head, and in a narrow notched ridge, running parallel with the rim at a distance of 2 cm. These strips are further tightened by a rattan strip running midway between the rim and ridge and knotted around each group.
Depth, 10.4 cm. Diameter of head, 43 cm.
(B-S.)

322. DEN-DEN-DAIKO. "Fan drum." White monkey-skin, on hoop. Japan
To the hoop—26.6 cm. in diameter—a wooden handle—17.9 cm. long—is securely fastened. The drum emits a very clear and incisive note. The *aelyau* of Greenland is similar, but is made of whalebone and bladder, and is struck on the rim.

323. TABL SHAMEE. Terra-cotta. Antelope-skin (raw) . . . . Algeria
The head is drawn over the basin-shaped body by flat braces. On one side is a broad strap of leopard-skin (with hair on the lower side) by which the drum is suspended from the neck. Opposite this strap is a broad fringe of leather thongs, each bearing a cowrie shell.
Depth, 16 cm. Diameter of head, 28 cm.

324. OZEE. Wood, lacquered. Parchment . . . . Burmah
Over the top of the goblet-shaped body, decorated in black and red lacquer, the painted head is drawn taut by leather braces passing under a wire hoop at the base of the bowl.
Height, 35 cm. Diameter of head, 17.7 cm.

325. DARABOUKKEH. Earthenware. Parchment . . . . Egypt
The funnel-shaped body of this toy bears a head secured by cement.
Length, 15.3 cm. Diameter of head, 14.2 cm.
This drum is held under the left arm, and tapped and rubbed by the fingers of the right hand. This form of drum, in larger sizes, is used by the Nile boatmen and in places of amusement.

326. DARABOUKKEH. Earthenware, decorated. Parchment. . . . . . Egypt
In every particular similar to the preceding, but larger, and decorated in colors with minature representations of musicians of ancient Egypt, copied from paintings in the tombs.
Depth, 45 cm. Diameter of head, 33 cm.

327. THONE. Daraboukkeh type . . . . Siam
Body of earthenware stained black, head of fish-skin. Strap tension.
Depth, 20.5 cm. Diameter of head, 12 cm.

328-9-330-1-2. DARABOUKKEHS from Morocco, Tunis, Egypt, Algeria, and Syria, which, in essentials identical, illustrate the vogue of the type. The body of No. 328 is of terra-cotta, of 329 of earthenware, those of 330 and 331 of wood beautifully inlaid, while that of No. 332 is of etched brass. The heads are all of parchment, with the exception of that of No. 330 which is of the skin of the Bayard-fish.
The depths run from 21 to 43 cm; the head-diameters from 16 to 22.5 cm.

333. THONE. Terra-cotta, inlaid with mirror-glass. Parchment....Siam
This very beautiful drum carries a painted head.
Depth, 37 cm. Diameter of body, 25 cm.; of head, 18 cm.

334. DONBEK. Wood, ivory inlay. Parchment...............Persia
In addition to the ivory the inlay includes bits of metal, stone and wood, set in geometric patterns. The head is secured by cement. This specimen is said to have been made at Shiraz about 1800. The sides of the upper part are perpendicular instead of curved.
Height, 30.5 cm. Diameter of head, 21 cm.

335. DARABOUKKEH. Pottery. Parchment ....Algeria
The gracefully modeled body is inlaid with arabesques of mother-of-pearl and ivory, outlined with lead wire. A string of small globular brass bells runs under the semi-transparent head. They serve the same purpose as the "jingles" of the tambourine.
Height, 36 cm. Diameter of head, 18 cm.

336. DARABOUKKEH. Olive wood, inlaid. Parchment..........Persia
The inlay, of mother-of-pearl, is in a stem and leaf design.
Height, 30.5 cm. Diameter of head, 21 cm.

337. TOMBAH. Dumb-bell type. Wood. Parchment..Sierra Leone, Africa
The heads are braced by cords of twisted rawhide. It bears a shoulder band of red cotton cloth. The *a-tabule* and *fanke* are drums of the same type and habitat, the *kalangu* being its representative in the Haussa Tribe.
Length, 45 cm. Diameter at head, 17 cm.; at middle, 7 cm.

338. TOMBAH. Wood. Soft, white leather........Sierra Leone, Africa
In this drum the heads are looped to hoops of bent withes braced together with hempen cord. Otherwise similar to the preceding.
Length, 31 cm. Diameter at heads, 12.5 cm.; at middle, 7.5 cm.
Nos. 337 and 338 are held under the left arm, and increasing the tension, by pressing the cords running longitudinally, changes the pitch of the drum.

339. DRUM. Wood. Raw parchment ....Malaysia
The conical body carries two heads with hoop and brace tension.
Length, 30 cm. Diameter, 6.5 to 12.5 cm.

340. DRUM. Dumb-bell type. Wood, decorated with bones. Parchment . . . . Dahomey, West Africa
In addition to the bones (which are not human) the body is grotesquely decorated with feathers and emblematic designs in colors. The heads are also rudely decorated. Hoop and strap tension.
Length, 58 cm. Diameter at heads, 26 cm.; at waist, 14 cm.

341. SIDE DRUM. Wood. Raw skin . . . . West Central Africa
Two heads are braced on the cylindrical body by cords running to thick hoops of some vine. A slender strip of the same vine is wound 13 times about the body. Snares of cord are stretched over one head.
Length, 18 cm. Diameter of heads, 31 cm.

342. DRUM. Wood. Raw parchment . . . Benin-Hinterland, West Africa
Quite like a modern drum in shape, but smaller. It serves in Soudanese railway stations as a signal.
Length, 24 cm. Diameter, 15 cm.

343. DRUM. Cocoa palm. Raw skin . . . . Soudan, Africa
The body is bucket-shaped and the heads are braced by rawhide thongs.
Length, 24 cm. Diameter of heads, 15 and 20 cm.

344. DRUM. Similar in material and source to No. 343.
Length, 28 cm. Diameter of heads, 14 and 19 cm.
The barrel contains some hard substance, and by shaking this drum it may be used as a rattle. This is a common constructive procedure among primitive peoples. The resemblance of these drums to such a North American Indian type as the *pur-pi-shuk-pi-po-ya* of the Hopi Tribe (Morris, p. 147, No. 630) is obvious and is one of the perplexing coincidences which are constantly met with in identification.

345. SIDE DRUM. Wood. Raw skin . . . . North Central Africa
The body is of the European type. The heads are tightened by cords so knotted together as to resemble the European method of tension.
Height, 24 cm. Diameter of heads, 20 cm.

346. TABL BALADI. Wood. Hide . . . . Egypt
The body is cylindrical, and the heads are secured by hoop and thong tension. One head is struck with a padded drum-stick and the other with a thin rod which touches the entire surface.
Length, 25 cm. Diameter of heads, 25 cm.

347. JINDAIKO. Wood. Parchment . . . . Japan
The short body is decorated with inlaid colored beads, in the middle by a band of brocade, and two long tassels.
Height, 16.3 cm. Diameter, 16.6 cm.

348. CAI TRONG CAI (*cai*—large). Wood. Hogskin...........Anam
The heads are fastened to the barrel-shaped body by round-headed copper nails. A narrow band of braided straw encircles the body at each end, running just inside the rows of nails.
Length, 41.5 cm. Diameter at heads, 33.7 cm.; at middle, 42 cm.

349. TSURI-DAIKO. Wood. Parchment ....Japan
The heads are fastened to the body (a very shallow cylinder) by close rows of round-headed nails. The body and heads are elaborately decorated with representations of the three-clawed dragon. The *tsuri-daiko* is generally suspended in an ornate frame of lacquered wood and is beaten with a pair of leather padded sticks. This example is a trifle smaller than the usual "hanging drum."
Depth, 9.5 cm. Diameter of heads, 33 cm.

350. TSURI-DAIKO. Brass, lacquered. Parchment ....Japan
Similar to No. 349 but with heads of greater diameter, viz., 43 cm.

351. DAIBYOSHI. Lacquered wood. Parchment ....Japan
The heavy heads are fastened to the body by cords which run through twelve holes in the rim to braces attached to hoops. The lacquer-work is very beautiful. It is called the "grand time-beater" from its function in the *kagura* orchestra. *O-Kakko* is an alternative designation. When in use it is borne in a small stand, the whole height being 68 cm.
Length, 50.1 cm. Diameter of heads, 46 cm.; of body, 30.5 cm.

352. JORAGHAI, or YORAGHAI. Wood. Skin ....India
A small *dhol* is fastened to the larger drum, which hangs from the neck by a rawhide cord. The larger drum is beaten with a stick, the smaller with the hand. The tension of the larger drum is secured by hoops and leather thongs. The thin parchment head of the smaller drum is cemented on and the entire body is enveloped in loose parchment.
Length of larger drum, 50.5 cm.; of smaller, 46 cm. Diameter of heads, 18 and 28 cm.

353. DRUM. Wood. Parchment ....Caffaria, South Africa
The heads are secured to the barrel-shaped body of wood by narrow strips of rattan which are fastened with small nails.
Height, 25.5 cm. Diameter at heads, 16.7 cm.
This drum has wandered far from the home of its type—India.

354. DHOLAKA. Wood. Parchment ....India
The heads are fastened to hoops around which run cord braces which are tightened by means of sliding iron rings.
Length, 49 cm. Diameter at heads, 21 cm.

PLATE IV.

CASE V. NOS. 316 TO 365 (RIGHT TO LEFT)

355. GENDANG PRANG. Wood. Parchment............West Borneo
The grotesquely painted heads of this war-drum are fastened by strips of rattan running from the hoop in zig-zag lines along the body, aided by two cords. It is carried by a cord of twisted rawhide.
Length, 42 cm. Diameter of heads, 22 cm.; at middle section, 32 cm.

356. KOU. Wood. Hogskin ....China
The body is painted red, and to it the heads are fastened with iron nails. Iron ring for hanging.
Depth, 16.5 cm. Diameter of heads, 27.4 cm.

357. CAI BOM. Wood, covered with thongs..................Anam
The barrel-shaped body is completely covered with rawhide thongs, which tighten the heads. These are weighted with a circular patch of some compound into which rice enters. A rawhide handle rises from one side.
Length, 46 cm. Diameter at heads, 24 cm.; at the middle, 34 cm.

358. KOU. Wood. Hogskin ....China
A spiral wire spring serves as a snare.
Depth, 8.2 cm. Diameter of heads, 28 cm.
(B-S.)

359. KOU. In this duplicate of No. 358, one head has been removed to display the snare ....China
(B-S.)

360. TSURI-DAIKO. Metal body and head..................Japan
The frame (of wood) is entirely covered with choice Cloisonné and surmounted by the *Kwa-yen*, or "flame ornament." The drum rests on a carved and gilded block, representing the waves of the sea. The whole symbolizes "Dai Nippon," "great Japan"—the "Land of the Rising Sun." This type is used in their temple worship. Five years were spent by the artist in the production of this remarkable example of Japanese art.
The head is struck in the exact center by two sticks with leather-covered knobs. The right, or "male stick," is called *obachi;* the left, or "female stick," *mebachi.* When not in use the sticks are placed in rings on the side of the frame (Piggott, p. 192).
Depth of drum, 28 cm. Diameter of heads, 48 cm. Height of frame, 216 cm.

361. BUDBUDIKI. Wood. Parchment ....India
The body, of hour-glass form, is decorated in colors, and the heads are fastened by gut cords. Beaten by balls which, attached to cords, strike the heads when the drum is swung. This is an important asset of the snake-charmer, and juggler. This specimen was brought from its home by the Russian painter, Vereshchagin.
Depth, 9.6 cm. Diameter of heads, 12.7 cm.

362. DAMARU. Two children's skulls. Human skin . . . . Thibet
This gruesome specimen comes from a Buddhist monastery. The heads are painted green. A long strap of vari-colored strips of cloth, ending with tassels, hangs from the point where the two skulls join. This drum is used in the Lamaistic ritual.
Greatest diameter of skulls and heads, 12.5 and 16.5 cm.

363. HURUK. Wood. Parchment . . . . India
With the exception of the hoops, which are of greater diameter than the body, it resembles No. 361.
Depth, 15.5 cm. Diameter of heads, 21 cm.; of body, 14.7 cm.

364. DHOLA. Wood. Raw parchment . . . . India
The staves forming the body are held together by two hoops of twisted rattan. The heads are drawn over the ends of the body and braced with hempen cords. Two wooden drumsticks are used.
Length, 40.5 cm. Diameter of head, 23 cm.

365. DHOLAKA. Similar to No. 354 . . . . India
Length, 40.7 cm. Diameter at heads, 18.5 cm.

366. DHOL. Wood. Parchment . . . . India
The heads are drawn over projecting hoops; otherwise it is typical.
Length, 36 cm. Diameter of heads, 27.5 cm.; of body, 20 cm.

367. DHOLAKA. Similar to No. 354 . . . . India
Length, 41.6 cm. Diameter of heads, 18.2 cm.

368. TAMBOUR. Wood. Parchment . . . . Tunis, West Africa
The body is covered with parchment decorated with a band of gilt running zig-zag. The heads bear a narrow band of red around the rim and figures of men and animals on the face.
Depth, 8.3 cm. Diameter of heads, 30.4 cm.

369. KO-TSUZUMI, or OTO-TSUZUMI. The "younger" or "shoulder" drum. Dumb-bell type. Wood. Parchment . . . . Japan
The body is elaborately lacquered in black and gold. The heads, fastened to hoops extending beyond the body and decorated with black enamel, are braced by red cords running through six holes at the rims. Used in the dance and in the orchestra, in each emphasizing the rhythm. It is held over the right shoulder by the left hand and beaten with the fingers of the right. The *tsuzumi* and *taiko* (or *daiko*) are differentiated through the method of fastening the head; the former with cords, the latter with nails.
Length, 26 cm. Diameter of body at head, 10 cm.; of head, 20 cm.

370. MRIDANGA. Turned wood. Parchment . . . . India
The body, slightly enlarging at the center, bears two heads of unequal size, held in place by hoops and flat braces of raw hide. The tension is so regulated, by wooden rollers under the straps, that the two heads are a fourth or fifth apart in pitch. The smaller head is weighted by a circular patch of some composition. The larger head is beaten with the left hand, the smaller with the palm, finger tips and wrist of the right. As its invention is ascribed to Brahma, it is commonly used to accompany dignified singing, or the *vina*.
Length, 53.5 cm. Diameter of heads, 16 cm. and 18 cm.

371. TABLA. Turned wood. Parchment . . . . India
The nearly cylindrical body suddenly contracts at the base. Braced like the *mridanga*.
Length, 25 cm. Diameter of head, 18 cm.

372. CAI TRONG CAI. A replica of No. 348. . . . . Anam

373. TSURI-DAIKO. Wood, lacquered. Parchment. . . . . Japan
The barrel-shaped body bears elaborate decorations in black and gold. On the center of heads appears the symbol *mitsuto-moye*, surrounded by rays symbolizing the dawn, both in gold against a black background. Ring for hanging.
Depth, 19 cm. Diameter of heads, 31.5 cm.

374. DRUM. Wood. Parchment . . . . Anam
The shallow cylindrical body with slightly convex sides is lacquered red and black. In the center of the head appears the symbol of the source of existence. It has an iron ring by which it may be hung. It may also be placed on the tripod which, for physical reasons, is placed under No. 318. No available data on Anamese instruments suggests the name of this drum. *Toung-yah*, sometimes used, appears to have no justification.
Depth, 18 cm. Diameter of heads, 43 cm.

375. CAI TRONG COM. Wood. Rawhide . . . . Anam
The cylindrical body is lacquered red and the weighted heads are braced by thongs of rawhide.
Length, 53.3 cm. Diameter of heads, 19 cm.

376. UTA-DAIKO, or SHIMEE-DAIKO. Wood. Parchment. . . . . Japan
The shallow cylindrical body bears black and gold lacquer. The gilded heads are bound to projecting hoops and braced with orange-red cord. It is supported on a low frame of wood, lacquered black, and is beaten with two beveled drumsticks of hard wood. Used in the *geisha* dances. Structurally it is a species of *tsuzumi*.
Depth, 14.5 cm. Diameter of heads, 34.5 cm.; of body, 25 cm.

377. KO-TSUZUMI. A replica of No. 369 .... Japan

378. MRIDANGA. Similar to No. 370 .... India

379. PAKHBAG, or PAKHABAGA. Wood. Parchment .... India
The slightly conical body bears two heads with the method of tension displayed in the *mridanga*.
Length, 50 cm. Diameter of heads, 20.4 and 35 cm.

The beautifully carved and decorated standard in the middle of the Case was purchased by Mr. Stearns at the Paris Exhibition of 1900 in order that he might secure No. 375.

Other instruments included in this purchase are distributed according to their classifications. See Nos. 304-312 (Case IV) No. 987 (Case IX) and Nos. 1212-1214-1251-1252 and 1253 (Case XII). Nos. 374 and 375 hang in their original positions.

380. KAKKO. Wood, lacquered. Monkey-skin .... Japan
The heavy body, lacquered black, bears two heads of monkey-skin coated with white pigment and drawn over widely projecting hoops. The heads are braced by thongs of black leather running through eight metal eyelets set in short straps of leather. The *kakko* rests on a low stand, lacquered in black and gold, and is beaten with slightly knobbed sticks.
Length, 32.2 cm. Diameter of heads, 25 cm.; of body, 14 cm.

381. E-TSUZUMI. The "elder" or side drum. Wood. Parchment.. Japan
Similar to No. 377, but lacquered in bands of red and black separated by lines of gold.
Length, 29.5 cm. Diameter of heads, 17.5 cm.; of body, 11.5 cm.

382. SHU-KOU, or SHU-KU. Wood. Parchment .... China
In form closely resembling the *den-den-daiko*, it differs in that it has two heads, which are nailed on.
Depth, 6.5 cm. Length, with handle, 43 cm. Diameter, 22 cm.

382A. RATTLE DRUM. Wood. Rawhide .... Malaysia
In principle this has much in common with the preceding, as well as with No. 344. The keystone-shaped body carries two heads secured by rawhide thongs which are tightened by bamboo wedges. The heads are crudely decorated after the manner of No. 355. It has an elaborately carved wooden handle, the carvings representing four human heads, turned in opposite directions, and a conventionalized elephant's head surrounded with an intricate scroll design. The carving is polished and partially picked out with lime.
Length, 63 cm.; of body, 29 cm. Greatest width, 21 cm. Depth, 14 cm.

383. TAIKO (generic name for drum). Wood. Parchment.......Japan
Heads secured by closely placed, round-headed nails. Iron ring for hanging.
Length, 20 cm. Diameter at heads, 10 cm.; at middle, 15 cm.

384. DRUM. Wood, with braided straw. Parchment....Source unknown
The edges of the heads are drawn over the body and cut into many semi-triangular strips with blunted ends. Through these run braces of fine hempen cord, which, after being knotted together, run in a double line around the body. The drum is exceedingly light.
Length, 27.5 cm. Diameter at heads, 42 cm.

385. LANDKNECHTS-TROMMEL. Wood. Parchment.......Switzerland
The long cylindrical body of this drum, which probably is of the seventeenth century, is painted in colors and bears three coats of arms. The hoops are unusually wide and are decorated with two rows of triangular designs in dark red and green, displayed against a background of deep orange. Cord tension.
Length, 72 cm. Diameter, 37.7 cm.

386. TAMBOURIN DE PROVENCE. Wood. Dogskin ....France
This drum, of the eighteenth century, is a fine example of the type known in England as the *Tabor*. The body, a long cylinder, is carved in vertical lines in low relief. The heads, fastened to round hoops, are braced by cords. The drum, suspended from the left arm, is beaten with a stick by the right hand, while the left manipulates the finger holes of the *galoubet* (*churula*), or pipe. Thus we have the "pipe and tabor" so constantly referred to in early literature.
Length, 79 cm. Diameter of heads, 38 cm.
Used with the "Galoubet"—No. 493 (Case VI).

387. SIDE DRUM. Wood. Parchment ....Holland
The barrel bears a coat of arms, and the inscription—"Haarlem 1572." The heads are fastened in the modern manner, and snares, tightened by a thumb-screw, run across the lower head.
Length, 33 cm. Diameter of heads, 38 cm.

388. TAMBOUR. Side-drum. Brass. Parchment. Modern.......France
In every particular representative of the drum of the middle decades of the nineteenth century.
Length, 39 cm. Diameter of heads, 32 cm.

388A. SIDE DRUM. Brass. Parchment .... United States
This drum was used by the donor (Mr. Irving K. Pond) in the first University orchestra. This organization included Mr. W. H. Murphy, Mr. Frederick K. Stearns, and other prominent Alumni. Besides the special interest accruing from the above facts, it is a splendid illustration of the evolution of the drum, and represents the penultimate stage.

Depth, 19.5 cm. Diameter of heads, 40.5 cm.

A comparison of these military drums will show the principle displayed in the evolution of this type. The barrel has been shortened until frequently it is a mere rim, while the diameter of the head has steadily been increased.

388B. BASS DRUM. Wood. Parchment .... United States
(University Musical Society.)

This is an example of the modern type, in which the exaggerated diameter, found in drums *circa* 1860, has been done away with.

Length, 35.4 cm. Diameter of heads, 72.3 cm.

The ethnological and sociological implications of drums are of great interest, and an appreciation of the relations they sustain to individual and communal life will lead one to view a collection of primitive instruments of this type with a feeling far removed from mere curiosity.

In an African village, the birth of a child is heralded by the beating of drums; the youth is lured to the performing fakir in the village square by the same rhythmical note; the oarsmen in their canoe races are stimulated by the hubbub of violently beaten drums; the hunters' departure and return are alike occasions for the display of the noise-producing power of drums; drums take the place of the organ in their wedding ceremonies; and, when summoned before a tribunal, the agonized cries of the victim under the inevitable torture are stifled by the strident tones of the drum, to the beat of which he is carried to his grave. Livingstone relates that scores of children in the slave caravans die of *nostalgia*, for, as they listen to the beat of drums in the villages they skirt, they are overcome by memories of happy days forever passed.

In Aztec Mexico the hollow roll of the drum *huehuetl* at midnight heralded a human sacrifice at sunrise, and no one knew who would die under the sacrificial knife. In Abysinnia the early Christians were called to the church by a drum, which, after functioning as a bell, was removed to the chancel and covered with a cloth, when it served as the altar. In Jamaica the convicts who were employed by the government in building roads, etc., were called together by the roll of a drum. In the record of 3rd Voyage of Sir Martin Frobisher (1587) given in "Voyages to the N. W." (Foxe and James),[1] we find in "Articles to be observed in the Fleete" the following:

[1] Hak. Soc., 1894, Vol. 1, p. 53.

"That every ship in the fleete in the Time of Fogs, which continually happen with little wind and calmes, shall keepe a reasonable noise with Drum and Trumpet, or otherwise to keepe themselves cleere one of the other."

While poets have sung the praises of the violin, the harp, the lute, and flute, and other instruments, it has been reserved for George Meredith to apostrophize the drum, specifically the bass-drum.

"There is no instrument whose sound proclaims such vast internal satisfaction as the drum. I know not whether it be that the sense we have of the corpulency of this instrument predisposes us to imagine it supremely content: as when an alderman is heard snoring, the world is assured that it listens to the voice of his own exceeding gratulation. A light heart in a fat body ravishes not only the world but the philosopher. If monotonous, the one note of the drum is very correct. Like the speaking of great Nature, what it means is implied by the measure. When the drum beats to the measure of a common human pulsation, it has a conquering power: inspiring us neither to dance nor to trail the members, but to march as life does, regularly, and in hearty good order, and with a not exhaustive jollity. It is a sacred instrument." "Sandra Belloni," Ch. IX.

Of the significance of the drum in modern life little need be said. As in the life of the savage, it expresses and incites military ardor, it speaks of death, and, in the orchestra it becomes eloquent. The modern drum, with the exception of the kettle-drum, which may be tuned, in its essentials is in advance of the earliest types only in its greater perfection of structure.

CASE VI.

CLASS II. Section A. One Vibrating Membrane with Resonator. Drums.

Section C. One Vibrating Membrane with Shallow Resonator (Rim) in which are Metal Discs. Tambourines.

Section D. Membrane, or Membranes, Vibrating Sympathetically. Pan bomba. Mirliton.

In one-headed drums of the Alaskan type (No. 389), the barrel is shortened, often to a mere rim. The insertion of metal discs in the rim converts this type into a Tambourine. (No. 396.) Striking the head of the Tambourine, or shaking the instrument, sets these discs in vibration, producing a pleasing sound thoroughly justifying their technical name—"Jingles."

389. DRUM. Wooden rim. Rawhide .... Tlingit Indians, Alaska

In this drum, of Chilkat origin, the head is fastened to the narrow rim by tacks and thongs of rawhide crossing each other at right angles. Unlike most of its type it is not decorated, nor does it have the usual handle.

Depth of rim, 3.3 cm. Diameter of head, 40 cm.

Used on all important occasions, it is also held to be invested with a supernatural power somewhat akin to that of the tambourine.

The *chau-i-yuk* of British Columbia, and the *cha-yakh* of Siberia are of this type.[1]

390. KETOBONG. Wooden rim. Skin .... Borneo

The head is drawn over the bowl-shaped body and braced with numerous narrow strips of rattan fastened to a ring of the same material at the base. A spiral coil of rattan serves as a snare. Used at marriage festivities at Kriang, Borneo.

Depth, 13.5 cm. Diameter at head, 33.8 cm.; at base, 19 cm.

391. KHANJANI, or KHANJARI. Wooden rim. Parchment...... India

The slightly tapering body is cut from a single block of wood and painted (striped) in colors. The head is cemented on.

Depth of rim, 4.5 cm. Diameter of head, 20.3 cm.

392. KHANJARI, or KHANJANI. Similar to No. 391 .... India

Depth, 6 cm. Diameter at head, 18.2 cm.; at open end, 15.7 cm.

---

[1] Morris, p. 91.

393. TAMBOUR. Brass. Parchment . . . . Italy
To a large drum, with brass body and one head braced in the European manner, a long staff is fastened in order that it may be carried in theatrical processions.
Depth, 20 cm. Diameter of head, 77 cm. Length of staff, 204 cm.

394. DAFF, or DEFF. Wooden frame. Oiled parchment. . . . . Algeria
The heads carry emblematic designs in dull red, and a leather strap, ornamented with cowrie shells, runs about the edge, and at one corner is looped to form a handle.
Thickness, 2.8 cm. Width, 33 cm.

395. DARA. Tambourine. Wooden rim. Parchment. . . . . Syria
The head is fastened to the rim by cords led through holes in its lower edge. Iron links on the inner surface act as "jingles."
Depth of rim, 7 cm. Diameter of head, 43 cm.

396. TAMBOURINE. Wood. Parchment. . . Tobago Island, Brit. W. Indies
Three groups of metal discs are inserted in the rude rim.*
Depth, 9.4 cm. Diameter, 43 to 47 cm.

397. TAMBOURINE. Wooden rim. Parchment. . . . . Italy
The shell of black walnut, with parchment head and five pairs of small brass cymbals, is fastened to a painted wooden shield. This, together with a small bowl-shaped gong, is attached to a long wooden rod painted to represent a spear. Used on the stage.
Depth, 4.8 cm. Diameter, 18 cm. Length of pole, 207 cm.

398. JHANJH-KHANJANI. Wood. Parchment . . . . India
This is a development from No. 391, through the use of two pairs of metal discs placed at opposite sides of the frame.
Depth, 7.5 cm. Diameter from 15 to 18.5 cm.

399. TYMPANUM. Wooden rim, with brass bells. Parchment. . . . . . Italy
At equal intervals on outer surface of the hoop are six small brass bells hung upon projecting wires. Reproduction from a wall-painting at Pompeii.
Depth, 10 cm. Diameter, 38 cm.

400. TAMBOURINE. Wooden rim. Parchment . . . . Italy
The shell of this very old specimen is set with eight pairs of small brass cymbals. The head is tightened with a hoop and metal screw-braces.
Depth, 9 cm. Diameter of head, 39 cm.

401. TAMBOURINE. Wooden rim. Parchment . . . . Italy
This specimen has ten pairs of discs.
Depth, 9.1 cm. Diameter of head, 41.9 cm.

---

* In these descriptions, "discs" refer to flat plates of thin metal, while "cymbals" indicate plates with a concave surface.

402. TAMBOURINE. Wooden rim. Parchment . . . . Cyprus
The rim is decorated with pictures of clowns and harlequins.
Depth, 8.5 cm. Diameter of head, 38 cm.

403. REBANA, or ADOK. Wooden rim. Parchment . . . . Sumatra
The body contracts at the open side and contains a rattan snare and three pairs of loose discs. The head is secured by ornamental nails.
Depth, 7.8 cm. Diameter of head, 33.5 cm.; of open side, 28.5 cm.
(B-S.)

404. TAMBOURINE. Usual materials . . . . France
The head bears the inscription "Marie Josephe de Saxe, Dauphine de France, 1767." On the obverse side is a portrait, presumably of the Dauphine. The rim carries five double pairs of cymbals.
Depth, 7.5 cm. Diameter of head, 44.5 cm.

405. TAMBOURINE. Wooden rim. Parchment. . . . . Italy
The head bears the portrait of an Italian peasant girl.
Depth, 9.5 cm. Diameter of head, 45 cm.
Signed—"M. Reli."

406. ABENDAIR. Wooden rim. Parchment. . . . . . Kabyle Tribe, Algeria
The oiled parchment head is decorated with the portrait, in oils, of the daughter of a Kabyle chieftain, signed by the artist, "C. Vincent."
Bandar and *bendeyr* are alternative Arabian names for the native *abendair*, pl. *ibendiren*.[2]
Depth, 5.6 cm. Diameter of head, 37.2 cm.

407. BANDAR, or BENDEYR. Similar to No. 406. . . . . Algeria
The painted shell carries a band of leather, decorated with brass ornaments and rosettes of cowrie-shells. The head is decorated with floral designs and Arabic characters. A snare of four cords of gut runs over the head, and a leather tassel bearing cowrie-shells strikes the head when the tambourine is in motion, taking the place of the usual metal cymbals.
Depth, 8.7 cm. Diameter of head, 39.8 cm.

408. RIQQ. Wooden rim. Parchment . . . . Algeria
The rim is painted red and the head is decorated with flowers and the figure of a peacock. Usual discs.
Depth, 5 cm. Diameter of head, 30.4 cm.

409. TAR, or REK. Wooden rim. Parchment . . . . Egypt
The shell is entirely covered with a checkered inlay of mother-of-pearl, ebony, and ivory. The translucent head is cemented on the body. Five double pairs of cymbals are set in rim.
Depth, 6.4 cm. Diameter of head, 23.2 cm.

---

[2] Sachs, p. 1.

410. TAMBOURINE. Wooden rim. Parchment................Spain
The head is decorated with a street scene, and from the rim (with "jingles") hangs a network of colored balls and yarn.
Depth, 4 cm. Diameter of head, 22.7 cm.

411. TAMBOURINE. Wooden rim. Parchment..........United States
Depth, 4.5 cm. Diameter of head, 20 cm.

412. TAMBOURINE. Similar to No. 411................United States
Depth, 4.5 cm. Diameter of head, 24.6 cm.

The Tambourine is widely distributed, being found in every quarter of the globe. It is the chief asset of the Siberian *tadibei* or *shaman*, who takes it with him for protection on his frequent visits to Erlich's realm (Hades). The natives believe that he cools off the denizens of that torrid zone by bestowing on them unlimited quantities of spirituous liquors.

The *shaman* already mentioned imposes his will on the natives by causing the tambourine to speak in terms which he alone can interpret. He does this by affixing a lump of magnetic ore to the under side of the head, and alternately engaging and releasing it by a magnet, which he holds with the middle fingers of the hand with which he supports the instrument.

In the modern orchestra the tambourine is used to suggest "local color," or to accentuate certain sensuous motives.

NOVEL TREATMENTS OF VIBRATING BODIES.

In the instruments hereinafter noted, novel treatments of a Vibrating Body (Class I), and a Vibrating Membrane or Membranes (Class II) are displayed. The first occurs through Friction, the second through Sympathetic Vibration.

CLASS I. Sections A and F.

"Violone" ....United States
This instrument is shown in Case III, No. 245 as a steel-harmonica, but the bars may be sounded by drawing a resined violin bow on the curved ends as well as by percussion, hence its alias, "Violone."

413. NAGELGEIGE (Eng. *Nail-violin*, or *Semi-lunar;* Fr. *Violon de fer;* Ital. *Violino di ferro*) ....Germany
The twelve iron pins arranged on a semi-circular sound-box may be set in vibration by a resined violin bow.
Compass:—Normal minor scale from a′ to c‴, with f sharp′ and e‴ added.
Diameter of sound-box, 20.2 cm.; depth, 4.3 cm. Length of pins, 3.5 to 7 cm.

414. VERRILLON, or MUSICAL GLASSES .... United States
Height of glasses, 14 to 16.5 cm. Diameter, 6.4 to 9 cm.
This process of tone-production was first described by Phil. Härsdörffer* in *Math.* u. *philos. Erquickstunden*, Nürn, 1677, II., 147, quoted by Sachs, p. 409.

415. MACARONI STICKS. Wood .... United States
Length of rods, 52.5 to 108 cm. Diameter of each, 1.2 cm.

416. TOY MACARONI STICKS. Incomplete set........... United States

CLASS II. Section D. Sub-Section I. Vibration induced by Friction.

417. CACCARELLA. Earthenware. Membrane........... Naples, Italy
A small earthenware body, shaped like a flower-pot, has its top covered with a membrane through which runs a reed which rubbed with resined fingers induces vibration. It figures in the Piedigrotta festival, and is a type whose distribution is world-wide.

418. CHICHARRA. A resined string induces vibration............ Spain
This toy represents a division of the type in which a string is substituted for a rod.
Diameter of (oval) body, 5.5 by 6.5 cm. Height, 4.4 cm. Length of string, 40.6 cm.

419. PAN BOMBA. Membrane and rod .... Spain
This is a miniature example of the following instrument. The earthen pot-shaped body is 3.8 cm. in diameter, 3.6 cm. in height, while the rod is 12 cm. long.

420. PAN BOMBA. Membrane and rod .... Spain
Height of body, 17 cm. Diameter, 13 cm. Length of rod, 40.4 cm.

421. PAN BOMBA. Similar to No. 420. Tin body .... Italy
Height, 19 cm. Diameter, 15 to 19 cm. Length of rod, 29 cm.

Sub-Section II. Sympathetic Vibration induced by the Singing Voice.

422. MIRLITON (*Flûte eunuque;* Ger. *Eunuchenflöte*) .... France
A cylinder of bamboo, 27 cm. long and 2.3 cm. in diameter, is covered with blue paper with a band of red at each end. This surface bears a continuous spirally-wound strip of white paper on which are printed a number of amorous couplets. Near each end is a mouth-hole into which one hums, thus inducing the vibration of the membranes closing the ends of the tube. This principle is also utilized in certain Oriental flutes, and dominates all the instruments in this rubric.

---

* It may be of interest to students of the history of literature and of music to know that this man was the author of the absurd set of rules regarding versification, which, published in 1647, is known as the *Nürnberger Trichter* (Nuremberg Funnel). Through it the author said the German Art of poetry and rhyming could be poured in six lessons. Ambitious poets take notice!

423. "KAZOO." Wood, with membrane. . . . . .United States
Length, 10.8 cm. Diameter, 1.8 cm.

424. "VOCOPHONE." Pasteboard with membrane. . . . . . . .United States
Length, 22.4 cm. Diameter 2.3 to 4.2 cm.

425. SING SCHALMEI. Tube of nickel-plated tin. . . . . .Germany
A small membrane under the mouth-piece is set in vibration by humming, or singing, into the slightly conical tube, which ends in a bell.
Length, 22.5 cm. Diameter, 1.2 to 3.8 cm.

426. SING SCHALMEI. Similar to No. 425 . . . . .Germany
Length, 34.5 cm. Diameter, 1.2 to 6.7 cm.

427. "ZOBO CORNET." Brass, with membrane. . . . . .United States
The tube has an oval funnel-shaped mouth-piece and a flaring bell.
Length, 28.7 cm. Diameter of bell, 13.6 cm.

UNIQUE PROCESSES OF TONE PRODUCTION.

(a) The Voice Modified by a Resonance Chamber (Nos. 428-9);
(b) Reinforced by a Conical Tube (Nos. 430-1-2).

428. SINGING DISK . . . . .England
Convex discs of tin placed edge to edge. Diameter, 7 cm.

429. "COR DE CHASSE." Boxwood discs, 6.8 cm. in diameter. . . .France
Length, 60.4 cm. Diameter of mouth-piece, 3.4 to 6.5 cm.; of bell, 14.4 cm.

430. SPEAKING TRUMPET. *Zinc* . . . . .Italy
Length, 45.6 cm. Diameter of mouth-piece, 5 to 7 cm.; of bell, 14.2 cm.
In the speaking trumpet we find the same principle of tone-reinforcement that characterizes the modern ubiquitous megaphone.

431. SPEAKING TRUMPET. Copper . . . . .England

432. SPEAKING TRUMPET. Type used by firemen. Copper. United States
Length, 44 cm. Diameter of mouth-piece, 5 to 7 cm.; of bell, 16 cm.
A silver plate runs "Presented to Robert A. Jones by His Friends, February 3, 1864."
Of the following, No. 433 falls in Class I; Nos. 434-435 belong in Class III.

433. BUMBASS (Fr. *Basse de Flandres;* Eng. *Bladder and Strings*) . . Ger.
A staff 137.6 cm. long, terminating at the upper end in peg-box and scroll, at a point 33.6 cm. above the lower end carries a wooden disc, 17.8 cm. in diameter. On this a small inflated bladder is held by the pressure of a taut gut string, 93.8 cm. long. Above the scroll two small cymbals are fixed, and on the back of the staff just below the scroll a wire lyre with cross-bars is attached by a coiled wire spring. Six small bells are hung on these bars.

As not infrequently a mixture of races accentuates the least desirable qualities of each, so in this composite instrument, we find a vulgar exploitation of the principle of the vibrating plate, or mass of metal, and of the vibrating string. The string is rasped or struck forcibly as the metal parts are set in vibration by thumping the staff on the ground. Used originally by strolling beggars. The *bumba*, with two bladders and strings, in use in Iceland as late as the seventeenth century, and the Anamese *cai xinh tien* are analogous instruments. An instrument of this type, but with two strings, is mentioned by Phil. Hainhofer, in his "Dresdener Reisetagebuch" (1629) as a "new invention."[3]

434. PHONOGRAPH TOP. Paper cone. Metal disc.......United States
Passing the tip of the cone lightly over the knobs on upper side of plate as the top is rotating, produces a series of tones.
Length, with handle, 20.2 cm. Diameter of plate, 11.2 cm.
Signed—"Worden."

435. SINGING TOP. Wooden cylinder with slit in one side, and a rod running through and extending at either end..............Java
When the top is rotating rapidly it induces the vibration of the column of air enclosed in the body of the top, producing a musical tone.
Length, 23.6 cm.; of body, 11.1 cm.; of slit, 3 cm. Diameter of body, 4 cm.; of slit, 4 mm.

At this point it must be stated that the types so far considered have less musical value than those included in the succeeding classes. The purely rhythmical, or more strictly speaking, metrical, appeal made by the most primitive rattle differs only in degree from the lure of the castanet, and its appeal, is, after all, to the same feeling—or instinct. With a few notable exceptions it may be stated that the types represented in Class I have not developed as have the instruments whose process of tone-production places them under different rubrics.

CLASS III. INSTRUMENTS WITH VIBRATING COLUMN OF AIR.

Section A. Vibrating Column of Air enclosed in a Vertical, Cylindrical Tube, with no lateral Openings.

When, how, and where, prehistoric man discovered that blowing across the open mouth of a tube, the other end of which was closed, produced a pleasing sound, is an unsolved mystery. That initial discovery was followed by another, that binding together tubes of varying lengths made possible the production of a series of such sounds, else Pan were without his pipes. In this instrument we may see the first representative of Class III, viz., the Syrinx (Eng. *Pandean-pipe;* Fr. *Flûte de Pan;* Ger. *Pansflöte*).

[3] Sachs, p. 63.

The "Syrinx" is a combination of reeds, bamboo joints, wooden, metal, or stone tubes, bound together. The upper ends of these tubes are arranged on a plane, while the lower are stopped, either by some foreign substance, or by a natural joint. The column of air in each tube is set in vibration by blowing across the top. This is the only process known to Nature whereby a column of air is so set in vibration as to produce a musical tone. The word "Ugab" (Genesis IV. 21), incorrectly translated "Organ," refers to this type.

Dr. Curt Sachs makes a distinction between the Syrinx and Pan's-pipe, the limit of the former being nine tubes, while in the latter the number of tubes is not restricted, but in this contention he stands quite alone.[4]

436. SYRINX. Twenty-five bamboo tubes.......Amazon Indians, Brazil
Pitches:—f, f sharp, g, b, g sharp, c sharp′, a sharp′, d sharp′, b′, f′, d sharp′, g sharp′, f′, a sharp′, f sharp′, g sharp′, a sharp′, d sharp″, b′, f sharp″, d, g sharp″, e″, g″, and g sharp″.
Longest tube, 25.6 cm.; shortest, 5.7 cm. Width of instrument, 35.3 cm.*

(B-S.)

437. SYRINX. Twenty-one tubes of cane.................Fiji Islands
Pitches:—a sharp′, c″, d″, d sharp″, f″, g″, g sharp″, a″, b″, c‴, d, d sharp‴, e‴, f‴, f sharp‴, g‴, g sharp‴, g‴, a‴, a‴, and a‴.
Longest tube, 17.9 cm.; shortest, 4.5 cm. Width, 27.3 cm.

438. SYRINX. Nineteen reed tubes, giving major scale from e to a″...Italy
Longest tube, 13.8 cm.; shortest, 4 cm. Width, 18.5 cm.

439. KOVE. Three bamboo tubes (d sharp′, g sharp, d′)..New Hebrides
Length of tubes in order, 29.9, 17.4, 17.2 cm.

440. SYRINX. Nineteen reed tubes, decorated........Funchal, Madeira
The tubes, arranged in a semi-circle, give the major diatonic scale from e to a″. Made by a Portuguese peasant, Manuel Viera.
Longest tube, 24.3 cm.; shortest, 11.5 cm. Outer circumference, 16.7 cm.

441. SYRINX. Eight tubes of reeds...Bogota Indians, Bogota, S. America
Longest tube, 11.2 cm.; shortest, 5.8 cm. Width, 7.9 cm.

442. SYRINX. Five tubes. In structure similar to No. 441......Ecuador
Longest tube, 6 cm.; shortest, 2.3 cm. Width, 6.2 cm.

(B-S.)

---

[4] Sachs, p. 367.
* In these measurements "width" represents the length of the plane.

443. FIEOULD. Ten holes bored in a flat wooden body..........France
Used by the shepherds of Arbeost (Dép. Hautes-Pyrénées).
Length of body, 10 cm. Width, 6.2 cm. Thickness, 1.9 cm. Depth of holes, 3 to 9 cm.
The *sioulet christedou* is of the same structure and habitat, and its characteristic signal is used by Charpentier in Act II of "Louise."[5]

444. SYRINX. Three bamboo tubes giving d, f, g sharp...........Java
Length of tubes in order, 28.3-24.1-20.3 cm. Width, 5 cm.

445. BUEBALABALA. Five bamboo tubes giving a diatonic series from f sharp ....New Hebrides
Longest tube, 24.2 cm; shortest, 15.2 cm. Width, 5.7 cm.

446. "ZAMPOGNA." Five brass tubes. Diatonic succession e to b....Italy
Longest tube, 12.3 cm.; shortest, 8.4 cm. Width, 7.2 cm.
Inscribed—"In mi magg. primo lavero."
Zampogna, the name given to this metal syrinx, really is that of a flute, or *schalmey*, used by Italian shepherds.

447. "ZAMPOGNA." Nine brass tubes. Key of C, e″ to f‴ ....Italy
Longest tube, 13 cm.; shortest, 6 cm. Width, 13.5 cm.
Inscribed—"In Fa magg. Sulla scena."

448. "ZAMPOGNA." Nine tubes. Major scale—f sharp to g sharp″..Italy
Longest tube, 13.1 cm.; shortest, 5.8 cm. Width, 13.5 cm.
Inscribed—"In sol magg. In orghestra."

448A. SIGNAL WHISTLE. Wood ....W. Africa
The tube—19.5 cm. long and 2 cm. in diameter—has a conical bore and ends in a flat projection bent to an angle of 30°. It is blown across the top producing c sharp″ and, by stopping the lower end, a′. A similar whistle is shown by Ankermann (p. 37, Fig. 65).
(John R. Effinger.)

Section B. Vibrating Column of Air in a Vertical Cylindrical Tube with lateral Openings.

Section C. Vibrating Column of Air in a Vertical Cylindrical Tube with lateral Openings and Mouth-piece.

Section B defines a type in which the breath is directed against a knife edge on one side of the upper end of the tube, while the performer presses the other side firmly against the chin. This is the "Vertical" type.

[5] Sachs, p. 347.

PLATE V.

CASE VI. NOS. 413 TO 641 (RIGHT TO LEFT)

In the instruments included in Section C, the tone is produced by blowing into a mouth-piece which is so constructed that the air is directed against a knife edge. The vibration thus induced sets the enclosed column of air in vibration . In whistles and flutes *with finger holes* the length of the vibrating column may be changed by manipulation of these holes, and modified by the manner of blowing. The Beaked Flute (Fr. *Flûte à bec, Flute douce;* Ital. *Flauto a becco;* Ger. *Schnabelflöte*) is the leading representative of this Section, which also includes the Whistle, the Flageolet and the Nose Flute. (Fr. *Flûte nasale;* Ger. *Nasenflöte*). The last-named type (blown from the nostrils) is common among primitive peoples as well as in the Orient, specifically India, where its use is conducive to the maintenance of caste.

The Flute (Fr. *Flûte;* Ital. *Flauto;* Ger. *Flöte*) is of great antiquity, and the types represented by the instruments in these sections were known and in use from a very remote date.

A musical asset of the Egyptians, Greeks, and Romans, this instrument is still a potent factor, especially in the orchestra. Though the lower-pitched flutes, like the Great Bass Flute, whose lowest tone was F, have been overwhelmed by instruments of greater sonority, the two existing representatives of this formerly very large family are numbered among the most useful members of the modern orchestra. It has an extensive compass (c′ to c′′′′), and blends well with other instruments even though its tone is somewhat lacking in warmth.

Originally the bore of the Flute was cylindrical, but *circa* 1780 it became conical. The typical modern instrument is cylindrical with a parabolic "head," i. e., the section containing the mouth-hole.

449. TRIPLE WHISTLE. Terra-cotta .... Mexico
The bodies are conventionalized bird forms, the beaks furnishing the mouth-pieces. Serpent decoration. The two whistles that can be blown give f′′ and d′′′.
Length, 8.6 cm. Width, 10.4 cm.

450. WHISTLE. Terra-cotta. From the native cemetery at Nicoya, Mexico
Length, 10.5 cm. Width, 7 cm.

451. WHISTLE. Terra-cotta. Globular form, serpent-decoration.. Mexico
By gradually uncovering the finger holes the chromatic scale from b′ to e flat′′ is produced. Length, 10.8 cm. Width, 8 cm.
(B-S.)

452. WHISTLE. Earthenware in form of a watering-pot.......... Spain
Height, 10 cm. Diameter with spout (the whistle), 9.5 cm.

453. WHISTLE. Earthenware. Toy, in rude animal form........ Egypt
Height, 8.5 cm. Length, 9 cm. Tone exceedingly shrill.

454-455. SILVADORES. "Whistling vases." Pottery. . . . . Peru
Two hollow globular vessels connected by two transverse bars, the lower of which is also hollow. If, after a small quantity of water has been poured into the right vessel, one blows directly into it, the pressure of the water forces the air through the small whistle in the top of the left vessel and a tone is produced. These vases are generally found in Inca graves and are of a very ancient type.
Height, 17.5 and 13.5 cm. Width, 18.8 cm. Diameter, 9.4 cm.
Height, 13 and 13.5 cm. Width, 21 cm. Diameter, 10.8 cm.
(B-S.)

456. BEAKED FLUTE, or WHISTLE. Terra-cotta . . . . . . Ancient Mexico
The conical tube has four finger-holes, by means of which the following tones may be produced:—c‴, c sharp‴, e‴, f sharp‴, and a‴. The unglazed body, 20 cm. in length, is decorated in narrow bands of black.

457. BEAKED FLUTE, or WHISTLE. Terra-cotta. . . . . Mexico
The cylindrical tube, 22 cm. in length, and ending in a bell, 5.5 cm. in diameter, has four finger-holes. Elaborately decorated, with thin flanges on either side, and a human figure. The native name is *pito*.
(B-S.)

458. BEAKED FLUTE, or WHISTLE. Terra-cotta . . . . . . Arizona Indians
By closing the seven finger-holes in succession e flat‴, d″, c‴, b flat″, a″, g″, and g flat″, are produced. The tone is soft and pure.
Length, 22.5 cm. Circumference, 8 cm. Diameter of bore, 1.5 cm.

459. WHISTLE. Cedar. Produces e . . . . Tlingit Indians, Alaska
Formed by binding two sections—24.5 cm. long—together with cords.

460. WHISTLE. Bottle-shaped body of cedar, giving f. . . . . Alaska
Length, 26.8 cm. Greatest circumference, 23 cm.; least, 11.3 cm.

461. DOUBLE WHISTLE. Cedar . . . . Tlingit Indians, Alaska
Three sections of cedar, 31.6 cm. long, with nearly square cross-section, 4.6 cm. in diameter, are bound together by cotton strips.

462. SCHNABELFLÖTE. Carved wood. Five finger-holes. . . . . . Germany
This instrument is very old and cannot be played. Length, 29.8 cm.

463. FETISH WHISTLE. Carved goat's horn. . . . . Zanzibar, Africa
A carved serpent, human heads, and other figures form an effective decoration. Three finger-holes in the inner curve, but the only tone that can be produced is f sharp. Lengths of curves, 30 and 22.2 cm.; greatest diameter, 6.1 cm.

464. WHISTLE. Glazed Pottery . . . . China
The whistle is a figurine of a monkey, 3.1 cm. in height.

465. DOUBLE WHISTLE. Glazed Pottery . . . . China

The figurines represent two billing swans. Whistle in each tail, giving g sharp. Height, 4.7 cm.

466 to 471. DOG WHISTLES. Glazed earthenware. . . . . Germany

These whistles, representing dogs, call for no special description. In length they range from 1 to 5 cm. The tones are indescribably shrill.

472-473. CUCKOO-CALLS. Glazed earthenware . . . . Germany

The first, representing chanticleer, with whistle in tail, and one finger-hole, gives f sharp′ and d sharp′, and is 8.4 cm. high. The second, is a typical peasant boy, 10.5 cm. tall, and has a whistle in the back.

474. BIRD-CALL. Wood . . . . Switzerland

Oblong wooden whistle with sliding piston and giving the chromatic scale from e″ to c sharp.‴.

Length, 13.6 cm. Diameter, 2.5 cm.

475. BIRD-CALL. Wood . . . . Switzerland

The round body, slightly swelling in the middle and decorated with poker work, has a whistle mouth-piece at one end while the other represents the head of a bird. One finger-hole. Pitches:—g″ and f″ sharp. Length, 16.5 cm.

476. DOUBLE WHISTLE. Wood. Used in orchestra. . . . . Italy

A wooden box, 26.5 cm. long, 10.5 cm. wide, and 5.5 cm. deep, is divided into two "Melodia" organ pipes, with air reservoir at the bottom, in which are two holes for blowing. The pitches are g″ and c″.

477-478. BIRD-CALLS. Wood . . . . Switzerland

The first terminates in a spotted egg through which the head of a chick breaks as the piston is operated. The second, displays an elongated egg with whistle body running through, while the chick, already grown up and roosting on a pivot, turns hither and thither as the whistle is blown. The first whistle gives four tones and the second one. Length of No. 477, 19.7 cm.; of No. 478, 16.2 cm.

479. VOGELPFEIFE. Brass . . . . Germany

The whistle carries the figure of a canary bird. The piston is attached to a handle of black wood. Compass:—d‴ to c⁗.

Length, extended, 23.2 cm.; closed, 14.5 cm.

480. BIRD-CALL. Wood . . . . Switzerland

The body, 17 cm. long, bears at lower end a painted wooden bird which turns as the piston is pressed. Pitches:—a sharp″ and b″.

481. "MAGIC FLUTE." Tin . . . . United States

482. OCARINA. Soprano in F . . . . France
The conical body with mouth-piece at one side, made of earthenware painted black and decorated in gilt, has nine finger-holes. This vaudeville type has not inconsiderable musical possibilities which, however, are seldom realized.
Length, 11.8 cm. Diameter of mouth-piece, 6 cm.

483. OCARINA. Alto in D . . . . Austria
Similar in every respect to the preceding but larger. 15 cm. long and 8 cm. in diameter.
Signed—"H. Viehn, Vienna."

484. OCARINA. Tenor in A . . . . France
In the larger end of the body, of brown earthenware decorated in black, a piston is introduced by means of which the pitch may be raised a semi-tone. Nine finger-holes.
Length, with piston closed, 20.3 cm.; extended, 8.3 cm. Diameter, 12 cm.
Signed—"Fabricateur, A. E. Mezzetti, à Paris."

485. OCARINA. Bass in G sharp . . . . France
Length, 30.2 cm. Diameter, 21 cm. Eight holes.
Signed—"Compagnie General de L'Ocarina."

486. TRANSVERSE WHISTLE FLUTE in E flat. Tin. . . . . Germany
As the player blows through a hole in the side it appears to be a transverse flute, but the tone is produced as in the whistle. In the inverted conical tube are six finger-holes. Length, 33.8 cm.
Signed—"Kirchhoff, Leipzig."

486A. TRANSVERSE WHISTLE FLUTE. Tin . . . . United States
Cylindrical tube. Six finger-holes. Pitched in C. Length, 43.2 cm.
Signed—"Kirchhoff, Leipzig."
(Mrs. Lucy Granger.)

487. TRANSVERSE WHISTLE FLUTE. Nickel-plated brass. . . . Germany
Pitched in E flat. Wooden mouth-piece. Six holes. Length, 35.7 cm.

488. VERTICAL WHISTLE FLUTE. Nickel-plated brass. . . . . . Germany
Six holes. Conical tube. Length, 28.1 cm.

489. REVOLVER VERTICAL WHISTLE FLUTE . . . . Germany
This instrument consists of seven cylinders bound together. By transferring the mouth-piece to the appropriate cylinder, seven different pitches—c, d, e flat, f, f sharp, g, and a—are made available.
Length, 33.3 cm.; with mouth-piece removed, 25 cm.

490. BEAKED FLUTE. Wood. Native name unknown. . . . South America
The slightly flattened, curved body, of ten longitudinal sections bound together with bands of gut, shows six finger-holes on outer curve.
Compass, from g′ to e‴, with many intervals imperfect. Lengths of curves, 44.5 and 41.8 cm.

491. VERTICAL FLUTE. Wood . . . . Poma Indians, California
The irregularly curving cylindrical body, 50 cm. long, is made from a branch of the buckeye (*Aesculus, Cal.*), or horse-chestnut. Two groups, of two finger-holes each, are so placed that the pitches vary according to which end is blown into.[6] Decorated with burnt bands, the ends being charred in deference to a myth regarding the tribe's acquisition of fire from another tribe.
The Poma Indians call this flute *du cim* (*doo a thim*), "to be blown upon or into," and the Ke'ya (Ukiah), *wal wal*, from the multiplicity of notes.[7]
(John P. Stanley.)

492. SHEPHERD'S PIPE. Vertical type. Wood . . . . Greece
The body is a thin wooden tube, 25.4 cm. long, with bevelled edge at the top. Six finger-holes in the front and one in the back.
(Francis W. Kelsey.)

493. GALOUBET, or CHIRULA. Beaked flute type . . . . France
This flute, of the eighteenth century, has a narrow cylindrical tube of boxwood, 38.5 cm. in length, with two holes in front and one behind. It has a compass of two octaves and is used with the *tabor*, or the *tambourin à cordes* (Case XI, No. 1168). According to Mistral, the name came from the celebrated jongleur Galaubet,[8] an assumption contested by Sachs who suggests *churula* as the more probable origin.[9] It is of the same type as the early German *schwegel.**

[6] Charles Kasson Wead, in "History of Musical Scales," pp. 427, ff., gives an exhaustive treatment of the principles involved in primitive and indigenous instruments.

[7] These names are given by Mr. John M. Hudson who has lived for years in these tribes. In a letter to the donor he also gives the myth referred to as related by the Indians.

This myth is of the "Uncle Remus" type and runs as follows: "At one time we had no fire. Hunters from the mountains declared they saw smoke away beyond. We chose delegates to visit that place and get fire for us. We sent the Jack-rabbit, mole, gopher, etc., etc., (according to who tells this story) to steal the fire. They arrived at a big Tcâné (underground house) and were invited in. A big fire was in the center and they warmed themselves for the first time by *Ho* (artificial heat). Now ——— was a great flute-player and by request played so sweetly that all the hosts fell asleep; ——— grabbed two coals and ——— snatched another and ran out and up the mountain. The people awoke and pursuing, caught them. The gopher hid his coals in the ends of the flute, while the mole escaped underground; the Jack-rabbit hid his under his tail (which is singed to this day) but it burned him and died out. One of the coals fell out of the flute and was lost at the time. After being searched they returned home and forever had fire, and to this day the charred flute-ends show where the first fire was carried.". . . "Generally the robin is regarded as the patron of the flutist and his mark is etched between the holes." This flute bears the above-mentioned device.

[8] Mistral. *"Lou Tresor dou Felibrige,"* Vol. II, p. 14.

[9] Sachs, p. 151.

* In Kastner's *Les Danses des Morts.*, Plate VII, Figs. 50 and 51, Death is represented playing the *schwegel*. The drum in Fig. 50 is silent, for with his right hand he holds a staff bearing a banner. In Fig. 51 there is no drum.

494. MANJAIRA. Vertical type. Six finger-holes. . . . . Syria
Length, 30.4 cm. Diameter, 1.7 cm.

495. NOSE FLUTE. Cane . . . . Nias Island, Malaysia
The body is of cane with back formed to fit the nostril. Four finger-holes. Length, 29 cm. Diameter, 2.2 cm.

496-497. NOSE FLUTES. Bamboo. Played together . . . . . . Jeypore, India
The bodies are 13 cm. long and 2.3 in diameter. In playing, one is blown from each nostril.

498. ALGHOZA. Beaked flute. Bamboo . . . . India
The tube—31.3 cm. long and 2 cm. in diameter—is decorated in incised lines. The lower end is nearly closed by a node. Five finger-holes give f‴, e″, d″, c″, and a′.

499-500. SHEPHERD'S PIPES. Vertical type. Wood . . . . Greece
The tubes, 33.2 and 29 cm. in length respectively, and terminating in rude bells, have six finger-holes each.
(Francis W. Kelsey.)

501. BEAKED FLUTE. Bamboo . . . . Philippine Islands
The mouth-hole of this flute, a bamboo tube—33.8 cm. long—is 2 cm. below a node at upper end. A pair of slightly hollowed bamboo splints, fitting together and projecting 1.8 cm. beyond the closed end, convey the breath to this hole. Six finger-holes give a diatonic series from g sharp″ to b‴, with c′ interpolated.

502. FLAUTO A BECCO. Wood . . . . Italy
Reproduction of ancient type by Pelitti, Milan, for use in the Pompeian Festival of 1883. Six finger-holes. One key. Length, 49.2 cm.

503. FLUTE DOUCE, Treble in A. Boxwood . . . . France
Inverted conical bore. Seven finger-holes in front. One in back. Length, 39.3 cm.
Signed—in a circle, with A in center—"Prosper Colas, à Paris."
The signatures of makers are given exactly as they appear on the instruments.

504. FLUTE DOUCE, Alto in G flat. Boxwood . . . . France
The body, with inverted conical bore, is in three pieces. It has seven finger-holes in front and one in back. Length, 50.2 cm.

505. SCHNABELFLÖTE. Alto in F. Boxwood . . . . Germany
Like most flutes, the body is in three sections and the bore is conical. Seven finger-holes in front, and one in back. Length, 49.5 cm.
Signed—"J. C. E. Saftler."

506. SCHNABELFLÖTE. Alto in F. Boxwood . . . . Germany
This flute is similar to the preceding, but 1.5 cm. longer.

507. SCHNABELFLÖTE, in A flat. Boxwood . . . . Germany
Of hard red wood, and typical in form and construction.
Length, 45 cm.
Signed—"J. L. Fischer."

508. SCHNABELFLÖTE, in B flat. Boxwood . . . . Germany
This eighteenth century flute is of stained wood, in three pieces. Four silver keys, giving c″, d″, f″, and g″. Of the nine holes, six are arranged as usual. The seventh, at one side, is raised, and the eighth is in the back. Connecting bands of silver. Length, 49 cm.
Signed—"Kruspe, Erfurt."

509. FLAGEOLET. Boxwood. Eighteenth century . . . . France
The tube, with inverted conical bore, carries black horn mountings. Four holes in front and two behind. One brass key. Lowest note b′.
Length, 49 cm.
Signed—"Jabard, à Lyon."

510. FLAGEOLET. Dark wood, with ivory mountings . . . . France
The tube has silver connecting-bands, and the bore is nearly cylindrical, slightly conical only at the bell. Three silver keys. Four holes in front and two behind. Lowest note b flat′. Length, 38 cm.
Signed—"D. Noblet, ainé."

510A. FLAGEOLET. Boxwood. Five keys . . . . United States
The body has silver mountings, and the mouth-piece section is of unusual length. By substituting section B, it becomes a piccolo. Six finger-holes, all in front.
Length, as a flageolet, 43 cm.; as a piccolo, 30.4 cm.
(Mrs. Lucy Granger.)

511. "FLOETUSE." Double Flute . . . . Germany
The tube contains two parallel conical bores, with seven holes in each, closed by circular silver keys. Of no musical value. Length, 43 cm.

512. OCARINA. Walking stick. In B. Metal . . . . France
A walking stick—91.5 cm. long—the lower half of which is lacquered bamboo, and the upper brass finished in imitation of that wood, has for its handle a metal *ocarina*. This section is also fitted with a mouth-hole and six finger-holes that it may function as a transverse flute in D.
Signed—"Ch. Mathieu, Paris."

513. STOCKFLÖTE. Ebony .... Germany
Of the five joints, three form a flute, with eight finger-holes, six in front, one in back, and one in the side. One silver key. The breath is directed into the tube through two small holes in the ivory top.
Length, 88 cm.

514. VENU. Vertical type. Bamboo .... Orissa, Bengal
A slightly conical bamboo tube artistically lacquered in black and dull gold forms the body, which has no finger-holes.
Length, 254 cm. Diameter, 2.5 to 3.2 cm.

515. DOUBLE BEAKED FLUTE OR FLAGEOLET. Boxwood.... England
This consists of two tubes, each 19.7 cm. in length, with inverted conical bore. The left tube has six finger-holes in front, one at the side, and four silver keys. The right tube has five finger-holes and four silver keys. Both tubes have a common air reservoir into which leads a flageolet mouth-piece. Length, 40.3 cm.
Signed—"Bainbridge, 35 Holborn Hill, London."

516. DOUBLE BEAKED FLUTE. Dark wood. Silver mountings.. England
The body has two parallel tubes 42.5 cm. in length. The left tube has five finger-holes and six keys, the right, three holes and six keys.
Length, with mouth-piece, 65.7 cm.
Signed—"D'Almain and Co., late Goulding and D'Almain.
Soho Square, London."
In Nos. 515-516 the breath may be diverted from one tube to the other by a valve operated by a key on the back of the instrument.

517. THIJ, or THITH. Nose flute. Bamboo .... New Caledonia
A curved body of bamboo, 101.2 cm. long with one hole at the end. But one tone, c sharp, can be produced. The name is given on the authority of Edge-Partington and Heape (Ethnological Album, Pacific Is., Series II, Pg. 68).

Section D. Vibrating Column of Air in a Horizontal (Transverse) Cylindrical Tube with lateral Openings and Mouth-hole (*embouchure*).

The Transverse Flute (Fr. *Flûte, Flûte traversière;* Ger. *Querflöte;* Ital. *Flauto, Flauto traverso*) is held at right angles with the body and the player blows into a mouth-hole near the end. The Fife (Fr. *Fifre;* Ger. *Schweizerflöte, Pfeife*), formerly used with the drum as an ideal incentive to patriotism, and the Piccolo (Fr. *Petite flûte octave;* Ger. *Pikkolo*), are pitched an octave higher than the ordinary flute.

As it is impossible to make an absolute differentiation of the instruments in this Case, each type will be defined, with the exception of Transverse Flutes, which, only in exceptional cases will be specifically designated.

518. TRANSVERSE FLUTE. Reed. Sounds but one tone. . Upper Amazon
Length, 76 cm. Diameter, 3 to 5 cm.

519. FLUTE. Wood. Sounds one tone only.
This flute is over two hundred years old. It was donated with the understanding that neither its source nor its uses should be divulged.

520. FLUTE. Bone .... Klamath Indians, Oregon
Four finger-holes. Length, 17 cm. Diameter, 1 cm. For particulars and descriptions of this type consult Morris, pp. 109-116.

521. VERTICAL FLUTE. Bone.............. Poma Indians, California
One finger-hole. Length, 9.2 cm. Diameter, 1 cm.

522. VERTICAL FLUTE. Wood .... Solomon Islands
Two finger-holes. Length, 18.2 cm. Diameter, 3 cm.

523. FLUTE. Wood. A primitive vertical type. . . . Gilbert Is., So. Pacific
The tube—length, 33.5 cm.; diameter, 2 cm.—is closed at each end by a node. Near the upper end is a whistle mouth-piece. Four finger-holes. Lowest tone, b flat′; highest, a flat‴.

524. VERTICAL FLUTE. Bone .... British Guiana
Pitches:—g′, f′, d″, and c‴.
Three finger-holes. Length, 16 cm. Diameter, 1 cm.

525. VERTICAL FLUTE. Wood. Name unknown[10]......... Venezuela
Finger-hole at each end. Length, 17.8 cm. Diameter, 3 cm.

526. TRANSVERSE FLUTE. Wood ..... Onama Indians, British Guiana
Tone produced by blowing through slit in back, while the hands, held over the open cutting in tube, govern the tone series by the fingers.
Length, 44.5 cm. Diameter, 3.2 cm.

527. VERTICAL FLUTE. Wood .... Poma Indians, California
In its possibilities this resembles No. 491.
Length, 30 cm. Diameter, 5 cm.

528. SARALA-VANCI. Beaked type. Bamboo .... India
The body, lacquered in black and gold, has seven finger-holes in front and one in back. Length, 30.2 cm. Diameter, 1.6 cm.

529. SIGU-NIHU. Nose flute. Reed .... Nias Tribe, Sumatra
The tube—39.8 cm. long and 1.6 cm. in diameter—is decorated with incised lines. Four finger-holes.

530. LAYA BANCI. Vertical type. Bamboo, lacquered .... India
Seven finger-holes. Compass, f′ to b″. Length, 36 cm.

---

[10] Mahillon (*Cat.* Vol. III, p. 314) gives a description and illustration of this flute, but gives neither name nor source. Miss Morris gives Venezuela as its source (p. 226, No. 3560).

531. LAYA VANCI. Vertical type. Bamboo, lacquered..........Bengal
Six finger holes. Lowest tone b′. Length, 35.6 cm.

532. FLUTE. Wood, painted...............Apache Indians, Arizona
The cylinder of soft wood is bored with six holes, and the breath is directed into the square mouth-hole by a peculiar mouth-piece of wood. It is painted in bands of red and green, and six strips of raw-hide bind the two longitudinal sections together.
Length, 50.4 cm. Diameter, 4 cm.

533. RYU-TEKI, or "Dragon's flute." Carved bamboo...........Japan
The cylindrical tube—41.7 cm. in length, and 1.4 cm. in diameter—is elaborately carved in conventional designs of the heavenly dragon. It has seven finger-holes. Used in the *bugaku* dance.

534. CAI ONG DIC. Cane..................................Anam
Compass of two octaves from b to b″. A membrane over the hole next to the "embouchure" (mouth-hole) imparts a reedy tremolo to the tone. The cylindrical tube is tipped at either end with ivory, and is wound at stated intervals with black lacquered cord. It has six finger-holes, in a group, and two near the end, which are, however, negligible.
Length, 62.7 cm. Diameter, 2.2 cm.; of bore, 1.5 cm.

535. Similar to No. 534, but 1.5 cm. longer...................Anam

536. TI TZÖ. Cane. Similar to 534.......................China
Length, 66.5 cm. Diameter, 2.3 cm.

537. SEI-TEKI. Similar to preceding instrument................Japan

538. YAMATO-FUYE. "Side-blowing flute," with case...........Japan
The beautifully decorated cylinder has six finger-holes and mouth-hole placed in slightly hollowed bands, stained a reddish brown. The entire surface, with these exceptions, is wound with black lacquered cord. The case carries elaborate designs of peacocks. *Fuye* is the generic name for flute in Japan. Length, 39.2 cm. Diameter, 2 cm.

539. TI TZÖ. Bamboo, decorated in incised floral designs........China
The designs are filled in with red, green, and yellow color, and the usual ivory ferules appear on the ends.
Length, 57.6 cm. Diameter, 2.1 cm.

540. SHAKUHACHI. Vertical type. Bamboo.................Japan
The body, somewhat irregular, bears an elaborate design in black at the section next to the mouth-piece end. Four holes in front and one in back. The *shakuhachi* is said to date back to 1335. A skillful performer can produce the entire Chinese chromatic scale.
Length, 87.2 cm. Diameter, 3.5 cm.

541. CANE FLUTE. Decorated with themes from 55 operas........Italy
Length, 80.2 cm. Diameter, 1.5 cm.
Signed—"Marco de Fumagalli Angelo, Fabrica-Bellagio, 22 Luglio, 1899."
(Francis W. Kelsey.)

542. SOULING KETJIL. Vertical type. Stained bamboo....S. E. Borneo
Compass of two chromatic octaves from b. Four holes.
Length, 54.8 cm. Diameter, 3.9 cm.

543. SEI-TEKI. In form, decoration, and source, similar to No. 537.
Length, 56.4 cm. Diameter, 1.7 cm.

544. SOULING, or SULING. Nose flute. Cane ....Java
The cylindrical tube is decorated with incised lines in artistic designs, separated by smooth bands of the polished surface. Six holes divided into two groups. Range of two octaves in a mixed series from d sharp′. Length, 50.8 cm. Diameter, 2 cm.

545. SOULING. Similar to No. 544 but larger ....Java
Compass:—a diatonic scale of two octaves, from c sharp.
Length, 55.7 cm. Diameter 3.2 cm.

546. NAY. Vertical type. Bamboo, decorated ....Egypt
The tube—55 cm. long and 2.2 cm. in diameter—is decorated in incised lines, and has six finger-holes. Lowest tone, a′.

547. NAY, or NAY GHIREF. Vertical type. Bamboo ....Syria
Six finger-holes in front, one in back. Lowest tone, b flat′.
Length, 54.6 cm. Diameter, 1.8 to 2.4 cm.

548. GÜESBA, or GSBA. Vertical type. Bamboo ....Algeria
The body—53 cm. long, and 2 to 2.3 cm. in diameter—is decorated in red incised lines. Six finger-holes. Lowest tone, g′.

549. HITO-YO-KIRI. In type and source similar to No. 540, but smaller. Lowest tone, d sharp′. Length, 52 cm. Diameter, 3.5 cm...Japan

550. SOULING. Similar in type and source to No. 544, but smaller. Six holes. Length, 50.2 cm. Diameter, 2 cm.

551. FANGO-FANGO. Nose flute. Bamboo.....Tonga Islands, S. Pacific
The tube—47.5 cm. long, and 2.7 cm. in diameter—has a breath-hole at either end; three finger-holes equi-distant from each other and from the breath-holes, and one in the back. The lowest tone is d. The compass is quite extended, but the manner of playing is quite complicated.

552. MANJAIRA. Vertical type. Bamboo. Five finger-holes.......Syria
This flute—44 cm. long, and 1.7 cm. in diameter—is played like the *nay*. Lowest tone, f′.

553. T'SOUNGYE, or T'OUNGYO. Bamboo, lacquered ....Corea
The breath is directed against a V-shaped notch at one end. The same procedure is followed in No. 525. The tube is 42 cm. long and 1.5 cm. in diameter, and has four finger-holes in front and one in back. The compass is indefinable, and the name given above is uncertain.

554. ROMAN FLUTE. Bronze, heavily patinated..........Ancient Italy
This fragment (in two pieces) is 19.4 cm. long and 2.3 in diameter. It has two holes. Its position in the complete instrument cannot be fixed, and it is obviously impossible to suggest any pitch. There is no doubt as to its antiquity.

555. BEAKED FLUTE.. Slate ....
......Haidah Indians, Queen Charlotte Islands, British Columbia
The tube is decorated with conventional carvings of grasshoppers and eagles. The six finger-holes are also set in ornamental carved bands in a leaf design. Length, 46.3 cm. Diameter of conical bore, from 1.5 cm. at mouth-piece, to 9 mm. at end. Unplayable.

556. BEAKED FLUTE. Same type, material, and source as No. 555.
It is decorated by carvings in high relief of the killer-whale and a *shaman*. Four finger-holes.
Length, 56.5 cm. Diameter, 9 mm. to 2.1 cm.

557. BEAKED FLUTE. Similar to No. 556.
Length, 50.7 cm. Diameter of conical bore, 1 to 1.7 cm.
These flutes are not products of primitive industry, but represent the lure of the "Lust for Gold."

Section D. Transverse Flutes. European.

Up to the improvements of Theobald Boehm (1802-1888) the evolution of the flute was gradual and ran along established lines. In his system the nodes of the vibrating column of air were scientifically fixed, and the holes were no longer of necessity placed where the fingers and occasional keys could open and close them, but were controlled entirely by a key mechanism. The bore again became cylindrical as in the original type.

As in the following examples the distinctions largely affect the dimensions and the number of finger-holes and keys displayed in the various examples, no further detailed descriptions will be given. It must be remembered that each key represents a hole.

558. FLAUTO TRAVERSO. One section missing ....Italy
Ivory mountings. Length of the two sections, 44.4 cm.
Signed—"Carlo-Palanca."

559. LIEBESFLÖTE (Eng. Fr. *Flûte d'amour;* It. *Flauto d'amore*) in A. Boxwood. One key. Eighteenth century..........Germany
The tone of this instrument is exceptionally sweet. Length, 76 cm.

560. CONCERT FLUTE in E flat. Dark wood. One key........England
Four sections. Ivory mountings. Length, 61.7 cm.
Signed—"Cahusac, London."

561. CONCERT FLUTE. Boxwood. One key ....England
The length of this very old instrument is 54.5 cm. Four sections.
(John P. Stanley.)

561A. CONCERT FLUTE. Dark wood. Four keys.............England
Four sections. Ivory mountings. Length 60 cm.
(Mrs. Lucy Granger.)

562. TENOR FLUTE in B. Wood. Five keys..............England
Four sections. Silver mountings. Length, 76.5 cm.
Signed—"Monzane and Co., 24 Dover St., London, 1816."

563. CONCERT FLUTE in F. Dark wood. Seven keys.........England
Three sections, silver mountings. Length, 54 cm.
Signed—"Monzane and Co., 24 Dover St., London, 1817."

564. CONCERT FLUTE in E flat. Boxwood. Eight keys.......England
Five sections. Ivory mountings. Length, 67.3 cm.
Signed—"Potter, Johnson's Court, Fleet Street, London."

565. CONCERT FLUTE in F. Dark wood. Eight keys.........England
Four sections. German-silver mountings. Length, 66 cm.
Signed—"J. H. Ebbelwhite, London."

566. CONCERT FLUTE in E flat. Boxwood. Seven keys.......England
Five sections. Ivory mountings. Length, 68 cm.
Signed—"Patent 6. Will'm Hen'y Potter, Johnston's Court, Fleet St., London."

567. CONCERT FLUTE in F. Dark wood. Nine keys..........England
Five sections. Silver mountings. Length, 70.2 cm.
Signed—"Payne, No. 13, Lft. Newport St., London."

568. QUERFLÖTE in E flat. Dark wood. Thirteen keys.......Germany
Three sections. Alabata mountings. Length, 81.6 cm.
Signed—"J. Roedel, Bremen."

569. QUERFLÖTE in E flat. Ivory and white metal. Nine keys..Germany
Two sections. Silver tip. Length, 71.5 cm.
Signed—"Meyer, Hannover."

570. FLUTE TRAVERSIERE. German silver. Sixteen keys........France
Modified Boehm system. Three sections. Length, 59.5 cm.
Signed—"G. Thibonville, Buffet à Paris."

571. FLUTE TRAVERSIERE. Glass. Four keys ....France
Four sections, the second interchangeable. Length, 62 cm.
Signed—"Laurent, à Paris, 1809."

572. SPARE SECTION (No. 2) for No. 571.

573. CONCERT FLUTE in E flat. Ivory. Eight keys.......United States
Five sections. Silver mountings. Length, 67.5 cm.
Signed—"P. H. Taylor's (252) Approved Pattern, C. Peloubet, New York."

574. CANNE-FLUTE. (Eng. *Cane flute;* Ger. *Stockflöte*). Wood. One key. Length, 71.2 cm. ....France

575. CANNE-FLUTE. Lacquered sheet iron..................France
Two sections. Length, 91.5 cm.
Signed—"Ch. Mathieu."

576. BASSFLÖTE in F. Stained wood. Four finger-holes and one key .... Germany
The pitch of this seventeenth century flute does not correspond to that given by Praetorius—B flat[11]—but he describes a rather larger specimen. It is blown through an S-shaped tube inserted at the top. It resembles the English "recorder," but is the bass of the German *blockflöte*. Length, 147 cm.

577. CZAKAN. Cane Flute in B flat ....Hungary
Ivory mouth-piece. Six finger-holes. Length, 137 cm.

578. STOCKFLÖTE in E flat. Early eighteenth century........Germany
Four sections. Brass mountings. Length, 83.5 cm.

579. CANE FLUTE. Japanned sheet iron......................Italy
Brass mountings. Six finger-holes. Length, 114 cm.

580. SCHWEITZERFLÖTE in B flat. Brass ....Switzerland
Six finger-holes. Length, 41 cm.

581. SCHWEITZERFLÖTE in B flat. Eighteenth century.......Germany
Black horn mountings. Six finger-holes. Length, 37.7 cm.
Signed—"C. Paul Walsh, Berchtesgarden."

---

[11] *Sytagma Musicum,* Pl. VII, p. 24.

582. FIFE in B flat. Boxwood .... United States
Brass mountings. Six finger-holes. Length, 35.9 cm.
(Mrs. Lucy Granger.)
"The trumpets, sackbuts, psalteries and fifes,"
Shakespeare, Coriol. V. 4

583. PICCOLO in E. Dark wood. One key .... England
Two sections. Six finger-holes. Length, 31 cm.

584. PICCOLO in E. Dark wood. Five keys .... England
Two sections. Silver mounted. Six open finger-holes. Length, 32 cm.
(Mrs. Lucy Granger.)

585. PICCOLO in E. Dark wood. Six keys .... England
Three sections. German silver mountings. Six open holes.
Length, 30.7 cm.

586. PICCOLO in E. Dark wood. Six keys .... England
Alabata trimmings. Length, 29.8 cm.

586A. PICCOLO in E. Boehm system .... England
Two sections. Alabata mountings. Twelve keys. Length, 30.8 cm.

586B. PICCOLO, and FLAGEOLET. Dark wood. One key .... England
By substituting a whistle mouth-piece for the usual one, this becomes a beaked flute, or flageolet. See 510A and B.
Length, as a piccolo, 30.1 cm.; as a flageolet, 28.1 cm.
C-Whistle mouth-piece; D-E-F-G-Flute mouth-pieces.

587. FLAUTOPHON, or "Flûte Harmonique" .... France
Thirty metal flutes on a wind chest, and a tube through which one blows. Tones controlled by 30 pistons.
Length, 60.5 cm. Height, 18.4 to 25.4 cm. Width, 1.6 to 3.1 cm.
Signed—"M. Baduel, Invent. Paris."

Section E. Vibrating Column of Air in a Vertical, Cylindrical Tube with lateral Openings, Modified by the Action of a Single Beating-Reed.

A Beating Reed (Fr. *Anche;* Ital. *Ancia;* Ger. *Blatt*) is a flat flexible strip of cane, or metal, which is dressed down to a thin edge at one end. The other end is fastened, leaving the reed free to vibrate, thereby alternately opening and closing a longitudinal aperture (somewhat smaller than the reed itself) which communicates directly with the column of air enclosed in the body of the instrument. In many, or most, Oriental types the reed is cut in a section of cane, one end of which is closed by a natural joint, while the other is inserted in the first section of the instrument itself. (See No. 608.)

588. BIRD-CALL. Gourd. Cane reed. . . . . Amazon Indians, Brazil
This bird-call from Matto Grosso consists of a brown globular gourd, 8 cm. in diameter, with a stem 3 cm. long, into which a beating reed, fashioned from a stalk of cane is inserted.

589-90-91. CORNETTA. Reed horn . . . . Argentina
Into the small end of a cow's horn, scraped thin, a flat beating reed is inserted. Two metal rings for carrying are also supplied.
Lengths of curves, 39, 29 and 30 cm. Diameters of open (oval) end, 6.5, 5.5, and 4 cm.
Nos. 589 to 594 hang from top of Case.

592. REED HORN. Gourd. Brass reed . . . . Italy
Long, bottle-shaped body with a slightly bent neck into which a brass single beating reed is secured. Apparently this is a modern adaptation of the *tromba di zucca*,[12] both in material and form, but it leaves much to be desired. Length, 69 cm. Diameter of open end, 11 cm.

593. REED HORN. Cow's horn, silver mounted. Brass reed . . . . Italy
The reeds sounds e. Length, 46 cm. Diameter at bell, 11.4 cm.

594. REED HORN. Goat's horn. Brass reed. . . . . Switzerland
The cap containing reed (sounding a) unscrews from body.
Lengths of curves, 30.5 and 41 cm. Diameter, 3 to 6 cm.

595. REED HORN. Lacquered brass. Brass reed . . . . Italy
The reed in the small end of the semi-circular tube sounds f.
Lengths of curves, 47.5 and 94.5 cm. Diameter of bell, 17 cm.

596. NACHTWÄCHTERHORN. "Night-watchman's horn" . . . . . . Germany
The reed covers a flat perforated disc. Brass rings for carrying. Tube of tin. Lengths of curves, 39.2 and 52 cm. Diameter, 3 to 15.5 cm.

597-598. PEDLAR'S HORNS. Tin. Brass reed. . . . . United States

599. TIBIA PARES. Wood. Cane reeds . . . . Italy
Two conical tubes of wood, painted to resemble ivory and ending in slightly conical bells, diverge from a single mouth-piece. The left pipe has three finger-holes, the right four. The two keys are an anachronism. Sachs gives 23 varieties of the *aulos* and 16 of the *tibia*.[13] Length, 59.5 cm. Diameter of bore, 1.4 to 2.2 cm; of bells, 6.5 cm.
Reproduction by Pelitti, Milano, of the ancient Roman type.

---

[12] Sachs, p. 393, who quotes from Bonanni's *Gabinetto armonico*, p. 86.
[13] Pp. 23, 386.

600. POONGI, or TUMERI. "Snake charmer's pipe." Gourd. . . . . . . India
This instrument consists of a globular gourd 10 cm. in diameter with a neck 18 cm. long. Into the lower end two parallel wooden tubes, each 24 cm. long, are fastened by wax. Into the upper end of each a beating reed is placed. The right tube has eight finger-holes, and a thumb-hole at the back. The left has four holes only.
Length, 48 cm.

601. Space reserved for a reproduction of an Ancient Egyptian Reed Pipe.
This pipe was to have been made and presented by Dr. T. Lea Southgate, one of the most reliable of English investigators. This niche will not be filled, as he died January 26, 1917, much to the sorrow of those who were so fortunate as to know him.

602. ARGHOOL, or ARGHUL. Cane. Cane reed. Incomplete. . . . . Egypt
Length, 20 cm.; of reed, 4 cm. Width, 1 cm.

603. ZUMMARAH. Cane. Cane reed. . . . . Egypt
Four open finger-holes. Length of tube, 21.2 cm.

604. ARGHUL. Cane. Cane reed . . . . Egypt
Into the upper end of the cylinder, 23 cm. long, and 1.5 cm. in diameter, a slender beating reed is fastened by a resinous gum. Seven finger-holes. Entire length, 30.2 cm.

605. ZUMMARAH. Two tubes and beating reeds of cane. . . . . Egypt
Into each tube—18 cm. long and 1.5 cm. in diameter—a beating reed, cut in a joint of cane, or reed, 5 cm. in length, is inserted. The right tube has five finger-holes, while the left acts as a drone, sounding f.
Entire length, 24.5 cm.

606. ZUMMARAH SETTAUIA. Two tubes and reeds of cane. . . . . . . Egypt
Each tube—21 cm. in length—has six finger-holes. Usual reeds. Brought from the Island of Aegina by the donor.
(James E. Church, Jr.)

607. ARGHOOL EL-ASGHA. "The little arghool." Cane. . . . . Egypt
The parallel tubes are of unequal length, 23.1 and 54.4 cm. respectively. The right tube has six finger-holes, while the left is a drone.

608. MEIJIWIZ. Two tubes and reeds of cane. . . . . Syria
Each tube—41 cm. long—has six finger-holes and typical reeds.

609. MEIJIWIZ. Similar to No. 608. Length, 33.3 cm. . . . . Syria

610. ARGHOOL EL-KEBYR. "The great arghool." Cane. . . . . Egypt
Like No. 607, the right tube (chanter)—30 cm. long—has six finger-holes. The drone is made up of several joints thus allowing a change of pitch. Length of drone, 37.8; with all the joints inserted, 70 cm. Like all examples of this general type it is decorated. Incised lines, bangles of thin gilded copper, and cords of various colors constitute the decorative materials used.
Brought from Cairo by Mrs. James Burrill Angell.

611. GHETE. Ebony, wound with leather. Large cane reed.......Egypt
The conical tube—48.5 cm. long ending in a long conical bell, 12.5 in diameter—has six finger-holes and a typical reed.

612. REED PIPE. Hard wood body. Cane reed.....Malay Archipelago
Seven open finger-holes, and the usual type of reed. Length, 38.1 cm. Diameter of bell, 7 cm. Were it not for the conical bore, this and the preceding instrument might be classified as clarinets.

613. REED PIPE. Boxwood. Ivory mountings. Cane reed in Cap....Italy
The cylindrical, elaborately decorated body—42.5 cm. long—ending in a nearly globular gourd bell, 5.5 cm. in diameter, has five finger-holes. Lowest note c. At the upper end is a capsule (an ovoid gourd), with blow-hole in the top, in which is a large beating reed. This is characteristic of many of the earliest European types.

The Clarinet (Fr. *Clarinette;* Ger. *Klarinette;* Ital. *Clarinetto*), invented c. 1690 by Joh. Chris. Denner of Nuremberg, soon found its place in the orchestra. It has a cylindrical bore and a single beating reed. It is pitched in A, B flat, C, and E flat. F, D, and D flat clarinets have been used in the past, and Mozart, in "Idomeneo," wrote for a clarinet in B natural. Its range is from e to c''''. The tones above g''' are uncertain. The compass of the Alto Clarinet (pitched in F) extends from e to g'''. The Bassett Horn (Fr. *Cor de bassette;* Ital. *Corno bassetto*) is also pitched in F, with a compass from c to c''''. Both of these instruments are now obsolete. As in all transposing instruments, the actual tone-series is determined by their pitch, not by their apparent compass.

614. KLARINETTE in F. Boxwood. Five keys..............Germany
Four sections. Horn and ebony mountings. Eight finger-holes. In this, as in the following examples, the total number of finger-holes always includes one at the back, and must be so understood in the descriptions. Length, 48 cm.
Signed—"G. Zenkler, Iun, S. In Adore."

615. CLARINET in B flat. Six keys ....England
Five sections. Ivory mountings. Seven finger-holes. Length, 63 cm.
Signed—"V. Metzler, London."

616. CLARINET in C. Boxwood. Five keys.................England
Length, 60.5 cm. Diameter of bell, 6 cm.

617. CLARINET in B flat. Dark wood. Nine keys ....England
Five sections. Ivory mountings. Eight finger-holes. Length, 65.5 cm.
Signed—"Key, London."

618. CLARINETTE in B flat. Cocos wood. Thirteen keys........France
Four sections. Silver mountings. Seven finger-holes. Length, 64.5 cm.
Signed—"Henry Gunkel, Paris."

619. KLARINETTE in E flat. Brass. Ten keys................Austria
Eight raised finger-holes. Length, 41.5 cm.
Signed—"Sulz, E. S. Wien."

620. CLARINETTE in C. Boxwood. Thirteen keys ....Belgium
Four sections. Ivory and ebony mountings. Seven holes. Length, 58 cm.
Signed—"Willame, Mons."

621. CLARINET in A. Dark wood. Ten keys............United States
Five sections. Ivory and silver mountings. Eight holes. Length, 68.3 cm.
Signed—"C. Christman, N. York."

622. KLARINETTE in C. Boxwood. Thirteen keys...........Germany
Four sections. Ivory mountings. Seven finger-holes. Length, 59 cm.
Signed—"Mollenhauer, Fulda."

623. KLARINETTE in A. Ebony, covered with German silver..Germany
Thirteen keys. Four sections. Seven finger-holes. Length, 68 cm.

624. CLARINET in B flat. Dark wood. Fifteen keys...........England
Four sections. German silver mountings. Seven holes. Length, 65.5 cm.

625. KLARINETTE in B flat. Modified Boehm system ....Germany
Eleven keys. Four sections. Brass mountings. Seven holes. Length, 66.5 cm.
Signed—"Sauerhering, Magdeburg."

It must be stated that, accoustically, the Boehm system can be fully applied only to the flute; therefore the term "modified Boehm system" must be understood as applying to some one of the many adaptations of his key-mechanism to other types of wood-wind instruments.

626-627. KLARINETTEN in B flat. Brass. Ten keys...........Austria
Each instrument has a body in one section, and eight raised finger-holes. Length, 56.5 cm.

628. CLARINETTO. Alto in F. Wood, covered with leather........Italy
Four sections, of which two are covered with leather. Ivory mountings. Seven finger-holes. No keys. Length, 83 cm.

629. ALT-KLARINETTE (Eng. *Tenor-clarinet*) in F. Boxwood..Germany
Fifteen keys. Four sections. Ivory mountings. Seven finger-holes. Length, 84 cm.
Signed—"Seidel, Mainz."

630. CLARINETTE-TENOR in E flat. Brass. Fifteen keys........France
The upper end of the tube is bent slightly backward, and the bell turns upward. The open thumb-hole in the back is the only one not covered by rings or keys. Length, 100 cm. Diameter of bell, 10 cm.
Signed—"Halari, Fournisseur de l'Empereur, à Paris."

631. CLARINETTE-TENOR in E flat. Dark wood. Seventeen keys. . France
Two sections. German silver mountings. Finger-holes as in the preceding. Length, 99 cm. Diameter of bell, 10 cm.
Signed—"Buffet, Crampon Cie, à Paris."

632. BASSETTHORN. Boxwood. Sixteen keys. . . . . Germany
The tube, bent midway at an angle, is in five sections. Ivory mountings. Seven finger-holes.
Length, 120 cm. Diameter of bell, 9.8 by 15.6 cm.
Signed—"F. Schölnast, Presburg."

633. BASSETTHORN. Boxwood. Fourteen keys. . . . . Germany
Five sections. Brass and ivory mountings. Bent at middle by a short elbow. Seven finger-holes. Late eighteenth century. Length, 106 cm.
Signed—"H. Grenser, Dresden."

634. BASSETTHORN. Boxwood. Eight keys. . . . . Germany
Body bent in middle. The bell projects from a three-sided block. Five sections. Ivory and brass mountings. Seven finger-holes.
Length, 120 cm.
Signed—"W. Hesse, Kammermusiker, Brunswig, 1789."

The Bass Clarinet (Fr. *Clarinette basse;* Ital. *Clarinetto basso;* Ger. *Bassklarinette*) was first constructed by Grenser, of Dresden, in 1793; lacking keys it was not successful. In 1807 Dumas developed an instrument with 13 keys, but it was unsuccessful. Streitwolf of Goettingen, in 1828, raised the number of keys to 17. It is pitched in B flat, one octave lower than the ordinary clarinet of that pitch. Buffet, of Paris, also constructed one pitched in C, with a compass from e to g‴.

In 1890, M. Albert, of Brussells, constructed a Contra Bass (or Pedal) Clarinet, pitched an octave below the Basset Horn. In 1891 Besson, of Paris, patented a form pitched in B flat, two octaves below the ordinary clarinet.

635. CLARINETTE BASSE in B flat. Dark wood. Twenty keys. . . . France
The parallel tubes, the smaller cylindrical, the larger slightly conical, are united at the lower end by a short brass elbow. The longer tube ends in a brass bell, the shorter carries the ebony mouthpiece and reed. No finger-holes. Length, 134 cm.; of model, 68 cm.
Signed—"A. Buffet, Jne. à Paris."

636. BASSKLARINETTE in B flat. Hardwood. Twenty-four keys. Germany
In construction similar to the preceding, excepting that the shorter tube bears the bell. Brass mountings. Three finger holes.
Length, 186 cm.; of model, 76 cm. Diameter of bell, 16.5 cm.
Signed—"C. Kruspe, Erfurt."

637. CLARINETTE BASSE in C. Dark wood. Twenty keys......Belgium
Two sections. Brass mountings. No open finger-holes. The original bell, which probably curved upwards, has been replaced by a straight bell, stamped "C. Roth, à Strasbourg."
Length, 128 cm.; of model, 80 cm.
Signed—"Sax. à Bruxelles."

638. CLARINETTE BASSE in B flat. Dark wood. Twenty keys....France
Two sections. Ebony mountings. No open finger-holes.
Length, 138 cm.; 74.8 cm. Diameter of bell, 16 cm.
Signed—"Buffet, Crampon, à Paris."'

639. CLARINETTE BASSE in B flat. Dark wood. Twenty keys....France
Two sections. White metal mountings. Two finger-holes.
Length, 132 cm.
Signed—"Buffet, Crampon et Cie, à Paris."

The Saxophone was first constructed by Adolphe Sax, of Brussels in 1844. It consists of a parabolic body of metal, with finger-holes and keys, to which a clarinet mouth-piece and reed are fitted. It has a great range, is facile in execution, and when not forced has a very sympathetic tone, which, however, can easily become very nasal and disagreeable. Although it has been utilized by Verdi, Bizet and others in the orchestra, it finds more favor with band-masters. The family consists of seven members, ranging from the *Saxophone sopranino*, in high B flat, down to the *Saxophone contrabasse*, in C or B flat. The same form of body was used by Desfontenelles of Lisieux in clarinets as early as 1807.

The compass of the various Saxophones runs as follows: High (in E flat, or B flat), to f‴. The Alto (in F or E flat); Tenor (in C); Baritone (in F) the same; while the Bass (in C, or B flat) runs to e flat‴ only.

640. SAXOPHONE. Soprano in B flat. Brass. Eighteen keys....Belgium
The straight conical body of brass—66 cm. in length, including mouth-piece—terminates in a slightly flaring bell, 7.5 cm. in diameter. No open finger-holes.
Signed—"C. Mahillon, Bruxelles."

641. SAXOPHONE. Tenor in C. Metal. Twenty keys..........France
At the lower end, the body is bent upon itself and ends in a small up-turned bell. No open finger-holes.
Length, 117 cm. Diameter of bell, 13.8 cm.
Signed—"No. 20669. Adolphe Sax, à Paris."

642. CANE CLARINET. Soprano in C. Wood. Five keys......England
Eight holes. Length, 83.5 cm.; of clarinet, 56 cm.
Signed—"Amman, C."

643. CANNE-CLARINETTE. High Soprano in B flat. Metal......France
The upper part forms a clarinet, 34 cm. long. Nine holes, of which two, as in the preceding example, are vent-holes.
Length of cane, 91 cm.
Signed—"C. Mathieu, à Paris."

644. AUTOMATIC CLARINET PLAYER ....Germany
Placed in a special Case, south of Case VII.

The figure is 197.5 cm. in height. The original gay habiliments vanished in the fire which destroyed its home, Barnum's Museum, New York, and, as the mechanism was wrecked, it is impossible to give any information as to its repertoire. The brass clarinet, in three sections, is 36 cm. long, and the diameter of the bell is 12.5 cm. The wind was furnished by a bellows run by clock work, which also governed the movement of the eighteen keys, of which two are in the bell section.

Friedrich Kaufman, of Dresden, (1785-1866), invented a number of such automatic players, and it is very probable that this automaton was made by his son, Friedrich Theodor (1823-1872), who developed the Orchestrion —in 1851—from an earlier instrument devised by his father.

The development of general musical appreciation is shown by the fact that, the automatic, or mechanical, musical instruments in vogue a few decades ago—with the exception of barrel-organs and music-boxes—could produce melody only. The modern self-players produce harmony as well. A comparison of a two-manual Orchestrelle with this clarinet virtuoso will enforce this statement.

CASE VII.

CLASS III.

Section F. Vibrating Column of Air in a Vertical Conical Tube with lateral Openings, Modified by the Action of Double Beating-Reeds.

A Double Reed consists of two thin strips of elastic wood, grass, or cane, so bound together as to stand slightly apart at the tips. The opening thus formed is periodically opened and closed as the reeds are made to vibrate by the breath of the player. These vibrations are communicated to the column of air contained in the body of the instrument, through a small tube on which the lower ends of the reeds are fixed. In primitive and certain Oriental types the reeds are of rude construction and are made from various materials. In European instruments they are made from the outer silicious shell of a tall grass (*Arundo Donax*), and are fashioned with extreme delicacy.

645. PI. Schalmei type. Hard wood, turned. Cane reeds.........Siam
The body, 41 cm. long, has its greatest diameter—4.5 cm.—in the middle. It has six finger-holes in groups of four and two, the former uppermost.

646. SO NA. Wood, with brass bell. Cane reeds...............China
A conical tube, with bell at the lower end and a pagoda-like reed holder at the upper, is bored with seven finger-holes and one thumb-hole in their usual positions. Length, 32 cm. Diameter of bell, 9 cm.

647. ZURNA. Wood. Mother-of-pearl inlay. Cane reeds........Persia
Finger-holes. One thumb-hole. Length, 36.3 cm.

648. MUKAVINA, SANAI, or SURNAY. *Chandannah* wood ....India
Cane reeds. Conical bore and bell. Seven holes. Length, 26.5 cm.
Also known as *holarcha surnai*, and *holarcha sur*. *Hanumunta ottu* is the name of a form with no finger-holes and which is used as a bourdon in connection with other instruments of this type.

649. ZAMR EL-KEBYR. "The large zamr." Wood. Cane reeds....Egypt
In the conical body, ending in a bell, seven equidistant finger-holes and two thumb-holes are bored. Seven small holes in the bell regulate the pitch, as any desired number may be closed with wax. The name given differentiates it from the *zamr el-soghair*, which is much smaller. Length, 60.2 cm. Diameter of bell, 9.3 cm.

650. ZAMR (pl. *zumur*). Similar in structure to No. 649.........Egypt
Length, 48 cm. Diameter of bell, 5.6 cm.

651. ZURNA, or SORNAY. Similar to preceding instrument.......Egypt
Length, 48 cm. Diameter of bell, 7.7 cm.

652. SCHALMEI. (Fr. *Chalumeau;* Ital. *Cialamello*) . . . . Germany
The body of this seventeenth century instrument is of ebony, in three sections which are connected by silver bands. The mouth-piece has an ivory tip. Six finger-holes. Typical reeds.
Length, 44.5 cm. Diameter of bells, 5 cm.

653. SHAWM in F. Dark wood . . . . England
Six finger-holes, one thumb-hole. One key. Length, 30 cm.

An aggravating peculiarity of double-reed instruments is indicated in "one of the 'proverbis' written about the time of Hen. VII on the walls of the Manor House, at Leckingfelde, near Beverly, Yorkshire."

"A shawme maketh a swete sound, for he tunyth the basse,
It mountithe not to hye, but kepithe rule and space.
Yet yf it be blowne with to vehement a wynde,
It makithe it to misgovern out of its kinde."[1]

654. SCHALMEI in F . . . . Germany
Two brass keys. Pear-shaped bell and usual finger-holes.
Length, 36.1 cm.

The *Schalmey* was the highest pitched instrument of the *Bomhart* family, corrupted in Germany to *Pommer*, the bass representative being called *Brummer*. The Alto Pommer is the direct ancestor of the *Cor Anglais*.

655. BOMBARDE in F. Ebony, ivory mountings . . . . Brittany, France
This is a modern evolution from the *bomhart* (Ger. Span. *bombarda*), mentioned by Praetorius (1618) and dating back to the thirteenth century. This specimen has six finger-holes, and one key, with double touch-piece. The early, popular name for trombone in the Netherlands was *bombarda*.
Length, 31.5 cm. Diameter of bell, 8.5 cm.

656. SCHALMEY in C. Ebony with German silver bell . . . . Italy
Seven finger-holes, one thumb-hole.
Length, 52 cm. Bell diameter, 9.7 cm.
Signed—"G. Pelitti, Milano."

657. DOUBLE-REED PIPE. Brass. (For theatrical use) . . . . Italy
Six finger-holes. Length, 68 cm. Diameter of bell, 8 cm.

658. DOUBLE-REED PIPE. Brass . . . . Italy
Six finger-holes. Length, 66 cm. Diameter of bell, 7.9 cm.

659. DOUBLE-REED PIPE. Bronze. Of early date . . . . Italy
Six finger-holes. Length, 52.7 cm. Diameter, lower end, 2.2 cm.

660. DOUBLE-REED PIPE. Brass. (Very crude type) . . . . Italy
No finger-holes. Length, 45.6 cm. Diameter, lower end, 1.9 cm.

---

[1] J. Eastwood and W. Aldis Wright, "The Bible Word-Book," p. 433.

PLATE VI.

CASE VII. SOUTH SECTION. NOS. 651 TO 704 (RIGHT TO LEFT)

661. TOURNEBOUT. Wood, covered with leather. Eighteenth century. Italy
The body is shaped like the letter J, and has six finger-holes and two pitch-regulating holes.
Length, 96 cm. Diameter at open end, 5.4 cm.

662. HICHI-RIKI. "Sad-toned tube." Bamboo. Cane reeds...... Japan
On account of the large reeds and character of bore, the tone resembles that of the clarinet. It is decorated on outer surface with bands of black lacquered cords, and the interior is colored red. The reeds are tightly pressed in the holder, *shita*, by dampened Mino paper. The cane for the reeds grows in Udono, is cut in mid-winter, and must be dried with great care.[2] The body has seven finger-holes, and two thumb-holes.
Length, 18.2 cm. Diameter of bore, 1 to 1.6 cm.

663. HICHI-RIKI. An exact replica of No. 652 .... Japan

664. CIALAMELLO. "Peasant's oboe." Brass, coin ornaments...... Italy
Besides the ten coins (portraits), the tube is ornamented with engraved lines. Bell of horn with ivory rim. Six finger-holes and one thumb-hole. Length, 33 cm. Diameter of bell, 4.7 cm.

The Oboe (Eng. *Hoeboy;* Fr. *Hautbois;* Ger. *Hoboe*) is derived from the *Schalmey*. It is pitched in C, but, by the use of certain keys, b natural and b flat are available. Its extreme compass runs from b flat to f‴. The upper notes are somewhat hazardous. Its varying effects, from pathos to a subtle jollity, have been utilized by all the great composers.

The *Oboe d' Amour* is pitched in A, and its hollow globular bell imparts to it a lovely quality. The *Oboe da caccia* (Fr. *Hautbois de chasse*) stands in F, or E. It was known generations ago as the *Faggotino* and was considered a bassoon pitched a fourth higher, rather than an oboe pitched a fifth lower. Its form, in the early type, resembled the former, rather than the latter instrument. These types are now obsolete and are not represented in the Collection.

The English Horn (Fr. *Cor Anglais;* Ital. *Corno Inglesi;* Ger. *Englisches Horn*) was developed from the "tenner hoboy,"[3] but not by Ferlendis, and in its first form was bent at an angle (No. 672). It was for this reason called *Cor anglé*, which, according to one theory, was corrupted into the present designation.[4] Another theory holds that its early and common use in England accounts for its name. It is pitched in F, and possesses a pathetic tone quality quite individual. Its compass extends from b to e‴.

[2] Piggott, p. 183.

[3] Galpin, "Old Eng. Insts. of Music," p. 166. Future quotations will give the name of the author only.

[4] Sachs' contention (p. 129) that *cor* and *anglé* are incompatible does not hold, as originally *cor* did not of necessity mean a curved horn, but was the generic name for a horn of any form or material; again, the acute accent over e in *angle,* to which he objects, was used as late as 1690, as is shown in Furetiere—*Dictionnaire universelle,* I, (no pagination). This statement is not to be construed as involving an endorsement of the theory, but rather to show that its rejection must be based on other grounds.

665. OBOE in C. Stained wood. Two silver keys............England
Three sections. Six finger-holes. Two holes in bell. Length, 58.3 cm.
Signed—"Cahusac, London."

666. OBOE in C. Boxwood. Three brass keys. Early date.....Germany
Three sections. Six finger-holes. Two holes in bell. Length, 55.5 cm.

667. OBOE in C. Similar to the preceding but 3 cm. longer.....Germany
Signed—"I. H. Rottenburgh."

668. OBOE in C. Boxwood. Eight keys......................Italy
Three sections. Six finger-holes. Two holes in bell. Length, 55.3 cm.
Signed—"G. Riva di Persiceto."

669. OBOE in C. Boxwood. Eleven brass keys...............Austria
Three sections. Ivory mountings. Six finger-holes. Length, 56.5 cm.
Signed—"S. Koch, Wien."

670. OBOE in C. Boxwood. Thirteen keys ....Germany
Three sections. Ivory mountings. Six finger-holes. Length, 55 cm.

671. OBOE in C. Dark wood. Sixteen keys. Modified Boehm system.
Three sections. Six finger-holes. Length, 59 cm....United States
Signed—"E. Baack, New York."

672. ENGLISCHES HORN. Dark wood. Bent model. Ten keys...Austria
Four sections. Pear-shaped bell. Six finger-holes. Length, 78 cm.
Signed—"S. Koch, Wien."

673. ENGLISCHES HORN. Boxwood. Bent model. Fourteen keys. Germany
Four sections. Six finger-holes. Length, 79.1 cm.

674. COR ANGLAIS in G. Curved model. Wood..............France
Two sections. Ten keys. Ivory mountings. Length, 79 cm.
Signed—"Triebert, à Paris."

675. COR ANGLAIS in F. Straight model. Dark wood..........France
Boehm system. Seventeen keys. Four holes. Length, 79.5 cm.
Signed—"Mangeaut, Brevelé, Paris."

676. "PETIT CASSON." Dark wood. Butt-joint. Thirteen keys..France
Three sections. Ivory mountings. Five finger-holes. Length, 104 cm.
Signed—"Triebert, à Paris."

The Hecklephon occupies a position midway between the English Horn and the Bassoon. It was first devised by F. Lorée of Paris, but is named after his rival, Heckel, the celebrated instrument maker of Biebrich, who began constructing it in various pitches in 1904. Pitched an octave lower than the Oboe it is sometimes called the Baritone-oboe. R. Strauss used it in the score of "Salome." Its compass runs from B to g″, in actual tones.

676A. HECKELPHON in C. Dark wood. Twenty-three keys. . . . . Germany
This beautiful example of the ultra-modern instrument described above, has a conical tube, 121 cm. in length, and from 5.5 to 3 cm. in diameter. In the upper end a curved metal tube carrying a reed is inserted while the lower end terminates in a globular wooden bell 10.1 cm. in diameter, in one side of which is a circular opening 2.5 cm. in diameter. The tube is in four sections and bears a very elaborate key-mechanism.
Signed—"Heckel, Biberich. Ges. geschütz. 3243."
(Loaned by the Chicago Orchestral Association.)

The Bassoon (Fr. *Basson;* Ital. *Fagotto;* Ger. *Fagott*), is pitched a twelfth lower than the oboe, but by the use of certain keys this original compass is extended to two octaves below. The tube is doubled on itself through a butt-joint. The conically-bored pipe is divided into five pieces. Reckoning from the player's lips they may be enumerated as follows: A. Crook, a curved tube of metal carrying the double-reed; B. Wing; C. Butt-joint; D. Bass-joint, extending upwards; E. Bell. (See No. 678.)

The instrument, dating from the sixteenth century, was evolved from the *pommer* with the Curtall, or Dulcian (Fr. *Doucaine*) as an intermediate type. Probably misled by the similarity in name, certain writers have seen its ancestor in the *Phagotus*, an instrument invented *circa* 1539 by Afriano, Canon of Ferrara. Cecil Forsythe gives a detailed description of this instrument in his "Orchestration," pp. 487-489. An interesting form, known as the Racket, or Sausage-Bassoon (Fr. *Cervelat;* Ger. *Wurstfagott*), so called from its resemblance to a section of Bologna sausage, is obsolete and is not in the Collection. The Bassoon has an extended compass:—BB flat to e flat″, and, in spite of certain inaccuracies not yet remedied, is one of the most useful instruments in the modern orchestra.

The Double-Bassoon (Fr. *Contre-basson;* Ital. *Contra fagotto;* Ger. *Kontrafagott*) is pitched an octave lower than the ordinary type.

677. FAGOTTO in C. Dark wood. Six keys (missing) . . . . Italy
The bell of this early eighteenth century specimen, is in the form of a dragon's head. Six finger-holes. One thumb-hole. Brass mountings. Length, 144.5 cm.

678. BASSOON in C. Six keys. Eighteenth century . . . . England
Dark wood. Brass mountings. Six finger-holes. Two thumb-holes. Length, 125 cm.

679. BASSOON in C. Dark wood. Thirteen keys . . . . England
Brass mountings. Six finger-holes. Two thumb-holes. Length 123 cm.
Signed—"Keys, London."

680. FAGOTT in C. Dark wood. Thirteen keys ....Germany
Brass mountings. Six finger-holes. Two thumb-holes. Length, 132.5 cm.
Signed—"Adler, Bamberg."

681. BASSON in C. Enamelled wood. Seventeen keys........Belgium
German silver mountings. Six finger-holes. Thumb-holes.
Length, 125 cm.
Signed—"Mahillon and Co., Brussells."

682. BASSON in C. Brass, nickel-plated. Seventeen keys........France
Five finger-holes. Thumb-holes. Length, 135 cm.
Signed—"A. Le Conte et Cie., Paris."

683. KONTRAFAGOTT in C. Wood. Eleven keys............Germany
German silver mountings. Four finger-holes. Length, 178.5 cm.
Signed—"Heckel, Biebrich."

684. KONTRAFAGOTT. Dark wood. Seventeen keys........Germany
This model was designed by Dr. W. H. Stone, F. R. S. It has a very extended range, is easy of manipulation, musically effective, but it has not been adopted to any extent. This may be owing to its size.
Brass mountings. No finger-holes. Length, 138 cm.
Signed—"Verfertigt von Ch. Geipel, Breslau."

685. CONTRE-BASSON. Brass. Seventeen keys ....Belgium
In form of a tuba. Length, 105 cm. Diameter of bell, 24 cm.
Signed—"Gautrot Marquette, breveté, s.g.d.g., à Paris."

686. SARRUSOPHONE. High Soprano in B flat. Brass. Nineteen keys, with modified Boehm system. Length, 47 cm.......France
Signed—"Gautrot Marquette Breveté, s.g.d.g.a., Paris."

687. SARRUSOPHONE. Tenor in B flat. Sixteen keys..........France
Signed—"No. 504, Henri Sax, Paris."
This instrument was invented in 1856 by M. Sarrus, a bandmaster in the French army, and perfected by Gautrot Marquet. Although it has many admirable characteristics, and has been made in nine pitches, it is not of great musical importance.

Section G. Vibrating Columns of Air in Tubes, Modified by the Action of Single and Double Beating-Reeds, with an Air Reservoir, or Bellows.

The Bagpipe (Fr. *Cornemuse, Biniou, Musette;* Ital. *Cornamusa;* Ger. *Sack-pfeife*), is of great antiquity. It was known to the Babylonians, is described in Sancrit treatises on music, and used by the Hebrews, Greeks and Romans (*tibia utricularis*). It was known at a very remote date as the *chorus*, but this designation was applied to a stringed instrument as early as the eleventh century. In the fourteenth century it was mentioned by Almeric de Peyrac as follows: "Quidam Choros consonantes; Duplicem chordam perstridentes."[5]

[5] Quoted by Sachs, p. 80.

It consists of a drone pipe (1300), or pipes (1400-1500), with cylindrical bore, and single reed; the chaunter, or melody pipe, with conical bore. and double reeds, and a wind chest, or bag. It exists in great variety.

The Bagpipe is of special interest in that it combines the clarinet type (drone) and the oboe (chaunter).

688. ZAMPOGNA. Goat-skin bag. Two drones ....Calabria, Italy
Two chaunters with five finger-holes each; the shorter with thumb-hole. Two holes above the bell for regulating pitch. The reeds are missing.
Length of chaunters, 27.5 and 45 cm.; of drones, 20 and 33 cm.

689. SOUQQAREH. Bag of skin. Reed tubes. Tunis............Africa
The bag, of the skin of some wild animal with the hair retained, is inflated through a tube of bone, decorated with incised lines (in black) and silver bands. The chaunters have a single beating-reed each, and terminate in upturned bells of horn. Each has five finger-holes.
Length of tubes, with bells, 22 cm.; of bag, 44 cm.

690. BOMBARD BRETONNE. Leather bag. Drone and chaunter...France
Seven finger-holes. Length of chaunter, 13.5 cm.; of drone, 33 cm.

691. MUSETTE BRETONNE. Velvet-covered bag ....France
Drones and chaunter. Six finger-holes, thumb-hole, and usual key.
Length of drones, 16 and 27 cm.; of chaunter, 23 cm.

692. CORNEMUSE. Velvet-covered bag. Drone and chaunter....France
The chaunter, of ivory, has seven finger-holes and one thumb-hole. The bag is inflated by bellows.
Length of chaunter, 33 cm.; of drone, 15 cm.

693. "BINIOU DE BERRY." Velvet-covered bag ....France
Drone and two chaunters. A beautifully decorated instrument. Two cylindrical drones and a conical chaunter of ebony, with ivory mountings, are fitted into a stock inlaid with mother-of-pearl, etched ivory, and various woods. The bag is inflated by a bellows.
Length of chaunter, 38.8 cm.; of drones, 30.5 and 78 cm.
Signed—"Bechonnet et Effiat, à Puy-de-Dome."

694. UNION PIPES Leather bag, and bellows, the latter with keys. Three drones, and two chaunters.....................Ireland
The drone keys were added in the eighteenth century.
Entire length, 98.9 cm.; of drones, 27.2, 35.8 and 77.4 cm.; of chaunters, 40 and 45.6 cm.; brass socket, into which drones and chaunters are fixed, 17.4 by 7.1 cm. Number of keys on drones, 2, 4 and 4.
The name given to this unique type has been thought by many to refer to the "legislative Union of Great Britain and Ireland in 1801," but Galpin suggests that it is a "mistaken rendering of the native *uilleann*, or 'elbow-pipes.' "[6]

[6] Galpin, p. 179.

695. BINIOU AUVERGNAT. Leather bag. Usual pipes.........France
The chaunter has six finger-holes and one thumb-hole.
Length of chaunter, 61.5 cm.; of drones, 47 and 120 cm.

696. PRACTICE CHAUNTER. Ebony, ivory mountings........Scotland
The cylindrical tube has seven finger-holes and one thumb-hole. It is used by learners only, for which reason it is very fortunate that its tone is soft and muffled. Length, 54 cm.
Signed—"R. Henderson, Glasgow."

697. GAITA ZAMORANA. Cloth-covered bag. Two drones, 17.5 cm., and 68 cm. long, and chaunter 29 cm. in length..........Spain
The covering is decorated with red borders, appliqué work, gilt braid, and brass buttons. The chaunter has seven finger-holes, a thumb-hole and three pitch-regulating holes.
The name is a survival of the Moorish supremacy in Spain. *Ghaida* is the Turkish name for bagpipe and a *schalmey* in Portugal is called *gaita*. *Gaita gallega, gaita grileira, gaita redonda,* and *gaita tumbul* are structural variants of the Spanish bagpipe.

698. BELLOWS for No. 694.

699. HIGHLAND BAGPIPE. Bag with cover of plaid cloth. Three drones and a chaunter ....Scotland
The pipes are of ebonized wood, with brass and ivory mountings. The chaunter has seven finger-holes, a thumb-hole and two pitch-regulating holes. Drones fitted with tuning-slides, as is the usual practice.
Length of chaunter, 41 cm.; of drones, 34, 42, and 73 cm.

700. CORNEMUSE. Bag with cover of plush. Drone and chaunter..France
The chaunter has seven finger-holes, a thumb-hole and two pitch-regulators. All the parts are made of ebony with ivory mountings.
Length of chaunter, 36 cm.; of drone, 27 cm.

Section H. Vibrating Column of Air in a Vertical Cylindrical Tube, Modified by the Action of a Free Reed.

A Free Reed does not rest on a block (single beating reed), nor on another reed (double-reed), but swings freely through an aperture slightly larger than the reed itself. The principle was known at a very early date in the Orient, and was first introduced into Europe by Kranzenstein, an organ builder at the Court of Catherine II, of Russia (1729-1796).

701. KELURI. A primitive free-reed instrument ....Borneo
It consists of an air reservoir of wood, on the top of which are arranged six tubes of cane, each of which contains a free reed, also of cane.

A mouth-piece—11.5 cm. long and 1.5 cm. in diameter—inserted in the hollow ovoid shell, whose dimensions are 6.5 by 12 cm., supplies the air. Length of tubes, 33 to 61 cm.

The *engkruri* (*engkerujai*) and *gurude*, also of Borneo, are of the *keluri* type, differing somewhat in details, while the *him*, or *heem*, an instrument of Laos origin, is its representative in Siam and Burmah.

702. KEN. Fourteen tubes of cane each containing a reed, also of cane, running through an air chamber . . . . Laos

Each tube has one finger-hole set in a lead plate. The holes in the longer tubes are stopped by the thumbs, in the shorter by the fingers.

The *ken* produces harmonies and frequently accompanies the *chlui*, or indigenous flute.[7] Length of chamber, 14.5cm.; of shortest tube, 67.3; of longest, 96.4 cm.

703. KHEN, or PHAN. Similar to No. 702, with plain finger-holes. . . Laos

Length of chamber, 16.3 cm.; of shortest tube, 69.5; of longest, 106.5 cm.

704. SHO. Air reservoir of dark wood carrying seventeen bamboo pipes, each containing a free reed of brass . . . . Japan

The reservoir is conical and is lacquered in black, silver, and gold. The short mouth-piece was originally faced with silver. The fourth, ninth, and tenth pipes are silver-mounted. The pipes are held in position by a metal ring, placed just below the middle. The pipes, beginning at the open space in ring and counting from right to left, are named, *hu*, *mo*, *kotsu*, *bok*, *jo*, *gyo*, *hichi*, *gou*, *ya*, *hachi*, *ichi*, *bei*, *ku*, *otsu*, *gei*, *jeu*, *sen*.[8]

705. SHENG. Bowl-shaped body of polished dark wood, with an ivory rosette at bottom. Seventeen tubes and reeds . . . . China

Length, 42.5 cm.; of pipes, 14 to 43 cm.

706. SHENG. Similar to the preceding but shorter . . . . China

To play the *sheng* the breath is drawn in. Nos. 704 and 705 are housed in the halves of the case in which the *sho* is placed when not in use. Nos. 705-6-7 are from the Beal-Steere Collection.

707. SHENG. Dismantled to show details of construction.

The mouth-piece, *chou or tsui* (A), is of wood, and the outer end is faced with an ivory plate. The air-chamber, *sheng tou* or *p'ao*, (B), is of *wu t'ung* wood scented with camphor and stained black. In form it is circular with convex sides. The top (C) is of hard wood. A horizontal partition, reaching from the bottom to a point half-way to the top, carries a solid drum of wood reaching to the top and leaving a space around it for the passage of

[7] Knosp, *Ueber annamitische Musik*, p. 164.
[8] Piggot, p. 186. Sachs gives a different order, p. 370.

the air. The pipes, *hsui chua*, or *ḳuan* (D), are of bamboo, and stand in holes around the top of the air-chamber. At the bottom of each pipe is a tapering foot of hard wood, of which one-half is above the air reservoir. In the lower part of the top a slit is made in which a thin brass reed, *huang*, is fixed. All the reeds face the air-chamber. Each pipe has a long narrow slit in the inner side, and a finger hole near the lower end. This hole must be closed if the pipe is to speak. In addition to the usual method of tone-production varying effects may be produced by direct blowing. The inverted pipe above (B) shows the reed and finger-hole; the longitudinal slit is seen in the pipe at the right.

The dimensions are, of A, length, 3.5 cm.; diameter, 2 cm.; of B, height, 6 cm.; diameter, 4 to 7 cm.; of C, same diameter as B; length of D, from 15 to 42.4 cm.; diameter, 9 mm. In addition to this description from Moule, pp. 89-90, detailed information may be found on pp. 90-95. *Cheng*, so frequently given, is the French spelling of *sheng*.

708. STATUETTE OF BAGPIPE PLAYER . . . . Italy

709. CEREMONIAL WHISTLE. Wood. Ribbon reed. Length, 23.5 cm.
The ribbon reed is fastened at both ends and vibrates in middle.
A reed not met with elsewhere[9] . . . . . Haidah Indians, B. Columbia

710. MITZ-SHIO-SHI. Three lacquered bamboo tubes . . . . Japan
The tones produced are fundamentals. Length of tubes, 6.6 cm.

711. SHO-SHI-BUYE. Six silver tubes. Free reeds. Twelve tones . . . Japan
Of more extended compass. Length of tubes, 8 cm.

712. CORNETTA. Brass, with reed, sounding f . . . . Argentina
Lengths of curves, 19 and 21.5 cm. Diameter of bell, 6.4 cm.

713. POCKET SIGNAL-HORN. Nickel-plated brass . . . . England
Two free reeds, sounding a flat, and f. Length, 7 cm.

714. SHO-SHI. Twelve bamboo tubes each containing a free reed and arranged in the order of a Japanese scale . . . . Japan
The length of these tubes, each of which has the name of its tone traced on the body in Chinese characters, runs from 11 to 18 cm.[10]

---

[9] For detailed information regarding this form of reed consult Galpin, "The Whistles used by Alaskan Indians, and Reed Instruments of the Am. Ind. of the N. W. Coast." Proc. Mus. Assn., 29th Sess., 1892, and Morris, pp. 78-87, including the valuable suggestions of Mr. E. H. Hawley, pp. 81, 82.

[10] See diagrams of Chinese scales—Case XVI.
An exhaustive treatment of this subject may be found in an article entitled, "Musical Scales of various Nations," by Alexander J. Ellis, in Jour. Royal Society of Arts, 1884-5, pp. 485-527.

PLATE VII.

CASE VII. NORTH SECTION. NOS. 691 TO 776 (RIGHT TO LEFT)

Section I. Vibrating Free Reeds Actuated by Bellows and Controlled by Keys, or Pistons.

The Accordion (Fr. *Accordéon;* Ital. *Armonica a manticino;* Ger. *Ziehharmonika*) was invented in 1829 by Damian of Vienna. Its essential constructive features are a pair of hand bellows, one side of which is attached to a key-board, with keys, varying in number from five to fifty, operating metal free reeds. Each key controls two notes with the inflation or deflation of the bellows. The Concertina (Ger. *Konzertina*)—invented by Sir Charles Wheatstone, June 19, 1829—is hexagonal in shape and has pistons, or "touches" on both ends of the bellows.

715. ACCORDION. Twenty-three keys .... England
Body dimensions 12 by 35.4 cm. Spread of bellows, 7 to 21 cm.
(Norman A. Wood.)

716. "MELODEON." Accordéon. Nineteen keys .... France
Body dimensions, 12 by 32.5 cm. Spread of bellows, 15 to 41 cm.

717. ACCORDION. Ten pistons controlling pallet valves. Two sets of free reeds, controlled by stops .... England
Body dimensions, 13 by 28 cm. Spread of bellows, 19 to 30 cm.
Signed—"J. H. Ebbelwhite, London."

718. ZIEHHARMONIKA. Twenty-one keys .... Germany
The body is beautifully inlaid with mother-of-pearl. Body dimensions, 8.9 by 30.4 cm. Spread of bellows, 6.5 to 27 cm.

719. PITCH-PIPE. Brass reed controlled by a bar of metal which changes the length of vibrating tongue. Compass from f′ to f″. (This comes under Section E) .... United States

720. KONZERTINA Twenty-seven ivory pistons .... Germany
Diameter, 16.5 cm. Spread of bellows, 14 to 35 cm.

721. ARMONICA A MANTICINO. Forty-eight porcelain pistons....... Italy
The deep, rectangular body is richly inlaid with various woods. The pallets, operated by pistons, are hidden by an elaborate fret-work. The pistons, or "touches," are arranged in four rows upon an upright finger-board. The bellows, fitted with an exhaust valve, have a spread from 32.5 to 86 cm., and the body dimensions are 16.5 by 30 cm.
Signed—"Tesio Jean."

722-723. TWO CONCERTINAS. Similar to 720.............. Germany

724. "ARIOPHONE," or "MYTHERIA." Ziehharmonika ...... Germany
Ten pistons controlling pallet valves. Two harmony keys and exhaust valve. Body dimensions, 16 by 32 cm. Spread of bellows, 35 cm.

725. ACCORDEON. Thirty-two mother-of-pearl pistons. Three stops, each controlling a set of reeds. Frame richly inlaid.......France
Body dimensions, 18.8 by 33.5 cm. Spread of bellows, 17 to 43 cm.

Sub-Section I. Vibrating Free Reeds Actuated by the Breath, (with or without keys).

726. BLAS-HARMONIKA. Brass. Thirty-three keys and reeds...Germany
The body is a thin plate on which are fixed tiny chambers, each holding a free reed. The instrument is blown through a flat, circular, wooden mouth-piece on the back, and the reeds are controlled by keys arranged in two banks at each end. A movable brass handle projects from either end..
Length, 19 cm. Width at ends, 12; in middle section, 10 cm.

727. MUNDHARMONIKA (Eng. *Mouth harmonica;* Fr. *Harmonica à bouche*) .... Germany
A cylinder 10 cm. long and 3 cm. in diameter, contains twenty reeds.

728. MUNDHARMONIKA, with gong. Twenty-four reeds .....Germany
Length, 13.5 cm. Width, 6.4 cm. Thickness, 2 cm.

729. MUNDHARMONICA. Thirty-three reeds ....Germany
The reeds are arranged in four equidistant rows on a cylinder 39.9 cm. long and 2.3 cm. in diameter.

730. "DAVID'S HARP." Mouth harmonica. Twenty reeds .....Germany
Length, 19 cm. Width, 3 cm. Thickness, 1.9 cm.
Signed—"Ch. Messner, Trossingen."

731. "ORGAN NIGHTINGALE." Mouth harmonica. Forty reeds.Germany
Same dimensions as the preceding.
Signed—"Weinhold Brothers."

732. MUNDHARMONIKA. Forty reeds ....Germany
Length, 14 cm. Width, 2.5 cm. Thickness, 1.8 cm.
Signed—"William Thie."

733. REED TRUMPET. Eight cylinders each containing a free reed operated by a key. Trumpet-shaped body. Length, 30 cm...Italy

734. "NEFER." Brass. Thirteen reeds. Operated by keys........Italy
The reeds are set in cylinders rising from a clarinet-shaped body of brass, with a bell and inverted cone just under the mouth-piece.
Length, 55.8 cm. Diameter of bell, 5.5 cm.

735. "HARMONIKA TROMPETE." Twenty reeds ....Germany
A mouth harmonica, with triangular cross-section, and 11 cm. long, is set on a widely expanding conical tube, 35 cm. long, and 3.2 to 11 cm. in diameter. The harmonica is of tin and the tube of nickel-plated brass.
Signed—"Gunter's Mund Harmonika Trompete."

736. HARMONICOR, HAUTBOIS JARDIN, or HARMONITROMPE....France
Twenty-five free reeds inserted in tubes, and controlled by pistons.
The silver-plated tubes, 7.5 cm. long are set on a cylindrical body of wood, 45 cm. in length, and secured by a metal band. A curved mouth-piece, 10 cm. in length, is placed at upper end of tube. The circular plates on the pistons are of black and white ivory (following the key-board sequence), and the compass runs from c to c″.

Sub-Section II Free Reeds with Air Reservoir Operated Mechanically; Reeds controlled by Pistons, or Keys.

737. HARMONIFLUTE. The body rests on a standard. The bellows operated by a treadle. A miniature keyboard, with compass of three octaves beginning with f, controls the reeds..........France
Body dimensions of accordion, 18 to 49.5 cm. Spread of bellows, 21.5 to 47 cm. Height with stand, 80 cm.
Signed—"Busson, Paris."

738. LAUDAPHONE (Ger. *Klavierharmonika*) ....France
Twenty-five free reeds controlled by a key-board. Air blown into the wind-chest through a rubber tube. Compass:—c to c″.
Length, 48 cm. Width, 14 cm. Depth, 10 cm.

739. BOOK ORGAN. Wood. Brass reeds..................France
Two bellows furnish the wind and fold down when the cover is closed.
Reeds operated by key-board. The form resembles the early Bible-regal. Length, 58.7 cm. Width, 23.3 cm. Depth, 13.5 cm.

740. LAP ORGAN. Wood. Brass reeds. Two Bellows....United States
The double row of pistons along the centre of the top control free reeds giving the chromatic scale from c to a″. The instrument is pressed down with the left elbow while the fingers of the right hand manipulate the pistons. Length, 38.7 cm. Width, 23.5 cm. Height, 23 cm.
Signed—"C. Austin, Concord, N. H."

741. ROCKING MELODEON. Double bellows ....United States
Similar to No. 741, *circa* 1850. Compass:—C to c‴.
Length, 56.7 cm. Width, 29.3 cm. Height (deflated), 28 cm.
Signed—"Abraham Prescott and Son, Concord, N. H."
(Francis W. Kelsey.)
(For examples of modern melodeons see Case XIV.)

742. MELOPHONE. Horizontal model. Ninety one free reeds. . . . France
Ninety-one ivory discs control an equal number of free reeds. Invented by Leclerc, of Paris, in 1834, it has not sustained itself. The deep guitar-shaped case, of maple, with a short ebony neck bearing the discs in closely set rows, is 76 cm. long, 29 cm. wide, and 18.5 cm. deep. The bellows are operated by a metal handle projecting from one end.

Signed—"Jacquet, Paris."

For vertical form see Case XV, No. 1375.

While, in the foregoing examples, pistons and keys in key-board sequence are employed, that fact does not place them in Class V, nor does supplying air with a bellows, militate against the present classification.

743. SPECIMENS OF VARIOUS TYPES OF REEDS: A—Reed cut from joint of grass; B—"Arghool" reed; C—Clarinet Reed and Mouthpiece; D—Oboe Reed; E—Bassoon Reed; F—Melodeon Reed; G—Trumpet (organ) Reed.

Sub-Section III. (a) Vibrating Column of Air in an Organ Pipe (Cylindrical or Conical); (b) Vibration Modified by the Action of a Beating or Free Reed.

As the various types of organ pipes illustrate the principles of tone production in Class III, so far set forth, the examples in the series 744-758 may be considered in the light of a summary. In "flue" pipes, whether of metal (No. 755) or of wood (No. 752), the tone production is analogous to that of the beaked flute. 752 is dismantled and will serve to illustrate the method of tone production. Air coming from a reservoir, where it is under pressure, is forced through the "foot" (A) into a chamber (B) which is closed at the top by the "block." Its only exit is through the aperture (C). This is closed by the "Cap" (D), which is hollowed on the under surface (E). The upward slope of the hollowed part directs the air over the serrated surface (F), against the sharp edge (G). By the interposition of a single beating, or free reed, the quality of tone is modified. In open pipes the vibrating length is determined by the distance from the "language" (G), to the top of pipe. In stopped pipes the top is closed by a cap, or stopper, and the vibrating length is double the distance from the "language" to top of pipe.

In modern organs extensive use is made of free reeds. They can be so voiced as to produce a very beautiful tone. Like the "Partition Mustel" (Case III, No. 249) and the "Celesta"—a key-board instrument also employing metal bars, figuring extensively in the modern orchestra—a free reed "stop" is always in tune. The ordinary beating-reed is frequently harsh, and the resemblance of certain reed "stops" to orchestral instruments, indicated by the "draw-stop" nomenclature, not infrequently makes a great demand on one's imagination.

744-5-6-7-8. STOPPED DIAPASON pipes from Positive Organ (Case XIV, No. 1347). Metal with small per cent of tin.......Italy
Lengths—23.5; 30.4; 45.6; 44.5, and 26.4 cm. respectively.
Vibrating lengths—12.8; 15.2; 15.7; 20.1, and 10.5 cm. respectively.
Diameters—2; 3; 2.2; 4.5, and 2 cm. respectively.

749-50-51. STOPPED DIAPASON. Wooden pipes.........United States
Length of pipes—38; 53.1, and 34 cm.
Vibrating lengths—15.2; 36.4, and 30.4 cm.
Diameters—4 by 4; 5 by 5.2, and 4.5 by 5.2 cm.

752. MELODIA. Wood ....United States
Length, 81 cm. Vibrating length, 60.8 cm. Diameter, 4 by 5.2 cm.

753. OPEN DIAPASON. Metal with less than 33 1-3 per cent of tin.. .... United States
Length, 46.1 cm. Vibrating length, 29 cm. Diameter, 3.8 cm.

754. HARMONIC FLUTE. Metal ....United States
A hole above the mouth causes the pipe to sound the octave.
Length, 19 cm. Vibrating length, 60.8 cm. Diameter, 3.2 cm.

755. OPEN DIAPASON. Metal pipes ....United States
No. 755 is of "spotted metal," containing more than 33 1-3 per cent of tin. Length, 80 cm. Vibrating length, 60.8 cm. Diameter, 6 cm.

756. OBOE. Metal pipe. Beating reed ....United States
Length, 41.6 cm.; of conical pipe and bell, 20.8 cm.; of reed-box, 20.8 cm.

756A. HARMONIC TRUMPET. Metal ....United States
Length, 42 cm.; of foot, 17 cm. Diameter, 8 mm. to 5.2 cm.
(Austin Organ Company.)

757. CLARINET. Metal pipe, closed at top. Beating reed..United States
Length, 58.2 cm.; of cylindrical pipe, 44.1 cm.; of reed-box, 14.1 cm.
Nos. 749-755 inclusive and 758 were donated by W. R. Farrand, Nos. 756-7 by A. Moeller.

758. SALICIONAL. String tone. Over 90 per cent tin.....United States
Length, 88.6 cm. Vibrating length, 66 cm. Diameter, 3.4 cm.

Section J. Vibrating Column of Air enclosed in an Animal Tusk, Horn, Gourd, or Wooden Tube, with embouchure in Body, and no lateral Openings.

The column of air in this type is set in vibration by the lips of the player, acting as a reed. The range is limited to the fundamental, octave, and twelfth. The embouchures display great variety, and are frequently definitive of source.

There are however, many exceptions as shown by Ankermann, who gives a by no means exhaustive list of embouchures, eight in number.[11]

11 *"Die afrikanischen Musikinstrumente,"* p. 43.

Three (*a-b-c*) show holes with no surrounding ridge, as in *d* and *i*, the latter of which forms a bed whose height is greater than the diameter of the horn at that point. In *c* and *d*, an oval projection on the under side is bored for a carrying-cord. In *e* and *f* the mouth-hole is in an anvil-shaped structure through which the horn appears to run. In *g*, a raised structure, with slightly constricted waist and sloping shoulders, encircles the horn and contains the mouth-hole. As a rule the mouth-holes are oval, although, occasionally, diamond-shaped holes are found. All of these are in the inner curve, wherein they differ from those in antelope horns, which are always in the side.

In the following descriptions, the type of mouth-hole will be indicated by italics in parentheses.

759. TRUMPET. Elephant tusk ....Ashantee, West Africa
Lateral mouth-hole (*b*) 43 cm. below tip. Lengths of curves, 107 and 117 cm. Greatest circumference 34 cm.; at mouth-hole, 14 cm.
Pitches:—f sharp and octave.

760. TRUMPET. Elephant tusk ....Ashantee, West Africa
The mouth-hole (*f*) is 5 cm. below tip. Lengths of curves, 69 and 75 cm. Greatest circumference, 27.5 cm.; at mouth-hole, 8.5 cm.
Pitches:—a flat, octave, and twelfth.

761. TRUMPET. Elephant ivory dyed with human blood........ ....Dahomey, West Africa
Mouth-hole (*c*) 6.5 cm. from tip. Lengths of curves, 39 and 42 cm. Greatest circumference, 15 cm.; least, 2 cm.
Pitches:—g flat, octave, and twelfth (flat).

762. TRUMPET. Wood. The skin of the leg of an antelope is drawn over the wood. Native name unknown.....Congo Region, Africa
Length, 64 cm. Diameter at bell, 8.5 cm.; at tip, 3.6 cm.

763. TRUMPET. Elephant ivory, polished...............West Africa
Vertical mouth-piece (missing).
Length, 64 cm. Diameter at bell, 7.6 cm.; at mouth-piece, 2.5 cm.
Pitches:—b (a trifle flat), b′ and e″.

764. TRUMPET. Stained ivory. Wound with rattan in parts...W. Africa
The native (Swahili) name is *barugumu*. The mouth-hole, on side, is 5.8 cm. from tip. Lengths of curves, 44 and 58.9 cm. Diameter, open end, 4 by 5.3 cm.
Pitches:—e, and e′.

765. TRUMPET. Large elephant tusk ....Benin, West Africa
Mouth-hole (*b*) 60.2 cm. from tip. Lengths of curves, 140 and 160 cm. Greatest circumference, 42 cm.; least, 14.3 cm.
Pitches:—G flat, octave, and d flat′ (flat).

766. TRUMPET. From the horn of some species of antelope......Africa
Lengths of curves, 46 and 49 cm. Greatest circumference, 20.4 cm.;

767. KANG-DUNG. "Leg-bone trumpet." The body is of the thigh-bone of a Buddhist Priest. Copper mouth-piece and bell...Thibet
The mouth-piece and bell bear symbolic designs. Strips of blue, red, yellow, and pink cloth hang from the bell.
Length, 22.6 cm.; of bell, 11.7 cm. Diameter of bell, 4.8; of mouth-piece, 2.8 cm.

As in Africa a flute made from the thigh-bone of an enemy is held to be of peculiar sweetness, and garlands of human skulls give added potency to their Fetish drums, so in this instance, the material from which this trumpet is fashioned makes its appeal more convincing. The copper bell has symbolical meaning. The apertures on either side represent the nostrils of a mythical horse, which conveys the souls of those found worthy, to their "happy hunting-grounds," while its tone is held to be the neighing of the aforesaid steed. The "Damaru" (Case IV, No. 366) also shows that, in the choice of material for other types, the Thibetan displays the refined tenderness exhibited by the African native.

768. OLIPHANT. Carved ivory ....France
The surface is covered with beautiful carvings, including medallion portraits of Francis I, Henry II, and Francis II. It has a cup mouth-piece. It is too large to have served as an actual hunting horn.
Lengths of curves, 105 and 120 cm. Greatest circumference, 31.5 cm.; least, 5 cm. Pitches:—g, g′, d″, g″.

769. BARUGUMU. Trumpet of antelope horn......Swahili Tribe, Africa
Oval mouth-hole, in the side, 8 cm. from tip.
Lengths of curves, 53 and 64 cm. Greatest circumference, 17; least, 6.6 cm. Pitches:—d flat, octave and fifth.

770. SHEPHERD'S HORN.. Body of ibex-antelope horn..........Syria
Embouchure at tip. Lengths of curves, 32.5 and 56 cm.
Greatest circumference, 19.4 cm.; least, 8 cm. Pitches:—d and d′.

771. TRUMPET. Goat's horn, highly polished ....Source unknown
Embouchure (in a polished mouth-piece) at tip.
Lengths of curves, 28 and 32 cm. Diameter, 1 to 4.5 cm.
The remarks on page 38 apply to the notation of the pitches of these trumpets, which must be taken as approximations only. The difficulty of producing the tones favors occasional recourse to the imagination.

772. TRUMPET. Horn ....Cameroon, West Africa
Oval mouth-hole in side, 5.4 cm. from tip.
Length, 34 cm. Diameter, 1.5, and 4 by 5 cm.
(G. Schwab.)

773. SHOFAR. Ram's horn. Used in the Hebrew ritual..........Syria
Mouth-hole at tip. Lengths of curves, 26.5 and 44.5 cm.
Circumference, 4.5 cm.

774. TRUMPET. Horn of Cape Buffalo ....South Africa
The mouth-hole, carved to represent a buffalo's head, is at the small end. This trumpet is carried by a braided rawhide cord.
Lengths of curves, 37 and 54 cm. Greatest circumference, 33.6 cm.; least, 7.4 cm. Pitches:—e flat and octave.

775. TRUMPET. Elephant ivory, colored with human blood..W. Africa
Mouth-hole (*d*) 3.5 cm. from small end.
Length, 33 cm. Diameter, 4.5 cm.
(G. Schwab.)

776. TRUMPET. Elephant ivory ....West Africa
The body is decorated by three raised bands carved on surface. The mouth-hole is of same type as the preceding.
Lengths of curves, 49.5 and 51 cm. Greatest circumference, 19.5; least, 9.5 cm. Pitches:—g flat and fifth.

In the measurements of these instruments, the shorter length of curve refers to the upper surface, as they are displayed in the Case, the longer to the lower. As the curves are frequently very irregular, to give the radii would entail needless complications.

As no accurate data regarding the native names or sources of most of these horns was secured at the time of their purchase, any attempt at fitting them appropriately would result in failure; therefore it has not been attempted. Among the native names for ivory horns we find *ḳpe* (Ewe tribe), *apunga* and *mpungi* (Loanga); for elephant tusks *rongo* (Loanga); for antelope-horns *barugumu* (Swahili), *gafa* (Gallas) and *ges* (Somali).[12]

[12] Sachs, pp. 231, 18, 262, 323, 32, 150, 156.

PLATE VIII.

CASE VIII. EAST SECTION. NOS. 784 TO 873 (RIGHT TO LEFT)

CASE VIII.

Continuation of Class III—Section J.

777. HUNTING-HORN. Cow's horn. Copper mountings......Germany
Lengths of curves, 30.4 and 34 cm. Bell diameter, 5.8 by 9 cm.
Formerly it had a lateral mouth-hole (*c*) which has been so imperfectly closed that it cannot be blown.

778. DERVISH-HORN. Cow's horn.............Soudan, North Africa
Lengths of curves, 33.5 and 44 cm. Bell diameter, 6 by 9.2 cm.

779. HUNTING-HORN in A flat. Cow's horn, carved............Italy
A coat of arms, a hunting scene, and geometric designs appear on the body. Diameter of bell, 5.7 by 7.7 cm.; of mouth-hole, 1.8 cm.

780. HORN in G. Ox-horn. German silver rings........South America
An ornamental carved band, in cameo-like designs, serves as decoration. Lengths of curves, 30 and 43 cm. Greatest diameter, 7 cm.
Pitches:—g, g′ and d″.

781. HUNTING-HORN. Cow's horn. German silver mountings..Germany
Lengths of curves, 30.4 and 40.9 cm. Bell diameter, 9.6 cm.

782. HUNTING-HORN. Cow's horn. German silver mountings.....Italy
Length, 66 cm. Diameter of bell, 10 cm.; of tip, 2.3 cm.
Signed—"Pelitti, Milano."
Most of these instruments are fitted with carrying-cords, and the diameters at tip do not vary much from that given for this specimen.

783. RAPPAKAI. Conch-shell trumpet (*Triton variegatus*)........Japan
The shell—33 cm. long, with 17 cm. as its greatest diameter—is carried in a netting of silk cord. It has a bronze mouth-piece, and sounds b and b′. It is sometimes called *hora-no-kai* and *horagai.* The Chinese have a similar shell trumpet known as the *hai-lo* or *lozeu,* while the Japanese *jindai rappa,* of clay, is said to have been the ancestor of the *rappakai.**

784. TRUMPET. Shell of *Turbinella pyrum* ....Nassau, Bahama Islands
Embouchure at tip. Length, 39 cm. Greatest diameter, 18 cm. Unplayable.

---

* Sachs, pp. 189, 189, 172.

785. JAGDHORN, or SAUHORN. "Boar-hunting horn." Brass. . . Germany
Covered with leather, with strap for carrying.
Length, 53 cm. Diameter of bell, 5.6 cm.
Signed—"H. Grenser, Dresden."

786. BARATAKA. Shell trumpet (*Cassis rufa*) . . . . Bengal
Tip embouchure. Length, 8.6 cm. Diameter, 6.3 cm. Pitch:—f sharp.
The conch-shell trumpet is widely distributed. It is used in war, in religious ceremonies, and, in Afghanistan, the *mir-sang* (pl. *sangûna*) calls to the bath, while in Persia, and among the Hindoos, it summons to prayer.

787. SHELL TRUMPET. (*Fusus probocei difero*) . . . . New Caledonia
Length, 41.7 cm. Greatest diameter, 14 cm. No tone obtainable.

788. LOKU. Trumpet of gourd . . . . Shavajé Indians, Brazil
Length, 106.4 cm. Bell diameter, 15.4 cm. Harmonics imperfect.

789. TRUMPET. Gourd. Length, 99 cm. Bell diameter, 28 cm. W. Africa
Pitches—d′ and a′. B, c′, d″, and f″, are also possible.

790. TRUMPET. Bamboo. . . . . Philippine Islands
Four pieces of bamboo of different lengths are fitted into each other at right-angles, giving an air column 99 cm. in length. Cup mouthpiece in body. Model length, 49 cm. Circumference of tubes, 1.5 to 18 cm. The term "model" refers to the appearance of an instrument as it hangs. In giving diameters the smaller is that of the tip, the larger that of the bell.

791. ALP-HORN. (Eng. *Alpine Horn;* Fr. *Cor des Alpes*). . . Switzerland
Straight tube of birch with upturned bell.
This form is used in the Canton Schwyz. It sounds a flat, a flat′, c″, e flat″, a flat″. Length of model, 102.2 cm. Vibrating length, 108 cm. Diameter, 2 to 12 cm.
Signed—"M. von Euw, Rigi Kulm."

792. ALP-HORN. Birch tube, twice folded on itself. . . . . Switzerland
This trumpet-like form dominates the Cantons of Uri, Unterwalden and Schwyz. Length, 102.2 cm.; vibrating length, 254 cm. Diameter, 2 to 12 cm.

The type of Alp-horn varies in the different Cantons.

Nos. 777-778-780-785-790-791-792 have cup mouth-pieces, several of very rude construction. Nos. 791-2 are of an elongated type. Their restricted range forbids the inclusion of these instruments in Section K.

Section K. Vibrating Column of Air enclosed in a Metal or Wooden Tube, ending in a Bell, with Cup mouth-piece and no lateral Openings.

The evolution from the various forms of embouchure, noted in Case VII, to the cup mouth-piece was inevitable. In this form the reed action of the lips is focussed and intensified. In some of the Oriental types the mouth-piece is a structural part (No. 797), but in European types the mouth-piece is removable.

When the air in a slightly conical tube of metal, expanding into a bell at one end, is set in vibration it produces a consecutive harmonic series, based on a fundamental whose pitch is determined by the length of the tube.

It is frequently very difficult to produce the fundamental, and some of the higher harmonics are of little value, as they are not in tune. In the trumpets preceding Nos. 821 the tube is straight. For convenience the tube is now bent on itself, a practice known to the Romans, forgotten for centuries, and reintroduced *circa* 1300. (See No. 821.) This bent form has existed in India from time immemorial.

793. RANA-CRINGA. "Trumpet of war." Colored brass. . . Nepaul, India
At five equi-distant points, the S-shaped body, is encircled by hollow double rings, also of thin brass and filled with shot or pebbles. It has a sharp incisive tone, which is now used for signaling, and in religious and civil ceremonials, rather than in war, as formerly.
Length, 126 cm. Diameter, 1.5 to 12 cm.

794. TRUMPET. Roughly hammered copper.................. India
The tube, 99 cm. in length, makes three complete turns. Native name unknown. Length of bell, 33 cm. Diameter, 9.5 cm.; of tube, 1.8 cm. Pitches:—E, e′, g sharp′, b′, and e″.

795. SONA-RAPPA, or DOSA. Brass .... Japan
The very narrow, conical tube—33.4 cm. long and from 4 mm. to 1.8 cm. in diameter—ends in a double bell with exaggerated flare. The first bell is 8.6, and the second 13.2 cm. in diameter. It has an extended compass, partly chromatic.
Lowest tone, G flat, highest, g flat″.
(B-S.)

796. KANG-T'UNG. Bronze, decorated .... China
Similar in form and decoration to No. 767 but with a longer bell. This is the Chinese form of the Thibetan *ḳang-dung*. Yellow bands hang from the bell. This color is symbolic of Buddhism.*
Length, 41.5 cm. Diameter of bell, 8 cm.

* Color-symbolism is an interesting phase of the study of instruments, for it opens up a wide field of investigation as yet comparatively unexplored. An esteemed colleague has collected a mass of material on the subject and, in the near future, will give to the world the results of his scholarly research.

797. ZABS-DUNG. Copper. Bulbous hollow rings encircle body... Thibet
This resembles the Chinese *la pa*, but is larger of body. Cup mouth-piece in body. Length, 161 cm. Least circumference, 8 cm.; greatest, at bell, 93 cm.

798. PHUNGA. "Instrument of the gods." Copper ..... Cashmere, India
The above name is given on the authority of Curt Sachs[1] as it is generally applied to a shorter and very narrow trumpet of brass. It is decorated with five wide bands of beaten brass encircling the body.
Length, 188 cm. Circumference, 3 to 31 cm. Pitched in E.

799. NAG-PHENI, or TURI. Brass, hammered and lacquered...... India
The conical body makes an S-shaped curve at mouth-piece end, and the body is encircled with rings as in the *rana-cringa.*
Length, 130.5 cm. Diameter of bell, 19 cm. Although it is in bad condition e, c sharp′, and a′ can be produced.

800. HAO T'UNG, or HUANG TEITH. Brass .... China
The peculiarity of this instrument is the bell, which is quite out of its usual proportional relation to the body. A form of wider diameter, and of wood, is used on funeral occasions, while a narrower type is used by the military. A similar Japanese instrument is called the *dokaku*. Length, 100 cm.; of bell, 37 cm. Diameter of bell, 14 cm. (B-S.)

801. TRUMPET in B flat. Terra cotta .... Ancient Egypt
Purchased in 1895 of Brugsch Bey at Gizeh Museum. Its date is said to be *circa* 300 B.C. (?). Length, 24 cm. Diameter, 3 to 8 cm.

802. CHA KIAO, or TUNG KEO. Brass, with upturned bell........ China
The upturned bell differentiates this from the *la pa*. The mouth-piece, a flat, circular plate of thin brass with a hole in the center, is typically Chinese. The *cha-kiao* is used in wedding processions. It gives A, e, a, e′, and a′. Length, 148 cm. Diameter of bell, 14 cm. (B-S.)

803. CORNU. Bronze, heavily patinated .... Ancient Rome
This purports to be a reproduction of a Cornu found in the Amphitheatre at Pompeii, and now placed in the Museum at Naples.
The conical tube—399 cm. in length—is bent so as nearly to describe a circle, of which a wooden shoulder bar—134 cm. long—forms the diameter. The bell is 13.4 cm. in diameter.

---

[1] Sachs, p. 297.

804. BUZINE. Bronze. Fifteenth, or sixteenth century .... Italy
The slightly conical body—131 cm. in length—ends in a bell 8.4 in diameter. Decorated with engraved bands and bars near the bell. This beautiful specimen might have served as the model for the representation of the *buzine*, Plate XLI, in "Old English Instruments," by the Rev. F. W. Galpin.
(Francis W. Kelsey.)

Like most of our modern instruments, the Trumpet (Fr. *Trompette;* Ital. *Tromba;* Ger. *Trompete*) can boast of an ancient origin. It has a compass from c to g″ (occasionally to c‴), giving the natural harmonic series.

805. TROMBA in E flat. Brass, painted .... Italy
The slightly conical tube—214.6 cm. long—carries two bosses, from the lower of which—51.1 cm. above the bell—it rapidly expands to the diameter of the upturned bell, 16.4 cm.

806. TRUMPET. Copper, in three sections .... India
Length, 42 cm. Diameter of bell, 6.8 cm.

807. RUF-HORN. Brass ornamentation. Eighteenth century .... Germany
Length, 31.4 cm. The bell is missing.

808. COACH HORN in D. Brass .... France
Length of tube, 121.6 cm. Bell diameter, 9.3 cm.

809. TROMBA in B. Bronzed brass .... Italy
The tube, whose model length is 123.7 cm., doubles on itself giving a vibrating length of 249.9 cm. An additional tube, also doubling on itself, and 49 cm. in length, may be added at upper end, thus increasing the vibrating length to 347.9 cm. and length of model to 172.7 cm. Used in the ballo "Excelsior."
Signed—"G. Pelitti, Milano."

810. COACH HORN in B flat. Brass .... France
Length of tube, 132.4 cm. Diameter of bell, 9.9 cm.
Signed—"F. Perinet, 31 Rue Copernico, Paris."

811. TROMBA in A flat. Brass .... Italy
At a point 34 cm. from mouth-piece the tube bends on itself three times, forming circles, 26.8 cm. in diameter. The model length—103.4 cm.—is thus increased to 183.8 cm. Diameter of bell, 16.2.
Signed—"G. Pelitti, Milano."

812. TROMBA in D. Brass, painted . . . . Italy
The tube—model length, 92.6 cm.—at a point 22 cm. from upper end bends in an oval—7.8 by 10 cm.—and expands to the flaring bell, 16.5 cm. in diameter.
Signed—"G. Pelitti, Milano."

813. COACH HORN in A. White metal, polished . . . . England
Length of body, 72 cm. Diameter of bell, 7.6 cm.

814. TUBA in B flat. Brass. Two keys . . . . Italy
This reproduction of a Roman type, by Pelitti, of Milano, shows a conical tube, 96.5 cm. long, gradually expanding to the bell diameter, 10.4 cm.

815. TROMBA. Alto in E flat. Brass . . . . Italy
The tube, by bending on itself twice, adds 51.5 cm. to the model length, 126.7 cm. Diameter of bell, 22.5 cm.

816. TUBA in D. In type and source similar to No. 814.
Length, 104 cm. Diameter of bell, 8.8 cm.

817. TROMBA in A flat. Brass . . . . Italy
Two circular bends in tube. Model length, 115 cm.
Diameter of bell, 13.5 cm.
Signed—"G. Pelitti, Milano."

818. TUBA in B flat. Somewhat smaller, otherwise similar to No. 816.

819. CORNU in B flat. Brass, bronzed. Two keys . . . . Italy
Reproduction of classic type. The keys, as in Nos. 814-16-18, are modern. Length, 262 cm.; of bar, 92.5 cm. Bell diameter, 14.5 cm.

820. CORNU in E. Similar to 819 . . . . Italy
Length, 204 cm.; of bar 77 cm. Bell diameter, 14.5 cm.

821. TROMPETE in E flat. Brass. Eighteenth century . . . . Germany
Model length, 38.5 cm. Vibrating length, 118.2 cm. Bell diameter, 8.3 cm.
Signed—"Michael Saurle in München."

822. TRUMPET in C. Brass, bearing Russian coat of arms . . . . Russia
As in No. 821, the tube makes one turn. The bell has a very slight flare. As the bell has steadily increased in this respect up to modern times, the flare of the bell is quite definitive of period. Model length, 40.2 cm. Vibrating length, 126 cm. Bell diameter, 7.7 cm.
Signed—"G. Eschenbach, St. Petersburg."

823. TROMPETE in D. Brass . . . . Germany
Length, 111.2 cm.; of model, 38.8 cm. Bell diameter, 10.5 cm.
Signed—"Lindenburg, Berlin."

824. TROMPETE in E flat. Seventeenth century . . . . Germany
The tube, with one turn, bears a boss, cords, and tassels. The bell is engraved with a floral design, a galloping horse, and the motto, "Ich."
Length, 221 cm.; of model, 70 cm. Bell diameter, 10.8 cm.
Signed—"Macht Johan Carl Kodisch, Nürnberg."

825. TROMPETE in E flat. Brass. Seventeenth century . . . . . . Germany
The tube makes one turn, bears a boss, also cord and tassels.
Length, 207.5 cm.; of model, 67.5 cm. Bell diameter, 123 cm.

826. CLAIRON in B flat. Brass . . . . France
In structure and decoration similar to the preceding instrument.
Length, 139.5 cm.; of model, 51.5 cm. Bell diameter, 15 cm.

827. CLAIRON in E flat. Brass . . . . France
The tube of this cavalry trumpet has two turns.
Length, 211 cm.; of model, 49.5 cm. Bell diameter, 13 cm.

828. TROMBA in C. Form of a Latin Cross . . . . Italy
To form the cross, at a point 25.5 cm. below the mouth-piece, and 59.4 cm. above the bell, the tube bends on itself five times.
Length, 282.1 cm.; of model, 88.6 cm. Diameter of bell, 13.7 cm.

Section L. Vibrating Column of Air enclosed in a Metal or Wooden Tube, ending in a Bell, (a) with lateral Openings, opened and closed by the fingers or keys; (b) with additional lengths of tubing incorporated in the structure, and controlled by valves, operated by pistons or keys; (c) with a movable tube (Slide) operated by the hand.

The group of instruments included in the series 829-836 dates back to the tenth century. The eleventh century witnessed the general introduction of finger-holes, whereby the possibilities of these instruments were extended.

Centuries later, the range of possible tonalities for brass instruments was extended by the use of "crooks." The "crook" is a section of tubing, which, inserted below the mouth-piece, lengthens the body. Thus a new fundamental is secured. These "crooks" were removable, and a constant source of annoyance. Later (*circa* 1826), three or more "crooks" were made part of the structure, which, opened or closed by means of valves, controlled by pistons, levers, or flat keys, made possible a chromatic series, covering the entire range of the instrument.

829. CORNO TORTO, or CORNETTO CURVO.. Wood, covered with leather. Six finger-holes. Early seventeenth century. . . . . . . Italy
The upper end of tube, shaped like a German peasant's tobaccopipe, is furnished with a bone ring in which the horn mouth-piece is set.
Length, 62.5 cm.; of model, 44 cm. Greatest diameter, 6 cm.

830. CORNETT, or ZINK. Same structure as No. 829, but with a very slight curve. Early eighteenth century . . . . Italy
Length, 41.5 cm. Greatest diameter, 4.9 cm.
The Middle Age spelling "Cornett" is endorsed by Galpin,[2] as it tends to prevent confusing the early instrument with the modern Cornet.

831. ZINK. (Fr. *Cornet à bouquin*). Typical construction. Early seventeenth century. Pitched in g flat . . . . Germany
The parchment-covered body, slightly curved, has six finger-holes and one thumb-hole in their usual positions.
Length, 56.6 cm. Greatest diameter, 3 cm.

832. CORNO CURVO (Ger. *Krummer Zink*). Typical structure. . . . . Italy
This early seventeenth century instrument has six finger-holes, and, like all the specimens in this group, is made of wood covered with leather.
Length, 43.2 cm. Greatest diameter of bore, 3.8 cm.

833. KLEINER ZINK (Ital. *Cornettino curvo*). Soprano, in B . . . Germany
Six finger-holes. Length, 35 cm. Diameter, 7 mm. to 3.3 cm.
Collected (in Hamburg, 1868) for the Rev. J. Beck, Sussex, Eng., by Mr. A. W. Frank, of the British Museum.

834. CORNO TORTO. Early seventeenth century. . . . . Italy
The elongated S-shaped body, has six open finger-holes and one closed by a flat brass key, also the usual bone ring for the mouth-piece.
Tenor in F. Length, 75.2 cm. Greatest diameter of bore, 5 cm.

835. CORNO CURVO. Six finger-holes and one key . . . . Italy
Bass in D. The tube has an octagonal cross-section.
Length, 92 cm. Greatest diameter of bore, 6.5 cm.

836. CORNO TORTO. Bass in C. Same date as No. 834 . . . . Italy
The semi-circular body has six finger-holes, and has the same quality of tone as the other members of the family, a tone that leaves nothing to be desired in the way of harshness.
Lengths of curves, 106.4 and 131.1 cm. Greatest diameter of bore, 9 cm.
The Serpent, Nos. 903-923 (top of this case) and 935, Case IX, belongs to this family. It was invented about the close of the sixteenth century by Guillaume, of Auxerre. It has persisted up to a comparatively recent date. It was incorporated by Mendelssohn in "St. Paul," and by Wagner in "Rienzi."

The Valved, or Keyed Trumpet (Fr. *Trompette à cléfs;* Ital. *Tromba a chiavi;* Ger. *Ventiltrompete*) gives a chromatic series within the same limits as the earlier type. A military instrument *par excellence*, it also fills an import-

[2] "Eng. Inst.," p. 189.

ant place in modern orchestration. It can be muted with good effect. The Bugle has a tube of greater diameter than the Trumpet, but has been almost entirely superseded by the Cornet, which structurally lies midway between these types. The compass of the Keyed Bugle runs from b to c‴; of the Cornet, from f sharp to a″ (c‴). With the exception of those pitched in C, these are all transposing instruments.

837. "AIDA" FANFARE TRUMPET. Bass in B flat. Brass, with German silver mountings. Three piston valves............Belgium
Length of model, 135 cm. Diameter of bell, 13 cm.

838. "AIDA" FANFARE TRUMPET in F. Brass. Two pistons....France
Length of model, 94 cm. Diameter of bell, 13.5 cm.

839. "AIDA" FANFARE TRUMPET in F. Brass. One piston......France
Length, 65 cm. Diameter of bell, 11.4 cm.
The quality of tone of these trumpets is very brilliant, and especially adapted for use in spectacular stage effects.

840. TROMBA A CHIAVI in A. Brass. Three pistons..............Italy
The serpentine body—88.5 cm. in length—ends in a moderately flaring bell, 9.5 cm. in diameter. Three fixed crooks—18, 32, and 39.7 cm. in length respectively—when opened by the appropriate pistons make possible the following vibrating lengths; 106.5, 120.5, and 128.2 cm. Combinations of the valves give corresponding alterations of the vibrating length. This is illustrative of the function of the valve, and may be applied to most of the instruments in this group.

841. BASS-TROMPETE in F. Brass. Four rotary valves.........Austria
The conical tube—167.6 cm. long, ending in a bell, 15.2 cm. in diameter—has four crooks in body, 76, 45, 27, and 12 cm. in length. This form of trumpet, used by Richard Wagner in certain scores, is by no means a modern invention. Length of model, 45.6 cm.
Signed—"Leopold Uhlman, K. K. Hof Instrumenten Fabrik in Wien."

842. TROMBA A CHIAVI in A. Brass. Three pistons............Italy
Length of tube, 76 cm. Diameter of upturned bell, 16 cm. Made for use in the ballet "Rodope."
Signed—"A. Abbate a figlio, Napoli."

843. VENTILTROMPETE in F. Three rotary valves..........Germany
Length of model, 46 cm. Diameter of bell, 11.6 cm.

844. TROMPETTE A CLEFS in A. Brass. Piston valves.........France
Length of model, 52 cm. Diameter of bell, 13.8 cm.
Signed—"No. 24330, Adolphe Sax, Breveté à Paris."

845. BUGLE A CLEFS. Soprano in E flat. Brass. Six keys.......France
Length of model, 40.5 cm. Diameter of bell, 13 cm.
Signed—"Müller, Breveté à Lyon."

846. BUGLE A CLEFS. Soprano in E flat. Brass. Six keys.......France
Length of model, 51.7 cm. Diameter of bell, 14.6 cm.

847. BUGLE A CLEFS. Soprano in D. Brass. Six keys ....Belgium
Length of model, 42.5 cm. Diameter of bell, 14.8 cm.
Signed—"Mahillon, jeune, Bruxelles."

848. KLAPPENHORN. Soprano in E flat. Brass. Six keys.....Germany
Length of model, 46.5 cm. Diameter of bell, 16.2 cm.
Signed—"Klüh, Mainz."

849. KLAPPENHORN. Alto in D flat. Brass. Eight keys......Germany
Length of model, 49.5 cm. Diameter of bell, 18 cm.

850. TROMPETTE A CLEFS.. Alto in E flat. Brass. Five keys....France
Length of model, 48 cm. Diameter of bell, 12 cm.
Signed—"Couturier, à Lyon."

851. POST HORN in G. Copper ....England
Length of model, 17 cm. Diameter of bell, 6.4 cm.

852. BUGLET in B flat. Brass, silver-plated................England
Length of model, 18 cm. Diameter of oval bell, 5.4 by 8 cm.
Signed—"The Buglet, Prize Medal, Keat and Sons, London."
On a raised shield also appears, "Thornton Heath, B.C."

853. CORNET in E flat. Brass. Three piston valves...........France
Length of model, 30 cm. Diameter of bell, 12 cm.
Signed—"Henry Gunckel, Paris. Lyon and Healy, Chicago, Sole Agents."

854. POCKET CORNET. Brass. Three piston valves..........England
Length of model, 22.5 cm. Diameter of bell, 9.8 cm.

855. FLUEGEL HORN, Soprano in B flat. German silver. Three rotary valves ....United States
Length, 35.5 cm. Bell diameter, 11.8 cm.
Signed—"Graves and Co., Boston."

856. CORNET in B flat. German silver. Three rotary valves..United States
Length of model, 40 cm. Diameter of bell, 12.2 cm.
Signed—"Hall and Quinby, Boston."

857. FLUEGEL HORN, Soprano in B flat. Brass. Three piston valves. .... England
Model length, 45 cm. Bell diameter, 14.4 cm.
Signed—"F. Besson, Breveté, 196 Euston Road, London."

858. CORNET in E flat. Brass. Three piston valves.......United States
Length of model, 30 cm. Diameter of bell, 11.8 cm.
Signed—"R. Wurlitzer and B'rs. Cincinnati, O."

859. CORNET in C. Brass. Three pump valves..........United States
Length of model, 31.5 cm. Diameter of bell, 12.5 cm.

860. CORNET in E flat. Brass, silver plated. Three valves..United States
Length of model, 30 cm. Diameter of bell, 12.4 cm.
Signed—"Superior Class, Conn and Dupont, Elkhart, Ind."

861. CORNET in E flat. Brass. Three pump valves.......United States
Length of model, 36 cm. Diameter of bell, 12.4 cm.

862. SAXHORN. Soprano in B flat. German silver. Three rotary valves. "Bell over shoulder" type...............United States
Length of model, 61.6 cm. Diameter of bell, 12.1 cm.

This type of instrument was patented in 1845 by Ad. Sax, from whom it takes its name. The family forms a homogeneous group, alike characterized by beauty and fulness of tone, as well as great security and ease in performance.

From the *subkontrabass tuba* (Ger.), the lowest, to the *Sax-horn sopranino*, the highest, is a tremendous range of pitch, and includes eighteen differently named representatives, although some of these are variants.

863. CORNET in B flat. Brass. Three patent lever valves........England
Length of model, 35 cm. Diameter of bell, 12.3 cm.
Signed—"By her Majesty's Sole Letters Patent, Köhler, Sole Maker, 35 Henrietta St., Covent Garden, London."
This is an example of the earliest application of the valve mechanism.

864. CORNET in B flat. Brass. Three piston valves.......United States
Length of model, 31.8 cm. Diameter of bell, 12.5 cm.
Signed—" 'Excelsior,' C. J. Whitney and Co., Detroit."

865. KORNETT in A flat. German silver mountings. Three double pistons. Length, 30.5 cm. Bell diameter, 12 cm.........Austria
Signed—"Anton Holly, W. Plzui."

866. KORNETT in B flat. Brass. German silver mountings. Three rotary valves. Length, 41 cm. Bell diameter, 12.2 cm....Austria
Signed—"Ignaz Sicwasser, K. K. Auschsl, Priv. Musik Instrumenten Fabrik in Wien."

867. SAXHORN. Alto, in E flat. Brass. Three pistons........England
Length of model, 53.3 cm. Diameter of bell, 15.5 cm.
Signed—"Henry Distin and Company, London."

868. SAXHORN. Alto, in E flat. Brass. Three pistons.........England
Length of model, 49 cm. Diameter of bell, 16.3 cm.
Signed—"Riviere and Hawkes, 28 Leicester Square, London."

869. SAXHORN. Alto, in E flat. Brass. Three pistons..........France
Length of model, 48.5 cm. Diameter of bell, 18 cm.
Signed—"Antoine Courtois, Breveté, Paris, V. R. H."

870. SAXHORN. Alto, in E flat. Brass. Three pistons..........France
Model length, 49 cm. Diameter of bell, 19.2 cm.
Signed—"Harry Wilson, Leeds, Made in France."

871. COR A PISTONS. Alto, in E flat. Brass. Three pistons......France
Length of model, 36.5 cm.; width, 37 cm. Diameter of bell, 17.8 cm.
Signed—"Michaud. Breveté, 10-11 Rue de Sartine, Paris."

872. COR A PISTONS. Alto, in E flat. Brass. Three pistons......France
Length of model, 37 cm.; width, 37 cm. Diameter of bell, 18.3 cm.

873. VENTILHORN in E. Brass. Three piston valves........Germany
Height, 43.5 cm. Width, 39.5 cm. Diameter of bell, 19 cm.
The valves in this horn are of the earliest type, invented by Bhülmel in 1816, sold to Stölzel, and patented by him in 1819. They were in use as late as 1853.

When valves were first introduced two only were used, but in 1829, Perinet, of Paris, raised the number to three, and in 1835, Müller, of Berlin, still further increased it to five. Another type of valve, the "ascending valve" (Ger. *Verkürzungsventile;* Fr. *Pistons ascendants*), instead of lengthening the vibrating length, as in the ordinary type, shortens it. First invented by John Shaw, of London, in 1824, it was perfected by the brothers, Adolph, and Alphonse Sax. Frequently, of five valves, three will lower the pitch and two raise it a semi-tone or whole tone.

The rotary valve" (Fr. *Cylindre à rotation;* Ital. *Cilindro rotativo;* Ger. *Drehventil*) was invented in 1832 by Joh. Riedt, of Vienna. At one time it was in great vogue, but now-a-days the piston valve has regained its former ascendancy. Mr. J. S. Johnson, of Grand Rapids, Michigan, has recently patented an improved form of this type which does away with certain obvious defects of the earlier form. In the valved orchestral horn, because the players were accustomed to "stop" with the right-hand, the valves were adapted for the left, and are so played today.

Models of the various types of valve, and also of mouth-pieces, may be seen in Case XVI.

French Horn (Fr. *Cor de chasse;* Ital. *Corno, Corno di caccia;* Ger. *Horn, Waldhorn, Ventilhorn, Inventions horn*). Used first in the chase; when introduced into the orchestra (*circa* 1757), its value was immediately recognized, although the tone of the earlier instruments was undeniably coarse and strident. About 1777, Hampel, of Dresden, discovered that inserting the hand in the bell produced a muffled tone at the same time altering the pitch. It was known thereafter as the "Hand-Horn." The application of valves did away with the multiplicity of crooks, and made possible the utilization of all its resources. In modern times it is generally pitched in F or E, while in early practice it was pitched in the key of the work in which it was used.

874. WALDHORN in F. Brass. Bell ornamented in repoussé work. Germany
Inner diameter of circle, 53 cm. Diameter of bell, 26 cm.
Signed—"Johann Gottfried Kerster in Dresden, 1775."

875. COR DE CHASSE in D. Brass .... France
Inner diameter of circle, 36 cm. Diameter of bell, 26 cm.
Signed—"A. Le Riche, Paris."

876. CORNO DI CACCIA in D. Brass .... Italy
Inner diameter of circle, 36 cm. Diameter of bell, 16 cm.
Signed—"G. Pelitti, Milano."

877. COR DE CHASSE. Brass. Ivory mouth-piece............. France
Inner diameter of circle, 24 cm. Two oblong crooks add 28 cm. to length of tube. Diameter of bell, 12 cm. A very unusual type.

878. WALDHORN in D flat. Brass .... Germany
Inner diameter of circle, 51 cm. Diameter of bell, 30 cm.

879. CROOKS (Fr. *Cor de rechange;* Ital. *Pompa;* Ger. *Stimmbögen*), by means of which changes of the fundamental are secured. Still other specimens may be seen in Case XVI.

880. COR DE CHASSE in G. Brass .... France
Inside diameter of circle, 30.4 cm. Diameter of bell, 26 cm.
Signed—"Raoux, Rue Serpent, à Paris. Fournisseur de S. M. L'Empereur et de S. J. Le Vice Roi d' Egypt."

881. WALDHORN in B flat. Brass .... Germany
Width of model, 50 cm. Diameter of bell, 28.3 cm.

882. COR DE CHASSE in D flat. Brass .... France
Length of tube, 421.5 cm. Diameter of coil, 22 cm.; of bell, 23.2 cm. The dimensions are designedly given in different terms to illustrate the form.
Signed—"Courtois Fréres, rue de Claire, à Paris."

883. WALDHORN in A flat. Brass .... Germany
Width of model, 59 cm. Diameter of bell, 27.5 cm.
Signed—"C. W. Durrschmidt, Neu Kirchen, in Sachsen."

884. COR. Brass. A form antedating the use of valves..........France
Five crooks (E-E flat-D-B flat and C) are so arranged that the mouthpiece can be placed in any one, while the others are prevented from sounding. The *cor omnitonique*, invented by C. Sax, père in 1824, attains the same end by means of a graduated slide.
Width of model, 37.5 cm. Diameter of bell, 13 cm.
Signed—"De la Abbaye, Breveté, Rue de Chartres, Paris."
Nos. 874 to 884 have no valves, but they belong to this family.

885. COR D'HARMONIE in A. Brass. Two pistons............France
Width of model, 33 cm. Diameter of bell, 26 cm.
Signed—"Antoine Courtois Mille-Mille Jr., Facteur du Conservatoire National, 88 rue de Marion, St. Martin, Paris."

886. VENTILHORN in F. Brass. Three rotary valves........Germany
Width of model, 36.8 cm. Diameter of bell, 26 cm.

The Trombone (Span. *Sacabuche;* Ger. *Posaune*) was known in England in the fifteenth century as the "Sakbut," in all probability a name derived from the Spanish designation. In the Trombone the diameter and flare of the bell are quite definitive of its period. (Compare Nos. 890 and 893.) The Slide provides a means for changing the fundamental through the seven positions used in performance. This makes possible a chromatic series of two octaves and a sixth, beside three additional very low tones called the Pedals. Of the four forms—Soprano, B flat; Alto, E flat; Tenor, B flat; Bass, F or E flat, the first is obsolete.

887. SLIDE CORNET, or SOPRANO TROMBONE, in B flat. Brass..England
In most details and measurements this might be considered the second instrument mentioned above. The principal deviation is in the diameter of the bell which is 4 mm. smaller than that of the typical instrument. Berlioz in his work on instrumentation (p. 151) speaks of it as an early German instrument unknown in France. It was used by Gluck in the Italian version of "Orfeo" under the name *Cornetto.* Strangely enough Virdung, Agricola and Praetorius do not mention it, and most authorities maintain a discreet silence regarding it. The Royal Collection at Charlottenburg displays two, but as Oscar Fleischer in his descriptions gives no measurements of any instrument—a most unpardonable procedure—that means of identification fails. This example may serve to illustrate the general features of the true Soprano Trombone.

Length, closed, 51 cm.; extended, 78 cm. Diameter of bell, 11.7 cm.
Signed—"Besson and Co. 'Prototype.' 198 Euston Square, London, England. C. Fischer, 6 4th Ave., N. Y. Sole Agent, U. States."
(Albert A. Stanley.)

887A. DISKANT-POSAUNE in F. Eighteenth century ....Germany
This instrument, whose name is something of a mis-nomer, frequently appears in German collections and is also listed as such by Angul Hammerich in the Copenhagen Collection. It must not be confounded with the real Soprano Trombone, and the size of the bore and structure of the mouth-piece prohibit its being called *Zug-Trompete* (Eng. *Slide Trumpet;* Fr. *Trompette à coulisse;* Ital. *Tromba da tirarsi*).
Length, closed, 71.5 cm.; extended, 102.5 cm. Bell diameter, 12.5 cm.

888. ALT-POSAUNE in E flat. Brass ....Germany
Length, closed, 84.5 cm.; extended, 113.6 cm. Bell diameter, 13.9 cm.
Signed—"J. A. Schmidt in Leipzig."

889. SACABUCHE, in E flat. Brass. Decorated bell ....Spain
Length, closed, 98.4 cm.; extended, 125.2 cm. Bell diameter, 6.3 cm.
Signed—"Trepaben, Barcelona."

890. TENOR TROMBONE in B flat. Brass ....Turkey
Length, closed, 108 cm.; extended, 121.6 cm. Bell diameter, 10.3 cm.
This is said to have been taken from the Turks, at Vienna, Sept. 13, 1683, when they were defeated by the Saxons under the Elector Johann George III.

891. TROMBONE TENOR, in B flat. Brass ....France
Length, closed, 113.4 cm.; extended, 172.4 cm. Bell diameter, 15 cm.
Signed—"F. Besson, Breveté S. D. G., Paris, 96 rue de Angouleme. Grand Prix, Paris, 1900; St. Louis, 1904; Liege, 1905."
(University of Michigan.)

892. TENOR TROMBONE in B flat (Valved). Brass. Three pistons.
Length of model, 73 cm. Bell diameter, 12.7 cm. ......England
Signed—"Henry Keats and Sons, 105 Matthais R'd. Stoke Newington, C. N., London N."

893. KONTRABASS-POSAUNE in F. Brass ....Germany
Length, closed, 128 cm.; extended, 205.2 cm. Bell diameter, 26 cm.
Signed—"Ed. Kruspe, Herzig'l'h. S. M. Hof Lieferant, Erfurt."
(University of Michigan.)

894. TROMBONE A CLEFS. Bass in F. Brass. Three pistons.....France
Length of model, 101 cm. Diameter of bell, 19.6 cm.
Signed—"Antoine Courtois et Mille, Paris."

895. VENTILPOSAUNE. Bass in F. Three rotary valves.......Germany
Model length, 113 cm. Diameter of bell, 19 cm.
Signed—"E. Kruspe in Erfurt."

896. Similar to No. 894, but with six pistons . . . . .France
Model length, 63 cm.; width, 66 cm. Diameter of bell, 15 cm.
Signed—"Seul Grand Prix. Paris, 1867. No. 39. 179 Noveau Trombone Sax. Adolphe Sax, 50 rue St. Georges, à Paris."

897. TROMBONE A COULISSE DOUBLE in G. Copper. Double slide. France
Model length, 60.9 cm.; width (to bell) 30.4 cm. Bell diameter, 17.6 cm.
Signed—"Schmittschneider, Inventer, Brevetē du Roi, Medaille d' Argent, 1823, Paris."
A very rare specimen.

898. GENIS. Alto horn in B flat. Brass, heavily patinated. . . . . Italy
The bell is decorated with a series of medallions.
Length of model, 73 cm. Diameter of bell, 17.4 cm.

899. BASSE-COR in B flat. Wood and brass. Six finger holes. One key. A fine example of the form. Dated 1810. . . . . France
Length of model, 93.2 cm. Diameter of bell, 17.2 cm.
Signed—"Coeffet e Gissin-Enri."

900. SAXHORN, Barytone in E flat. Brass. Three pistons. . . . . . France
Length of model, 56.7 cm. Diameter of bell, 16.2 cm.
Signed—"No. 40649, Ad. Sax et Cie, à Paris."

901. SAXHORN, Barytone in B flat. Brass. Three pistons. . . . . . . France
Model length, 63.4 cm.; width, 20.6 cm. Bell diameter, 20 cm.

902. BASSON RUSSE. Basshorn in C. Wood and brass. Bell in form of dragon's head. Six finger-holes. Three keys. . . . France
The vibrating length of this instrument, whose name is misleading, as it is neither a bassoon, nor Russian, is 258 cm.; of model, 100 cm. Diameter of bell, or in this instance, spread of jaws, 15 cm.
Signed—"Dubois et Couturier, à Paris."

OVER CASE VIII (RIGHT TO LEFT)

903. SERPENT in C. Wood, covered with leather. Six finger holes. Seventeenth century . . . . .Italy
The body of wood covered with leather, is in the shape of the figure 8, with mouth-piece section projecting from the top.
Length, 262 cm.; of model, 102 cm. Diameter of bell, 28.5 cm.

904. CORNO in B flat. Copper. Early date . . . . .Italy
The conical tube, 268 cm. in length, describes two close circles after which it expands into a long conical bell, 23 cm. in diameter.
Model length, 133 cm.; width, 69.5 cm. Diameter of bell, 15 cm.

905. TROMBA in B flat. One piston, transposing to G flat. . . . . Italy
Length of model, 86 cm. Diameter of bell, 22.8 cm.
Signed—"G. Pelitti, Milano."

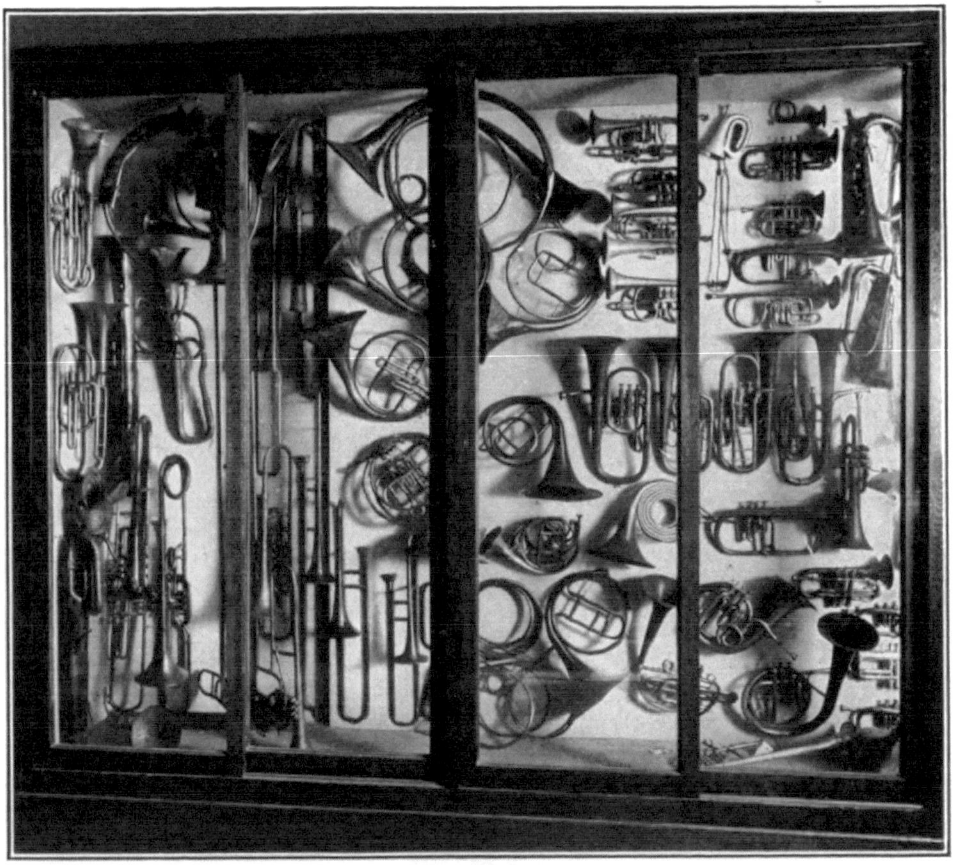

PLATE IX.

WEST SECTION. NOS. 862 TO 903 (RIGHT TO LEFT)

906. TROMBA A CHIAVI. Tenor in E flat. Brass. Three pistons. . . . . Italy
Length, 367 cm.; of model, 111 cm. Bell diameter, 18.5 cm.
Made by G. Pelitti for use in the opera "Messalina."

907. TROMBA A CHIAVI in F. Brass. One piston. . . . . Italy
Height of model, 69 cm.; width, 36 cm. Diameter of bell, 20 cm.
Signed—"C. Sambruna, Milano."

908. TROMBA in E flat. Brass . . . . Italy
The conical tube makes a double circular turn, 30 cm. below mouth-piece.
Length, 280.5 cm.; of model, 119 cm. Bell diameter, 12.5 cm.
Signed—"C. Sambruna, Milano."

909. TROMBA. Bass in A. Brass . . . . Italy
Two double circular turns, 25 cm. in diameter on opposite sides of body.
Length, 306 cm.; of model, 54 cm. Bell diameter, 15.5 cm.

910. TROMBA in A. Brass . . . . Italy
A boss, just below the bell, and two circles of tubing, serve as decoration. Length, 154 cm.; of model, 133 cm. Bell diameter, 12.8 cm.
Made by Pelitti especially for the opera "Regina di Cipro."

911. TROMBA in E flat. Brass. One piston, transposing to B flat. . . . Italy
The tube bends on itself bringing the mouth-piece in the middle.
Length of model, 119 cm. Diameter of bell, 12 cm.

912. TROMBA. Bass. Copper. Trombone form . . . . Italy
Length, 560 cm.; of model, 161.5 cm. Bell diameter, 14.8 cm.
Signed—"Pelitti, Milano."

913. PELITTONI FAGGATONA. Contra-bass in F. Brass . . . . Italy
The gilded body, fantastically curved for 333 cm. of its total length—807 cm.—terminates in a bell, 46 cm. in diameter. Model length, 294 cm.
Made, by Pelitti, Milano, for theatrical use.

914. TROMBA in G flat. Brass, painted. . . . . Italy
The body resembles a serpent in motion. The bell turns abruptly upwards. Length, 181 cm.; of model, 87 cm. Bell diameter, 14 by 16 cm.

915. TROMBA in B flat. Brass . . . . Italy
The tube has one circular turn and an S-shaped curve.
Length, 132.5 cm.; of model, 65 cm. Bell diameter, 12.2 cm.
Signed—"C. Sambruna, Milano."

916. TROMBA in F. Brass . . . . Italy
The tube bends closely on itself five times for 40 cm. of its model length, 74.7 cm., giving a vibrating length of 274.7 cm. Bell diameter, 10 cm.
Signed—"Pelitti, Milano."

917. "CAMPIONE." Trumpet in D. Brass . . . . Italy
The serpentine tube makes eight graceful bends.
Length, 217 cm.; of model, 116 cm. Bell diameter, 14 cm.

918. TROMBA-DOPPIA in D flat. Brass . . . . Italy
Two conical tubes, each making one full turn, unite in a single mouthpiece. Lengths, 106 and 116 cm.; of model, 53.5 cm. Bell diameter, 21 cm.

919. TROMBA in E flat. Brass . . . . Italy
A semi-circular tube, 194.5 cm. in length, ends in a French-horn bell, 23 cm. in diameter. Width of model, 87 cm.
Signed—"G. Pelitti, Milano."

920. TROMBA A CHIAVI in B flat. Brass. Three pistons . . . . Italy
Length of model, 94 cm. Diameter of bell, 22.6 cm.
Signed—G. Pelitti, Milano."

921. TROMBA A CHIAVI in A. Brass. Three pistons . . . . Italy
Length of model, 92 cm. Diameter of bell, 9.8 cm.
Signed—"C. Sambruna."

922. CORNO. Similar to No. 904 . . . . Italy
Length, 262 cm.; of model, 102 cm. Brass bell, 28.5 cm. in diameter.

923. SERPENT in C. Similar to No. 903 . . . . Italy

With the exception of No. 923, the instruments from 904 to 930 were designed for use in a series of pageants in connection with the Festival at Pompeii in 1883. In spite of their unusual forms all of them are playable and display the usual musical possibilities of their type, while several are reproductions of instruments used in early Roman ceremonials.

924. TROMBA A CHIAVI in B flat. Brass, painted. Three pistons. . . . Italy
The body, painted to resemble a reptile, ends in a bell representing a snake's head, with open jaws plentifully supplied with teeth.
Length of model, 88 cm. Width of open jaws, 13.9 cm.

925. TROMBA A CHIAVI in B flat. Brass, painted . . . . Italy
Similar to the preceding. Length of model, 85 cm. Spread of jaws, 19 cm.

926. TROMBA A CHIAVI in B flat. Brass, painted................Italy
The body, painted dull green, describes a circle and ends in a dragon's head. Length, 304 cm.; of model, 91 cm. Diameter of mouth cavity, 24 cm.

927. TROMBA A CHIAVI in E flat. Brass, painted ....Italy
Length, 69 cm. Width, 7 cm. Diameter of bell, 7 cm.

928. TROMBA A CHIAVI in D flat. Brass, painted ....Italy
Length, 70 cm.; vibrating length, 226 cm. Width, 58 cm.

929. TROMBA in E flat. Patinated brass. The bell is in the form of a lion's head in repoussé work ....Italy
Length, 63 cm.; vibrating length, 172 cm. Width, 46 cm.

930. TROMBA, Baritone in G flat. Brass, painted ....Italy
Length, 193 cm.; of model, 70.5 cm.
The conical tube bends once on itself. Bell turns outward. Six finger-holes. Length, 345 cm.; of model, 180. Bell diameter, 17 cm.

The last seven instruments, products of Pelitti's redundant fancy, flanked by No. 902 on the right, and No. 931 on the left, form a veritable dragon's den.

CASE IX.

(Continuation of Class III, Section L.)

931. OPHICLEIDE, Bass in B flat, with crook in A. Brass. Nine keys. Bell in form of a dragon's head..................Spain

The bell is exquisitely decorated in gold designs, against a dull-red background.

Length, 275 cm.; of model, 120 cm. Spread of jaws, 24 cm.

Signed—"Bernareggi, Ynstrumentista de Camara de S. M. a Barcelona."

The Ophicleide (Fr. *Ophicléide;* Ger. *Ophikleide*), a bass-horn of deep pitch, was invented by Halary of Paris, in 1817. Although it was adopted by leading composers, and despite the improvements of Labbaye (1822), after 1835 it was superseded by the Tuba.

932. SAXHORN. Baritone in B flat. Brass. Three rotary valves. Model length, 75.5 cm. Bell diameter, 19.6 cm....United States

933. OPHICLEIDE, Alto in E flat. Brass. Nine keys...........France

Length, 213 cm.; of model, 91 cm. Bell diameter, 18.5 cm.

Signed—"David, à Paris."

934. BASS-HORN in B flat. Wood and brass. Six finger-holes and four keys ....France

Model length, 95 cm. Bell diameter, 16.5 cm.

935. SERPENT in C. Wood, covered with varnished leather. Crook and mouth-piece of silver-plated brass. Six finger-holes. Seventeenth century. A perfect example of the type.........France

Length, 226 cm.; of model, without crook, 84.5 cm.

To all intents and purposes the Serpent has become obsolete. It has suffered the fate of many other representatives of Class III, and, like them, has given place to instruments of greater efficiency. The Rev. F. W. Galpin, Harlow, England, has mastered its technique, and is frequently called upon to play the part assigned it in Mendelssohn's "St. Paul," when that work is given in London.

936. SAXHORN. Baritone in B flat. German silver mountings. Elliptical model. Three rotary valves ....Germany

This instrument, of very beautiful tone quality, has a model length of 74 cm. Diameter of bell, 22.5 cm.

Signed—"J. Altrichter, Frankfort, A. O., Hof Instrumenten Fabrik S. Königl. Hoheit D. P. Prinzen Friedrich Carl V. Preussen."

937. "COR D' HARMONIE," in E flat. Brass. Three piston valves. . France
The tube is bent as in the preceding type. The bell resembles that of the orchestral horn. It is frequently used as a substitute for that instrument. Length of model, 72 cm. Diameter of bell, 27.8 cm.
Signed—"No. 21130. Adolphe Sax. Brevetė à Paris.
Fleur de la Mson Milre de l'Empereurs."

938. SAXHORN. Baritone in E flat. German silver. Four rotary valves.
Model length, 72 cm. Bell diameter, 18.6 cm. . . . . . United States
Signed—"J. Lathrop Allen, No. 17, Harvard Place, Boston."

939. SAXHORN. Baritone in B flat. Brass. Three pistons. . . . . . England
Length of model, 63.8 cm. Diameter of bell, 23.3 cm.
Signed—"Henry Potter and Co., 30 Charing Cross, London."

940. EUPHONIUM in B flat. Brass. Four piston valves, the fourth being a transposing piston . . . . England
Length of model, 68.5 cm. Diameter of bell, 25 cm.
Signed—"F. Besson, London."

941. SAXHORN. Bass in B flat. Brass. Three rotary valves. . United States
Length of model, 103.5 cm. Bell diameter, 19 cm.

942. SAXHORN. Baritone in B flat. Three pump valves. . . . United States
Length of model, 103.5 cm. Diameter of bell, 19 cm. Imperfect.

943. SAXHORN. Bass in B flat. Brass. Three rotary valves. United States
Length of model, 104 cm. Diameter of bell, 24 cm.
Nos. 941-2-3 are of the "Bell over shoulder" model. For several decades, beginning with 1860, this form was quite in vogue. The tone was directed backward, which was a distinct advantage for army bands.

944. SAXHORN. Baritone in F. Brass. German silver mountings. . France
Five rotary valves, four worked by levers, and the fifth, a transposing valve, by a thumbscrew . . . . France
Length of model, 103 cm. Diameter of bell, 21.3 cm.
Signed—"Gautrot, à Paris."
Made for Ganongia y cia, and taken to Funchal, Madeira, Feb. 18, 1836, for the use of the "A Sociedade Philharmonica des Artistas."

945. SAXHORN. Baritone in F. Brass. German silver mountings.
Three pump valves . . . . Germany
Length of model, 85 cm. Diameter of bell, 20.3 cm.
Signed—"A. Langhamer, Instr. in Bremen."

946. BOMBARDON. Bass in E flat. Brass. Three pistons. . . . . . . England
Length of model, 72 cm. Diameter of bell, 29.5 cm.
Signed—"F. Wallace and Son, Ltd., Paris and London, N. W."

947. EUPHONIUM in B flat. Brass. German silver mountings. Three rotary valves .... Austria

Length of model, 75 cm. Diameter of bell, 22.3 cm.

Signed—"K. K. Hof Instrumenten Fabrik, Leopold Uhlman und Sohn in Wien."

948. HELICON. Contrabass in E flat. Brass. German silver mountings. Three rotary valves .... United States

In all probability, the date of the invention of this instrument falls in the first half of the nineteenth century. It is circular in form and rests on the shoulders, the mouth-piece being in the circle. This particular example has a conical tube, wound once on itself, and then running in a series of long and short curves to the mouth-piece. The crooks controlled by the valves add 52, 23, and 76, or a total of 151 cm. to vibrating length. Lengths of curves, 340 and 397.5 cm.

Length of model, 91.2 cm. Diameter of bell, 29.8 cm.

949. HELICON. Contrabass in E flat. Brass. Three pistons ..... England

The tube, of greater diameter than in the preceding, winds twice on itself, and runs to mouth-piece as in No. 948. The additional lengths gained by these crooks are 55.5, 22.7, and 78, or a total of 156.2. Length of model, 118 cm. Diameter of bell, 39 cm.

Signed—"S. Arthur Chappel, 52 New Pond Road, London, N. W."

In a general way it may be stated that all the principles of tone-production embodied in the instruments in Class III were known to the ancients. Even the date of the introduction of finger-holes falls in the days of Egyptian supremacy.

The development of higher musical ideals has led to the perfecting of the various types, for, in this domain the economic law of supply and demand has been, and is, operative. The increase in virtuosity has led to improvements in the controlling mechanism, and a wider knowledge of the laws of acoustics has resulted in the removal of many obvious defects. Possibly no improvements are of greater value than the application of the Boehm System to the instruments known as "the wood-wind," and of valve mechanism to the group generically known as the "brass."

The somewhat exaggerated demands made by modern composers is resulting in the emergence of new instruments, some of which will be welcomed as valuable acquisitions, while many—possibly the most—will sink into "innocuous desuetude." It may be that a greater advance will be made by the rehabilitation of obsolete instruments, like the "Flute d'Amour" and the "Oboe d'Amour."

CLASS IV. INSTRUMENTS WITH VIBRATING STRING, OR STRINGS.

Section A. One Vibrating Plucked String. Monochord.

Section B. Vibrating Plucked Strings running free. Early Harp; Lyre.

Section C. Vibrating Plucked Strings running free, whose pitches may be changed (a) by hooks, (b) by mechanism. Haken-harfe—Modern Pedal Harp.

Section D. Vibrating Plucked Strings running close to Resonator. Couched Harp.

Section E. Vibrating Plucked Strings running over Frets and Bridges. Tamboura. Lute. Mandoline. Guitar.

That a string in a state of tension could be made to sound when forcibly plucked by the fingers, or a plectrum, was discovered at a very remote date. Closely following this initial discovery, came an appreciation of the fact that the resonance of the tone was sensibly increased when the string was stretched over a hollow box or gourd, and, again, that the quality of the tone was improved owing to the richness of the overtone series. Moreover, an extended knowledge of the scientific principles underlying this method of tone-production is revealed by the examples of these types of which we have records, and more concrete evidence in the instruments themselves.

Possibly no instrument can boast of so distinguished a history as the Harp. Whether it originated in so simple a type as the primitive musical bow with its one string, or not, we meet it in the earliest civilizations. In its fundamental essentials, the earliest form was identical with our modern instrument, with the exception of the devices for shortening the strings.

That David, through his skillful manipulation of its strings, could move the moody Saul, is one of the earliest recorded testimonials to its charm. The belief that it is the only instrument accorded a place in Heaven must have been based on a higher valuation of its musical worth than obtains at present, for we find its proper place as a member of the orchestra. Its graceful shape has always appealed to the artist, while it was a favorite instrument with Victorian novelists. It has a very extended compass, running from CC flat to e flat''''.

In the ancient and primitive Harp but one tone could be produced from each string. This may be taken as a general definition of the type. The graceful shape of the modern instrument was developed in the days of antiquity for structural reasons, and for the convenience of the performer, not from any scientific necessity. In many Oriental and primitive types the strings are not free, so they may be plucked by the fingers of either hand, but run closely over the resonance box. They may be defined as "couched" harps (see No. 1000).

950. GOURD RESONATORS, used in primitive string instruments to increase the resonance . . . . Cameroon, W. Africa

(G. Schwab.)

951. MUSICAL BOW. One string. Resonator ....St. Christopher Is., Brit. W. Indies
Like many of the instruments used by the negroes in the West Indies this appears to be a mixture of several African forms. Shorter than the *oüta* of S. Africa, it resembles it in its stringing; in other respects it is almost identical with the African *gubo*. The alternative term *cocolas*, given by the negroes, may be derived from *kokolo*, the name of a Congoese harp.
Length of bow, 102.4 cm.; of string, 92 cm.

952. GENDANG-BAWOI. Bamboo. Two fibre strings...........Borneo
Length, 47 cm. Diameter, 4.4 cm.

953. MAROVANY, or VALIHA. Bamboo. Eight strings cut from body. Alternative spelling *marouvana* ....Madagascar
Length, 58.5 cm.; of strings, 40 cm. Diameter of body, 4 cm.

954. MVET. Three imperfect specimens of type described under No. 956.
Lengths, beginning with the uppermost, 98.5, 96.4 and 99.8 cm.

955. VALIHA, or MAROVANY. Bamboo ....Madagascar
Sixteen strings, cut from body, are stretched over bridges of pith in positions indicated by bands of red yarn.
Length, 145 cm. Average length of string, 40 cm. Diameter, 6.7 cm.

956. MVET. Slightly bowed body. Four strings....Fr. Congo, Africa
The strings, cut from body, run over a high wedge-shaped bridge.
Length, 152 cm.; of strings (average), 100.2 cm. Diameter, 2.6 cm.

957. MVET. Alternative spellings, *mver*, *mverk* and *mvöt*........ ....French Congo, Africa
The body, with ovoid cross section, is 197.7 cm. in length, with a diameter of 1.5 by 3 cm. It has two gourd resonators, 13.5 cm. in diameter, placed in the middle under the bridge. Occasionally one is placed at each end. The strings are in bad condition.

958. GENDANG-BULU .... Sumatra
Section of bamboo, over which run three wire strings. Carved peg-head at one end and three long tuning-pegs at the other. Two low bridges.
Length, 78.5 cm.; of body, 52 cm. Diameter, 12.3 cm.

959. COUCHED HARP, or PSALTERY.......Name and source unknown
Body of bamboo, or reed, to which the upper section of a large bottle-gourd is attached. The tube is decorated with broad lines in designs quite like the *suling* (No. 545, Case VI). There is no authoritative data on which the existence of this instrument in Java can be securely based. The *sadiou* of Cambodia, a monochord with a wire string, is in every other respect similar. (Knosp, *Ueber annamitische Musik*, p. 159.)

960. UKEKE-LAAU, or UKEKE. (*uke*—to strike) . . . . .Hawaii
Flat narrow strip of light-colored wood over which run three gut strings. The first name is given by Mahillon,[1] the second, the one more generally used, by Balfour.[2] The player holds the instrument in his teeth and plucks the strings with his finger or a plectrum. The result is said by Mahillon to give great joy to the object of a lover's worship. Length, 57.6 cm. Width, 3.9 cm. Thickness, 9 mm.

961. ZEZE, or SESE. One string. Three frets. No resonator. . . E. Africa
The slightly rounded body, of a hard dark wood, has three rudely fashioned frets at one end over which runs the string, which is fastened to a peg at each end. It is possible to produce five tones. A very rude specimen.
Length, 48 cm. Width, 2.9 cm. Height of frets, 2 cm.
This instrument is in its present position for ethnological reasons, to which purely scientific classifications occasionally must pay deference. (See Case XII, Nos. 1186 and 1194.)

962. NGKRATONG. Wooden body. Four strings. . . . . Borneo
The irregular rectangular body carries four standards from one of which run four strings, which, braced against two others, end in the fourth. Rude decorations, including a bird at one end and a bird's tail at the other.
Length, 28 cm. Width, 10 to 17.2 cm. Height, 11.8 cm.

963. PSALTERY, or HARP. Wood. Palm-fibre. . . Atonga Tribe, Africa
Six palm-fibre strings run over a trough-like wooden body, ending in a handle and resting on a gourd resonator.[3]
Length, 61.9 cm. Width, 5.7 cm. Height, with gourd, 24.1 cm.

964. KINANDA. Typical cane-psaltery, gourd resonator. . Congo, Africa
Of fifteen lengths of cane, held together at the ends by transverse joints of the same material, twelve have very narrow longitudinal strips cut from body. These strips, tightened by a transverse length of cane forced under them at each end, produce a mixed tonal sequence, but of incisive quality. A similar procedure is followed on the under side, but the tension strip is in the middle. The structure, either side up, rests on an oval gourd resonator. With minor variations this description applies to the entire type.
Length, 36 cm. Width, 20.9 cm. Height, 17.1 cm.
Floss-psalterium, "raft-psaltery," is the designation of type given by Curt Sachs.[4]

---

[1] Mahillon, *Catalogue*, Vol. III, p. 346.
[2] Balfour, "The Natural History of the Musical Bow," pp. 81-83.
[3] Ankermann, *Af. Mus. Inst.*, p. 29, gives a full description and illustration of this instrument but assigns it no name.
[4] Sachs, p. 144.

965. INANGA. Wooden body. Eleven strings....Urundi Tribe, Africa
A string, generally of ox-sinew, *umurya*, runs through holes, *ututo-boro*, in the ends of the scow-shaped body. Authorities differ as to the number of strings, but it must be remembered that in indigenous types there is little standardization.
Length, 38 cm. Width, 15 cm. Depth, 7 cm.

966. CANE-PSALTERY. Thirteen joints of river reed. (Toy).....Egypt
Lengths of reeds, 21 to 30 cm.; width of each, 1.9 cm.

967. CANE-PSALTERY, or DULCIMER ....Dahomey, W. Africa
This most artistic psaltery has the same number of joints and structural characteristics as No. 964. The vibrating lengths are weighted by wrapping, or "over-spinning," with narrow strips of cane. Tension secured by wedges, which produce a buzzing sound.
Pitches:—b, d, -, -, b flat, g′, b′, g″, and a flat′.
Length, 50.5 cm. Width, 20.9 cm.
The definition, "couched harp," would apply to this, if the strings are plucked; if struck, as they frequently are, the instrument would figure as a dulcimer.

968. KORRO ....Mandingo tribe, N. W. Africa
The body, a half-section of gourd, is pierced by a wooden rod, of the length of which 10 cm. project at the rear and 64 cm. in front, forming the neck. Three bars, two longitudinal and one transverse, each 30.8 cm. long, run through and over the skin head. From the back of body eighteen strings of *garon* bark are led over a high bridge and fastened to gut rings on the neck. By pushing these rings along the neck the tension is increased: a favorite device. A sheet of tin, bearing the emblem "Palmer's Biscuits," buzzes to order.
Length, 118 cm. Diameter of gourd, 44 cm.; depth, 20 cm.

969. KASSO. Gourd. Fourteen gut strings.........Senegal, W. Africa
Similar to the preceding. Length, 91.2. Width, 41.1. Depth, 25.5 cm.

970. PSALTERY. Wooden body. Carved. Eight wire strings......Java
The body, stained a rich dark brown, represents a goose resting on its back with spread wings. At one end the neck is curved sufficiently to allow it to view its tail at the other extremity. The strings, fastened to iron pins at one end, run over the thin wooden belly to tall wooden tuning-pegs.
In principle it corresponds to the Javanese *ketjapi*, but in detail it is quite distinct. It may be a sophisticated variant.
Length, 98.8 cm. Width, 22.8 cm. Depth, 7.9 cm.

971. KASSO. Calabash body. Ten fibre strings. . . . . Senegambia, Africa
Calabash body, with antelope-skin. Ten strings from fibrous bark of the *garon* tree.
Length, 77 cm. Diameter of gourd, 30.4 cm.; depth, 20.9 cm.
As the strings run free, these and many of the instruments immediately following are of the harp family. The *kasso* is held against the body, with the resonator turned outward, and the strings are plucked by the fingers of both hands. The following naive description of the psaltery and harp and the difference between them, is interesting if not conclusive:
"This is the diversity and discord betweene ye harpe and the psaltery, in ye psaltery is an holow tree, and of that same tree the sound cometh upward; and the strings be smit downward, and soundeth upward; and in the harpe, the hollownesse of the tree is beneath."[5]

972. NANGA. Six-stringed harp . . . . Niam-Niam, Central Africa
Wood, covered with parchment. Base of post covered with lizard-skin. It is of the *ombi* type. Length, 47 cm. Height, 37 cm.

973. AGONG. Bamboo. Two strings, cut from body. . Philippine Islands
Of the *valiha* type. The strings—vibrating length, 41.7 cm.—are cut from the cylindrical body, 60.8 cm. long, and raised by low bridges at either end. The *krumba* of Nias Island is also of this type.

974. KISSAR. Lyre type . . . . Uganda, Central Africa
The body of hard wood resembles a shallow oval bowl. From the back, two posts of polished hard wood diverge as they are led up to a cross bar uniting them at the top. The belly is of lizard-skin. The six strings terminate in rings encircling the cross-bar. The strings are tuned by these rings as in the Greek *cithara.*
Length, 54 cm. Width, 31 to 40 cm. Depth, 8 cm.

975. HARP . . . . Upper Congo Region, Central Africa
Wood, with parchment belly. Five fibre strings.
Length, 55 cm. Greatest diameter, 29 cm. Depth, 10 cm.

976. OMBI, or BAMBUR. Leather covered body. Five fibre strings. Africa
The body is round, and the string-post is inserted directly into one end.
Length of body, 36 cm.; of string-post, 38.2 cm.
This instrument was collected by M. Casman.

977. KISSAR. Of ruder construction than No. 975. . . Soudan, N. Africa
The rawhide belly is round. The posts, bound with leather rings, are mere sticks. Length, 30.8 cm. Diameter of belly, 18. 5 cm.

[5] Eastwood and Wright, "Bible Word-Book," p. 389, quoting "Batman vppon Bartholome, fol. 423 b (ed. 1582)."

978. WAMBEE. Harp type. Wood. Five strings.......Congo, Africa
To the bottom of a scow-shaped resonance-box, five cane rods of graduated length, bound together in the middle and slightly curving upwards at the free ends, are secured. Five strings of tendril run from the back of the body to the top of these rods. This is the typical form of construction.
Dimensions of body, 14 by 22 by 6 cm. Length of rods, 70 to 74.7 cm.

979. NGOMO. Ombi type. Wood. Eight strings..Fan Tribe, Fr. Congo
The rectangular body, with slightly curving bottom, is covered with antelope-skin with the hair retained. A rudely carved head of a hippopotamus forms the arm of a T-shaped projection at the upper end. The curved string-post is inserted at the intersection of body and this projection. Eight tuning-pegs.
Length of body, 56 cm.; of post, 53 cm.; of carving, 8 cm.

980. WAMBEE. Wood. Five strings...........Cameroon, W. Africa
The body, open at both ends, has a triangular cross-section with the belly for its base. This belly projects beyond the upper end of body. Usual rods, in this case running along the apex of the inverted triangle.
Length of body, 25.9 cm.; of belly, 33 cm.; of rods, 40 to 63.3 cm.
(G. Schwab.)

981. WAMBEE. Similar to the preceding....Upper Congo, Cent. Africa
The body is rounded at upper end and also in its cross-section. The belly is slit at a point 8 cm. from lower end of body, leaving an aperture—9 by 15 cm. It is colored a pale orange-red. These examples are exceedingly rude in construction, but they "soothe the savage breast."
Length of body, 21.3 cm.; of belly, 28 cm.; of rods, 35 to 52 cm.
Collected by M. Casman.

982. KISSAR. Tortoise shell, decorated ....Ababa tribe, W. Africa
Seven strings. The decorations are a star and crescent done in red lines, the former being pierced with six sound-holes. From the posts hang tassels of cowrie-shells. Quite like the Greek *cithara* in form. Length, 55 cm. Width, 40 cm. Depth, 11 cm.

983. ROTTE, or ROTTA. Wood. Six strings ....Old German
The elongated narrow lyre-shaped body is 79 cm. in height and 21 cm. in width. From the slightly curved arm at the top the center section is open, diminishing at the round lower end, 42 cm. below the top. Six strings run from a peg at the bottom of the body to tuning-pegs in cross-bar. The latter are modern, as in the original they were missing.

The "Rotte" is an early application of the lyre type, though differing in form. This is an exact reproduction of the only specimen in existence. The original was found in the grave of a Suabian nobleman of the fifth, or seventh century at Oberflacht, Würtemberg, and is preserved in the Völkerkunde Museum, Berlin.

984. CITHARA. Wood. Eleven strings .... Italy

Copied from a wall-painting at Pompeii. This is an exact reproduction of the instrument shown in the *Apollo Citharoedus*, in the Hall of the Busts, No. 277, Vatican, Rome.

Length, 67; of body, 28; of cross-bar, 35 cm. Width, 28 to 22 cm.

985. LYRE. Wood. Six strings .... Italy

Reproduction of the ancient type by Pelitti, Milano.

Length, 56 cm. Width, 25 cm. Depth, 5 cm.

Most of the instruments in the following group are played with plectra, but, with exceptions which will be noted, they display the structure of the couched harp and produce but one tone from each string.

986. ICHI-GEN-KIN, or SUMA-KOTO .... Japan

Wood. One string. Four ivory flying birds on the body indicate the position of the principal tones. It may be classified as a monochord. It usually rests on a small table with four legs and is played with cylindrical plectra of ivory called *ḳuda*.

Length, 109.3 cm. Width, 8 to 11 cm. Thickness, 9 mm. to 1.3 cm.

987. CAI DAN BAU. Monochord harp .... Anam

The rectangular body, of wood, is open at the base. It is lacquered black, and wonderfully inlaid with mother-of-pearl in intricate designs. A wire string runs from one end of belly to a neck projecting at the other and bent to an angle of 30 degrees. It is played with a bamboo plectrum held between the thumb and fore-finger of the right hand. The left hand changes the curve of the elastic neck, thus producing many tones. The word *bau*, Anamese for gourd, indicates its use for a resonator.

Length of body, 80 cm.; of neck, 75 cm. Width, 11 cm.

It must be borne in mind that the instruments from Anam, Cambodia, and Siam, were made for exhibition at the Paris Exposition of 1900, and are much more elaborately finished than those in common use among the people.

988. NI-GEN-KIN. "Two-stringed kin" .... Japan

Body of *ḳiri* wood. Two silken strings tuned in unison (f sharp).

Length, 108 cm. Width, 11 cm. Depth, 3.5 cm.

989. ROKU-KIN, or ROKU-GEN-KIN .... Japan

Camphor-wood. Six fine silken strings. Tuned by movable bridges. The strings are alternately green and black.

Length, 92.5 cm. Width, 11.5 to 13.5 cm. Thickness, 2 cm.

990. MEGYOUNG, or MEGYUN (crocodile) .... Burmah
The rectangular body of wood, elaborately carved, gilded, and inlaid with bits of glass, is roughly imitative of the crocodile. The ends rise upward and bear, the one the head, with open jaws, the other, the tail. The base is flat. Over eleven bridges, three gut strings are drawn. Played with plectra. On account of its weak tone, it is becoming obsolete.
Length, 97.4 cm. Width, 10.5 cm. Height (at end), 24.1 cm.

991. SOUNG. Harp type. Wood. Thirteen strings......... Burmah
The boat-shaped body, 74 cm. long, 16 cm. wide, and 10 cm. deep, is lacquered and gilded. The gilded belly is of finely tanned buffalo-skin. From a ridge on the belly, thirteen cord strings run to rings encircling the lower part of the gracefully curved post—78.4 cm. long—the lower end of which forms the ridge, or midrib, just mentioned. The belly has four sound-holes.
A cut of this exceedingly beautiful instrument appears in the last edition of the "Century Dictionary."

992. HAN-KOTO. "Half-koto" .... Japan
The typical *koto* body is decorated with red silk tassels. It has thirteen strings running over adjustable bridges. Played with *tsume* (plectra).
Length, 91 cm. Width, 22 to 23.5 cm. Greatest depth, 6 cm.

992A. K'IN. Wood. Seven strings .... China
This instrument, of the psaltery type, is said to have been invented by Fu Hsi. The body, of *wu t'ung* wood, is 127 cm. long, from 14 to 20 cm. wide, and 6 cm. deep. The top (firmament) is slightly rounded and the bottom (earth) is flat. In its earliest form it had five strings, representing the elements; the present number is seven. These strings, of silk, run through jade pins at the bottom of the wider end, and are led over a bridge to the other end, where they are fastened to two large pegs at the bottom by means of which they can be drawn taut. The 13 studs on the face represent the 12 moons and the intercalary moon. The *k'in* is played with the fingers. It is no longer in general use, on account of the difficulty of manipulation, and functions only in ceremonials at court. This example has a case of bluish-green satin embroidered with Chinese characters in black. This case serves as a background for the instrument as it hangs.*

(Marvin A. Ives.)

---

* For detailed information regarding the *k'in* and its functions consult Van Aalst, "Chinese Music," pp. 59-62.

993. KOMOUNKO. Koto type. Kiri wood ....Corea
The body, 152 cm. long, 17.7 cm. wide at the ends, increasing to 20.3 cm. at the middle, has a flat base in which is a rectangular sound-hole, 17 cm. long, and 2.5 cm. wide. The top is rounded, increasing from 2.1 cm. at ends to 7.7 cm. in middle section.

Angus Hamilton, in "Korea," p. 166, speaks of the tone of the *komounko* as "a melancholy, discordant wail," only equaled by the bowed-instrument, *nageum* (?), whose lure he describes as follows: "The awful screech of this unhappy viol overwhelms me, even in recollection." He probably refers to the *haggum* (Case XII, No. 1247) which could easily qualify.

994. YO K'IN. Same type as No. 992 ....Japan
Lacquered wood, decorated with metal ornaments. Thirteen pairs of fine wire strings. The upper surface is convex.
Length, 68.8 cm. Width, 22.8 cm. Depth, 8 cm.

995. YAMADA-KOTO. An unusually fine specimen............Japan
Camphor-wood, lacquered and inlaid. Thirteen strings of silk running over adjustable bridges. Played with the fingers and ivory *tsume*. The body rests on four feet, from which it rises in a slight, graceful arch.*
Length, 189 cm. Width, 29 cm. Height, 15 cm.

996. YAMADA-KOTO. Miniature model in case ....Japan
Length, 39.2 cm. Width, 8.3 cm. Height, 5 cm.

997. SONO-KOTO. In structure similar to No. 995.............Japan
Wood, lacquered and inlaid. Thirteen strings of colored silk running over bridges. Reproduction, made for the Columbian Exposition (1893) by Lyon and Healy, Chicago, and presented to the University. It is the oldest form of the *koto*. (2000 B. C.)
Length, 190 cm. Width, 24 cm. Height, 17 cm.
The names of the various parts of the koto are: *koto no ji*—bridge; *koto no o*—strings; and *koto no tsume*, plectrum.[6]

998. CAI DAN THAP LUC, or THAP LUC ....Anam
The trapezoidal body—98 cm. long, and 13 to 21.5 cm. wide at the larger end—rests on two short legs. The sound-board is convex. A band of ivory, with incised designs in black, encircles the larger end of sound-board. Sixteen (*thap luc*) brass wire strings, fastened inside the body, run through holes in this board, extending from a low ridge over moveable triangular bridges to tuning-pegs at the

---

* Details of the various tunings of the *koto* are given by Polak in, *Die Harmonisierung indischer, türkischer und japanischer Melodien*, pp. 59-62.

[6] Sachs, p. 231.

smaller end. The wood is very light, both in weight and color, and, following the outline of the instrument, a band of some dark colored wood richly inlaid with mother-of-pearl serves as decoration. Played with the fingers.

It will be noticed that, as the bridges run parallel to the holes through which the strings are drawn the strings are divided into two groups. The one to the left gives the pentatonic scale of B from f sharp to f sharp‴; the group to the right a series, partly diatonic, partly chromatic, with constantly changing suggestions of tonality, all within the limit of a fourth (f-b). The instrument is a direct descendant of the Chinese *k'in*, which was invented between 2852 and 2737 B. C. The round upper surface represents the heavens, the lower flat surface the earth. Because the earth is under the heavens it rests on this flat surface, not because it is more practical. (See Knosp., p. 146.)

999. CHENG, or TCHENG. Similar to 998. . . . . China

This specimen is undecorated save at the ends. It is the diminutive form of the *she*, which, originally having fifty strings, now has but twenty-five.[7] Length, 97.5 cm. Width, 13.5 to 20 cm.

(B-S.)

1000. CHANK. Couched harp . . . . Persia

The upright body with string-post outlines a right-angle triangle. The hard, dark wood body is decorated with the head of an antelope and several curious designs in incised lines. The post terminates in a carved head of the same animal. The strings run from the bottom over and close to the resonance-box, to tuning-pegs set spirally in the string-post, which rises 47.6 cm. above the body. This is neither the typical modern, nor the ancient form, and the number of strings does not correspond.

Height, 96 cm. Width, 29.6 to 15 cm. Depth, 7.5 cm.

1001. HARP. Wood. Seven free strings of gut. . . . . Persia

The strings run free from the sloping side of the triangular body to the string-post, which projects from the upper part of the body, 47.6 cm., as in the preceding instrument. Ornamental triangular sound-holes.

Total length, 85 cm. Width, 5 to 31 cm. Depth, 7.5 cm.

These harps were exhibited at the Columbian Exposition and were obtained through the Persian Commissioner.

---

[7] Van Aalst, p. 66.

1002. HARP .... Philippine Islands
Bamboo body. Twenty-seven strings of twisted hemp. Tuning-pegs of split bamboo. This is the first example of the modern type. Rude as it is, in it is shown the chief structural advance over the original type, viz., the introduction of the front pillar, through which the rigidity lacking in the Egyptian type is secured. The body has three rectangular sound holes at equi-distant points in the back. Height of front pillar, 138 cm. Width—the distance from the top of resonance body to the tip of the front pillar—72.2 cm. This definition applies to the measurements of all harps.

1003. ARPA A NOTTOLINI (Eng. *Hooked Harp;* Fr. *Harpe à crochets;* Ger. *Hakenharfe*). Eighteenth century......... Italy
Body elaborately inlaid with ivory. Thirty-seven strings. Twenty-three strings can be raised in pitch by turning the hooks. The harp derives its name from this device, which, introduced in the second half of the seventeenth century, was the first step in the direction of the modern pedal mechanism. It still persists in certain localities. The front pillar ends in a carving of a female head, gilded. The sound-board is pierced with six groups of small sound-holes forming rosettes.
Height of front pillar, 144 cm. Width, 73.7 cm.

1004. HARFE. (Eng. *Harp;* Fr. *Harpe;* Ital. *Arpa*). Seventeenth century .... Germany
Rectangular body with straight pillar. Twelve strings.
Height, 60 cm. Width, 29.3 cm.; of sound-board, 32 to 54 cm.

1005. EARLY IRISH HARP, or "MINSTREL'S HARP" .... Ireland
This reproduction of the famous "O'Brien Harp"—not of King Brian Borumna—was made by Lyon and Healy of Chicago, for the Columbian Exposition in that city in 1893, and presented by them to the University. It has a curved front pillar and the cross-bar curves downwards instead of upwards as usual. The broad, tapering sound-board is pierced with four circular sound-holes, and is decorated with incised geometric designs.
Length of curved front-pillar, 94.5 cm. Width, 69.7 cm.; of sound board, 31 cm., at base, to 12 cm., at tip.
Nos. 1005 to 1010 are placed on top of Case.

1006. MODERN IRISH HARP. Bent front pillar. Thirty strings.. England
This harp, very appropriately painted green and decorated with shamrocks, is modeled on the old type. Small pivoted bridges of brass may be turned so as to raise the pitch of each string a semitone.
Height, 99 cm. Width, 57 cm.; of sound-board, 2.7 to 8.9 cm.
Signed—"J. G. Morley, London."

1007. HARPE A PEDALES. (Eng. *Pedal Harp;* Ital. *Arpa a pedali;* Ger. *Pedalharfe*) .... France
Wood, with elaborately carved head and front pillar. Thirty-eight gut strings. Seven pedals operate a hook mechanism which changes the pitch of the strings, a device first used by Hochbrucker in 1720.
Height, 165 cm. Width, 88 cm.; of sound-board, 35.5 to 8.9 cm.
Signed—"Naderman, à Paris, 1790."

1008. PEDAL HARP ....England
Semicircular body. Straight front pillar. Forty-three strings. Seven double-action pedals operate to raise the pitch a semi-tone or tone as desired. An eighth pedal operates a damper.
Height, 169 cm. Width, 91.2 cm.; of sound-board, 35.5 to 8.9 cm.
Signed—"F. Dizes' Patent Harp, London."

1009. HARP .... Cuba
Rectangular body. Straight front pillar. Sixteen gut strings.
Height, 107 cm. Width, 52.6 cm.; of sound-board, 18 cm.; of head, 32.5 cm.

1010. BANJO HARP ....England
Eighteen strings run over a banjo body. Five handles operate a mechanism by which changes of pitch are produced.
Height, 87 cm. Width, 45 cm. Depth, 9.5 cm.

1011. AEOLSHARFE (Eng. *Aeolian harp;* Fr. *Harpe d' Eole;* Ital. *Arpa eolia*) .... Germany
Semi-cylindrical body of wood. Eight gut strings. The wind causes the strings to give out their harmonics.
Length, 90 cm. Width of base, 23 cm. Depth, 13 cm. Circumference of upper part, 37 cm.

1012. HARPE D' EOLE. Trilateral body. Five gut strings.......France
Length, 103 cm. Width of sound-boards, 22 cm.

1013. ARPA DOPPIA or ARPANETTA (Eng. *Double Harp;* Fr. *Arpanette;* Ger. *Doppelharfe*) ....Italy
On each side of the body, seven gut strings are led from tuning-pegs at the top. It illustrates the early *spitzharfe* (Ger.), but the form is quite distinct.
Height, 58.2 cm.; of body, 41.8; depth, 12.5 cm.

1014. HARFE. Seventeenth century ....Germany
Rectangular body. Twenty-four gut strings.
Length, 71.1 cm. Width, 36 cm. Diameter of sound-board, 9.7 to 4.7 cm.

1015. HAKENHARFE. Seventeenth century .... Germany
Quadrangular body. Straight pillar. Thirty-four gut strings, of which twenty can be raised as in No. 1003.
Height, 146.3 cm. Width, 85.2 cm.

1016. HARP-LUTE .... England
Wood. Thirteen strings, of which three run over frets. Sometimes called "Dital Harp." The body—57.6 cm. in height—has a shallow, hexagonally vaulted back, is rounded at the base, and the sides slope from a width of 33 to 23.7 cm. From the left side of the top a pillar rises to a height of 26.7 cm. From the right side extends a fret-board 5.5 cm. in width to a height of 22.4 cm. The two are connected by the usual harp tuning-peg bar. Tuning-pegs of iron. The instrument is lacquered black and decorated in gilt.
Signed—"Angelo Ventura, 1829, London."

1017. HARP-LUTE .... England
Upright lute-shaped body. Fourteen strings. Eight of these are free, six run over double frets. Nos. 2-3-4 and 6 run through rings by means of which they may be raised in pitch. Nos. 5 and 8 may also be thus affected by levers. Identical with No. 1016 but smaller.
Signed—"C. Wheatstone, Inventor, London."

1018. SITAR, or SETAR. Tamboura type .... India
Gourd body, and wooden neck, elaborately decorated. Five fine wire strings run over fifteen frets.
Length, 89.9 cm.; of gourd, 17.8 cm. Diameter, 12.4 cm.
The group of East Indian instruments to which this belongs represents the "Tamboura" type which, with the exception of the stringing, is closely allied to the Lute. They are all beautifully decorated, and display marvellous ingenuity and skill in the manner in which the bodies, almost invariably of gourd, are incorporated into the structure. Withal the tone is very beautiful.

1019. BIN .... India
Bamboo. Seven tuning pegs from which run the same number of strings. Four run over high wooden bridges and twenty-two frets, the remaining strings, two on one side, and one on the other, are free. Two large gourds serve as resonators. A reproduction.
Length, 137.9 cm. Diameter of body, 12.7 cm.; of gourds, 30 cm.
(Lyon and Healy.)

1020. VIPANCHI-VINA . . . . India

Body of gourd with belly of wood. Neck and head of hard wood.

Five strings run over sixteen adjustable frets to T-shape pegs, two in front and three at left side of the head. The carving on belly and the decorations on the gourd resonators are unique in conception and delicate in execution.

Length, 127 cm.; of body, 28 cm.; width, 19 cm.; depth, 17 cm.

1021. NADECVARA-VINA. "The loud-toned vina" . . . . India

Flat, violin-shaped body of wood. Six tuning-pegs, two on flat surface of neck and four on the side, draw an equal number of wire strings over one ivory bridge and sixteen adjustable frets. The shape of the body is indicative of European influence.

Length, 123.7 cm.; of body, 28 cm.; width, 19 cm.; depth, 17 cm.

1022. TAMBOURA, or SITAR . . . . India

The body, of a large gourd with a flat wooden belly, is joined to a long neck, which tapers towards the head. From a projection at the base five wire strings run over the un-fretted finger-board to the same number of wooden tuning-pegs inserted in the sides of the neck. It corresponds exactly to no instrument described in the literature of the subject.

Length, 114 cm. Width of belly, 25.5 cm.; depth, 22 cm.

1023. CACHA-VINA . . . . India

Body of gourd with neck of elaborately carved wood. Five wire strings. Seventeen frets. Eight sympathetic strings run under a glass plate. Under the wooden belly is placed a second of tightly stretched parchment. The use of sympathetic strings is a very common procedure in India, as will be seen in Case XII.

Length, 122 cm.; of body, 28.5 cm.; width, 25.5 cm.; depth, 13.5 cm.

1024. SUR-VAHARA. "Beautiful toned" . . . . India

Body of gourd. Belly and neck of dark brown wood. Five tuning-pegs, and same number of strings, running over fifteen frets. Eight sympathetic strings. Said to have been invented about the middle of the last century, by Gutam Mohammed, Khan of Lakhnau.

Length, 152 cm.; of body, 45.6 cm.; width, 32 cm.; depth, 30 cm.

1025. TUMBURU-VINA . . . . India

Gourd body. Convex wooden belly. Four tuning-pegs. Four wire strings.

Length, 118 cm. Width, 32 cm. Depth, 30 cm.

There is a conflict of authorities regarding this instrument. Mahillon states that the strings were plucked, while Fétis places it among the bowed instruments. It is fair to state that the former authority carries the greater weight.[8] Tumburu was one of the *gandharva*, or musicians of Indra's heaven. The typical member of this group is played only by professionals and is called *dasiri tamburi.*[9]

1026. SOUTHERN-VINA . . . . India

Body of gourd and wooden belly. Two resonators of gourd, one at end of neck. From ten tuning-pegs, of which eight are distributed along the side of the neck, run an equal number of strings over two bridges, one on neck and one on belly, and over sixteen frets.

Fully described by Capt. Day; he assigns to it no native name.[10]

Length, 142 cm.; of body, 47.1 cm. Circumference of gourds, 62.9, and 11.4 cm.

1027. TARAFFEDAR SITAR . . . . India

Gourd body, with wooden belly and neck, both elaborately decorated. Six tuning-pegs. Six wire strings, and ten sympathetic strings.

The name assigned to this instrument is given by Capt. Day (p. 118) and been assumed because this example does not correspond in essentials to any other of the East Indian instruments.

Length, 142.8 cm. Circumference of gourd, 76 cm.; depth, 34 cm.

1028. PRASANARI-VINA . . . . India

Shallow gourd body. A neck of usual form carries five strings. A shorter neck, also carrying five strings, is attached to the longer.

Length, 113.5 cm.; of short neck, 67.9 cm.; of body, 25.4 cm. depth, 29 cm.

1029. RANJANI-VINA, or "The colorful vina" . . . . India

Body of wood resting on two large gourds. Five strings running over sixteen frets. Same type as the *mahati-vina.*

Length, 121.6 cm. Height, 31.4 cm. Circumference of gourd, 101.2 cm.

This form of *vina* is placed over the shoulder when played, and is the instrument most frequently illustrated in accounts of Indian music.

---

[8] Mahillon, *Catalogue,* I., pp. 154, 155; Fetis, *Histoire de la Musique,* II, p. 287.

[9] Day, "The Music and Musical Instruments of Southern India," which will be referred to in the future by the name of the author.

[10] Day, p. 111. On page 112 he gives the names of the various parts of the *vina.*

1030. RUDRA-VINA, or RABABA .... India

Body and neck carved from a single piece of hard brown wood. Parchment belly. Six strings. Length, 77 cm. Width, 25.2 cm. Depth, 13 cm.

Sachs and Mahillon are in direct conflict regarding this instrument, which is listed as above on the authority of the latter. The terms "Vina of the god Rudra" and "howling vina," applied to the instrument, seem to indicate an extra-European dissension.

1031. COMPOSITE SITAR .... India

Were one inclined to follow the modern fad and create a composite name, the fact that this trinitarian instrument is made up of an *esra*, a *sitar*, and a *tambura*, might suggest *es-si-tam*. It is a modern contrivance invented by Surpiar Ashraf Ali, from whom it was bought by Mr. Stearns in 1892, presumably under the name given above.

The body rests on three thin gourd resonators and the necks are united by a plate surmounted by a group of three birds carved in wood. A multi-colored portrait of some East Indian beauty, in style quite prophetic of the modern cigarette picture, affixed to one side, attests the modernity of this instrument.

Height, 133.9 cm. Circumference at base, 91.2 cm.; at plate, 50 cm.

1032. TANBUR .... Persia

A pear-shaped body with an extremely long neck, both of which are of ebony inlaid with mother-of-pearl in a very artistic manner. Seven fine wire strings. Thirteen frets.

Length, 130.5 cm.; of body, 42.5 cm.; width, 18 cm.; depth, 17 cm.

1033. SAZ. Tanbur type .... Algeria

Minature type. Slender neck with two flat heads. Wire strings. The entire instrument is covered with an inlay of tortoise-shell, mother-of-pearl, and ivory.

Length, 47 cm.; of body, 14 cm.; width, 7 cm.; depth, 5 cm.

In essentials the Lute (Fr. *Luth;* Ital. *Liuto;* Ger. *Laute;* Span. *Laud;* Port. *Alaude*) harks back to Egypt. Migrating to Arabia it was carried to Spain by the Moors, and soon became a favorite European instrument. During the fifteenth, sixteenth, and seventeenth centuries it was regnant. The French name *Luthier*, for violin-maker, is derived from the fact that during its vogue he also made lutes. Any doubts as to the pronunciation of the word in England are dispelled by the early spelling—"lewte." In the course of the lute's career it underwent minor structural changes but retained its essential characteristics, among which must be noted its unfortunate tendency to go out of tune with, or without, provocation.

In the form of the Mandoline (Ital. *Mandolino*) we see a derivative of the lute. There were two types in general use in Italy, the "Neapolitan," with four pairs of strings, and the "Milanese," or "Lombardy," with five. The tuning of the former is in fifths like the violin, in the latter it is variable. The modern mandoline in its form exaggerates the convexity of the lute, and, thus, is a recrudescence of the early Egyptian form, while in the two types mentioned above there were well defined differences in form. (Compare Nos. 1048 and 1056). Variants of the form will be described as they occur.

1034. KUITRA, or KOUITARA. Arabian lute . . . . Algeria

Deep body of wood. Four pairs of gut strings. A triangular sound-hole. All string instruments of this type have rather large sound-holes, necessitated by the fact that the strings are plucked.

As in all lutes, the peg-box is placed at an angle from the rest of the neck.

Length, 88.5 cm.; of body, 43 cm.; width, 27 cm.; depth, 17 cm.

1035. E'OUD, or UD. (Pl. *idan*). Early Arabian lute . . . . Egypt

Body of nineteen alternating strips of light and dark wood. Short neck similarly inlaid. Rosette sound-hole. Six pairs of gut strings.

Length, 90 cm.; of body, 50 cm.; width, 34 cm.; depth, 18 cm.

At the time it was introduced into Spain by the Moors it was known as the *alud*. This instrument, probably of Persian origin, is described by Al Farabi in the tenth century.

Quoting from "Mefatih ol alum," "The Brothers of Purity," an encyclopedia of the tenth century,[11] Sachs gives the names of the various parts of the *ud* as follows: *ain*—(eye), pl. *ayun*—sound-hole; *bamm* (Tk.)—the bass string, in the ancient four stringed *ud* woven from 64 silk threads, but later the only gut string; *had*—the highest string of the five-stringed type; *ibrik* (Ar.) or *raqabe*—neck; *mossena* (air), in the four-stringed type the next to the highest string, woven from 36 silk threads and giving g; *motsellets* (water)—the next to highest string in four-stringed type, giving d; *qasa*—the vaulted back; *reqme*—a small patch of green fish-skin, gummed on between string-holder and sound-hole; *shemsyat*—the two small sound-holes; *shemshat* (*shemsyat*) the large sound-hole; *zir* (pl. *ziran*), the highest string in the olden type, woven from 27 silk threads.[11]

---

[11] According to Kiesewetter (*Musik der Araber*, p. 8) this encyclopedia of twelve folio volumes was the work of an association of scholars known as the "Brothers of Purity." The names given by Sachs on the following pages are without doubt taken from this source, as there is a complete copy in the Imperial Library at Vienna. The pages run as follows: 5, 28, 173, 194, 315, 262, 262, 320, 369, 369, 431.

1036. E'OUD . . . . Egypt
In all essentials similar to No. 1035 but with five pairs of gut strings.
For this reason it is a modern recrudescence of an ancient type.
Both in this and the preceding example, the space given up to the peg-box, and the angle at which it is set, are greater than in the *kuitra*.
Length, 90 cm.; of body, 50 cm.; width, 34 cm.; depth, 17 cm.

1037. LIUTO . . . . Italy
Pear-shaped body of fluted strips of red wood. Flat sound-board, with ornamented rosette sound-hole. The neck—flat and inlaid with ivory—bends at an acute angle. Nine pairs of fine wire strings. A type made familiar by the great Italian painters.
Length, 110 cm.; of body, 52 cm.; width, 37 cm.; depth, 17 cm.

1038. MANDOLA. Eighteenth century . . . . Italy
Deep oval body. Circular sound-hole, inlaid. Six pegs carrying six strings of gut and overspun silk. Twenty brass frets.
Length, 91.5 cm.; of body, 41.5 cm.; width, 28.3 cm.; depth, 12.5 cm.

1039. MANDOLA. Same date as the preceding . . . . Italy
Deep oval body, beautifully inlaid. Circular sound-hole. Six pegs, carrying six strings of gut and over-spun silk.
Length, 93 cm.; of body, 47 cm.; width, 28 cm.; depth, 14.2 cm.

1040. LUTE . . . . England
Oval body of brown wood with ebony inlay. Five pairs of strings, two of gut, two of brass and one of steel.
Length, 76.5 cm.; of body, 39 cm.; width, 26.5 cm.; depth, 12 cm.
Signed in ink on base of instrument—"Hoffman, London, 1758."

1041. PANDORA . . . . Italy
Flat, shallow body of wood. Triple rose sound-hole. Nineteen fine wire strings run over five frets. Broad finger-board terminating in a graceful curve and a carved human head.
Length, 122.9 cm. Diameters of the three curved bouts—33.7, 44.2, 45.6 cm. Depth, 8.9 cm.

1042. ORPHEOREON. Form of a small Pandora . . . . Italy
Body of wood with sloping shoulders and sharp upper bouts. Two reversed and two inverted F-holes. Twelve gut strings. Broad finger-board with six frets.
Length, 109.2 cm. Diameter, at bouts, 35 cm.; at waist, 24.1; at base, 35 cm. Depth, 8.4 cm.
Signed—"Petrus Sabrianus, Neapoli, Annio 1534."

1043. CHITARRONE. Seventeenth century .... Italy
Pear-shaped body. Ornamental rosette sound-hole edged with inlay of ivory and mother-of-pearl. Finger-board and neck of black wood, inlaid with ivory. Two peg-boxes, of which the upper has eight pegs from which run open bass strings of gut, the lower, nine pegs with nine wire strings. Five gut frets.
Length, 164 cm.; of body, 50 cm.; width, 33 cm.; depth, 14 cm.

1044. ARCILIUTO (Eng. *Arch-lute;* Fr. *Archiluth;* Ger. *Erzlaute*) . . Italy
Oval body with vaulted back. Short, broad finger-board inlaid with ivory. Two peg-boxes, the lower containing twelve pegs from which run six pairs of strings, three of gut and three of over-spun silk. From the upper box extend six pairs of open over-spun silk strings. Seven brass frets.
Length, 113 cm.; of body, 48 cm.; width, 32 cm.; depth, 16 cm.
Signed—"1600, In Padova, Vuendilio Venere."

1045. BASS COLASCIONE .... Italy
Oval body. Rosette sound-hole with double-headed eagle in the center. Six wire strings. The long finger-board terminates in a scroll and carved lion's head. No frets. 1602.
Length, 191 cm.; of body, 65 cm.; width, 41.5 cm.; depth, 23 cm.
Signed—"In Padova, Michielle Harton."

1046. MANDOLINO. Lombardy model .... Italy
Oval body and sound-hole. Six strings. Twenty metal frets.
Length, 53 cm.; of body, 29 cm.; width, 22 cm.; depth, 12 cm.

1047. MANDOLINO. Eighteenth century .... Italy
Long, narrow lute-shaped body, ornately decorated. Flat neck, inlaid with tortoise-shell, ebony, and ivory. Four pairs of wire strings. Inlaid tortoise-shell plaque under the strings.
Length, 58 cm.; of body, 28,5 cm.; width, 15.5 cm.; depth, 11 cm.

1048. MANDOLINO. Neapolitan model .... Italy
Deep oval body. Purfled sound-board with oval sound-hole. Flat head. Eight mechanically operated metal pegs carrying four pairs of wire strings. On the sound-board is a tortoise-shell plaque.
Length, 60 cm.; of body, 30 cm.; width, 18.5 cm.; depth, 16 cm.

1049. PANDOURINA .... Italy
Long and narrow lute-shaped body. Rosette sound-hole. Finger-board beautifully inlaid. Six pairs of strings of which all are wire, with the exception of the second pair. Seven ivory frets.
Length, 54 cm.; of body, 25 cm.; width, 14.5 cm.; depth, 8 cm.
Signed—"Domenico Brambilla abitante in Milano nel Borga della Citadella in Porta Ticinese al segno della Tromba, 1759."

1050. BANDOLIN (Span. Port. *Bandolim*) .... Mexico
The carapace of an armadillo forms the body. Inlaid sound-board. Circular sound-hole. Five pairs of gut strings. Ten frets.
Length, 72 cm.; of body, 35 cm.; width, 22.5 cm.; depth, 8 cm.
According to MacCurdy, quoted by Miss Morris (p. 194) "The armadillo (*proapus novemcinctus*) is a dominant decorative factor full of symbolic meaning and is as characteristic of the Chiriqui as the lotus is of Egypt."

1051. BANDURRIA .... Philippine Islands
Body made from the base of a cocoanut. Sound-hole inlaid with mother-of-pearl. Four pairs of wire strings. Seventeen metal frets.
Length, 51 cm. Width, 18 cm. Depth, 8 cm.

1052. MANDOLINE .... Madeira
Flat pear-shaped body with slightly convex back. Four pairs of wire strings. Seventeen brass frets.
Length, 57 cm.; of body, 29 cm.; width, 21.5 cm.; depth, 6 cm.
Signed—"Augusto M. Da Costa."

1053. MANDOLINE .... Possibly from Mexico
Body made from the entire shell of a turtle. Sound-holes in lower corner. Four pairs of strings. Seventeen metal frets.
Length, 68.5 cm.; of body, 25 cm.; width, 18.5 cm.; depth, 11.5 cm.

1054. MANDOLINO .... Italy
Lyre-shaped body with rounded back. Four pairs of wire strings. Circular sound-hole. Seventeen metal frets.
Length, 60 cm. Width, 21.5 cm. Depth, 6 cm.

1055. MANDOLINE .... France
Body of unusual shape. Machine head, with eight pegs carrying four pairs of wire strings. Seventeen frets.
Length, 62 cm.; of body, 34 cm.; width, 21 cm.; depth, 11.5 cm.

1056. MANDOLINO .... Italy
Oval body with vaulted back. Mechanical peg-head. Four pairs of of wire strings. Eighteen frets.
Length, 44.5 cm.; of body, 29.1 cm.; width, 21.6 cm.; depth, 12.5 cm.

1057. MANDOLINE .... Egypt
Oval body with marquetry back. Mechanical head. Four pairs of wire strings. Seventeen frets.
Length, 60 cm. Width, 19.5 cm. Depth, 11.5 cm.
The presence of a mechanism defines a mandoline as modern.

1058. MANDOLINO . . . . Italy
Oval body. Purfled sound-board. Machine head. Three pairs of gut, and an equal number of over-spun silk strings. Twenty metal frets. One oval and two F sound-holes. V-shaped head.
Length, 61 cm.; of body, 32 cm.; width, 21 cm.; depth, 14 cm.
Signed—"Luigi Embergher, Roma, 1890."

1059. MANDOLINE . . . . United States
Body in the shape of a six-pointed star. Oval sound-hole. Machine head. Usual stringing.
Length, 57.5 cm. Width, 24.3 cm. Depth, 5.3 cm.

1060. TANBOURICA, or TANBOURITZA . . . . Croatia, Austria
Pear-shaped body. Sound-board pierced by four groups of small holes. Four wire strings passing over thirteen and sixteen wire frets, respectively, are fastened to tuning-pegs in front of neck.
Length, 57.5 cm.; of body, 16.5 cm.; width, 10.7 cm.; depth, 6 cm.

1061. TANBOURICA, or TANBURICA . . . . Croatia, Austria
Similar to the preceding, excepting that it has a machine head and one small circular sound-hole. The title given is in general use.
Length, 52.5 cm.; of body, 16.5 cm.; width, 11.5 cm.; depth, 5.6 cm.

1062. SAZ . . . . Egypt
Pear-shaped body of some soft wood. Four wire strings. Twelve gut frets. Groups of small holes in belly.
Length, 70 cm.; of body, 25 cm.; width, 13 cm.; depth, 12 cm.

1063. TANBOUR BAGHLAMAH. "Child's tanbour" . . . . Turkey
Lute body of exaggerated depth. Beautifully inlaid. No sound-hole. Six wire strings pass over thirteen frets.
Length, 59 cm.; of body, 19 cm.; width, 12.5 cm.; depth, 14.5 cm.

1064. TANBOURICA Croatia, Austria
Length, 51.5 cm.; of body, 18.5 cm.; width, 11 cm.; depth, 6 cm.

1065. TANBOURICA . . . . Slavonia
Violin-shaped body. Flat head. Two pairs of fine wire, running over 18 and 20 frets respectively. This type is played with a thin oval plectrum of tortoise-shell, or ivory.
Length, 50.5 cm.; of body, 13 cm.; width, 8 cm.; depth, 3.5 cm.

1066. TANBOURICA . . . . Slavonia
Guitar-shaped body. Usual number of frets and strings.
Length, 55 cm.; of body, 18.5 cm.; width, 13.5 cm.; depth, 3.4 cm.
Signed—"Terezija Kova ac—Graditeljica Tambura,
Skladiste Glasbila u Zagiebu. Ilica 47."

1067. TANBOURICA. Similar to preceding instrument . . . . Slavonia
Length, 52 cm.; of body, 16 cm.; width, 10.5 cm.; depth, 3.5 cm.

1068. MANDOLINE .... United States
Aluminum body. Machine head. Four pairs of wire strings.
Length, 60.8 cm.; of body, 36 cm.; width, 20 cm.; depth, 15 cm.

1069. MANDOLINE. Porcelain body. Four pairs of wire strings.. Germany
Length, 60.8 cm.; of body, 36 cm.; width, 20 cm.; depth, 14 cm.

1070. "GIBSON" MANDOLINE .... United States
The instrument, with an oval body, back of polished dark wood, and belly of light-colored wood, has the characteristic mandoline neck, but the back is not vaulted. Typical mandoline stringing, The modern makers of guitars and mandolines have taken many hints from the early makers and are making many curious, but not always effective combinations.
Length, 62.8 cm.; of body, 33.9 cm.; width, 25.1 cm.; depth, 4.2 cm.
(Gibson Guitar and Mandoline Co., and University Music House.)

Of the tone quality of the Arabian Lute we get a naive opinion in "Covel's Diary," 1675. ("Private Musick" to accompany dancing.) "Turkish and Arab lutes of five, eight, sometimes but four strings, with a little neck, a yard (at least) or more in length. Several sorts, all not worth a louse."[12]

Lane says, "A kind of mandoline, called the *tambour*, is used at concerts in Egypt, but mostly by Greeks and other foreigners."[13]

---

[12] "Early Voyages and Travels to the Levant," Hak. Soc., 1893, p. 4.
[13] "Modern Egyptians," Vol. II, p. 331.

CASE X.

CLASS IV.

Section E. Vibrating Plucked Strings running over Frets.

The instruments in this Case cover a wide range but show unmistakable points of contact. With a few exceptions they have flat bodies. A few, at the beginning, illustrate the structural principles embodied in the last group in Case IX.

1071. TANBOURIZA. Similar to No. 1065, but larger.........Slavonia
Length, 81 cm.; of body, 37 cm.; width, 19.1 cm.; depth, 6.5 cm.

1072. MANDO-LYRA .... Italy
Flat lyre-shaped body. Purfled sound-board and sound-hole. Machine head. Four pairs of wire strings.
Length, 59 cm.; of body, 34 cm.; width, 28 cm.; depth, 7 cm.
Signed—"Liugi Sartosio, Napoli."

1073. "KAKOKA." Flat body. Long neck. Six strings...Source unknown
A beautifully decorated instrument, but its name is uncertain, and it is of doubtful antecedents.
Length, 149 cm.; of body, 43 cm.; width, 41 cm.; depth, 2.7 cm.

1074. "PAPEHA" .... Source unknown
This product of some one's fancy comes under the same condemnation as No. 1073.
Length, 67.2 cm.; of body, 29 cm.; width, 25.2 cm.; depth, 3.4 cm.

1075. CAVONTO ....Island of Rhodes, Mediterranean
Deep body. Four pairs of wire strings.
Length, 102 cm.; of body, 35.5 cm.; width, 25 cm.; depth, 13 cm.
Signed—"Ata-key—. . . . o k . . gah."

1076. MACHETE. Mounted on a stand ....Madeira
Deep, flat pear-shaped body. Twelve pairs of wire strings played with a plectrum. In its form, this type vibrates between the vaulted body of the lute, and the flat back and constricted waist of the guitar.
Length, 72.5 cm.; of body, 28 cm.; width, 27.2 cm.; depth, 8.7 cm.
Height, with stand, 71 cm.
Signed—"A. Da Costa, Funchal."

1077. BANDURRIA. Cittern type .... Spain
Flat, oval body, the back and sides of which are made of black wood, and inlaid with a floral design in light-colored wood. Fourteen wire strings and the same number of frets. Played with a shell plectrum. Pitches:—f sharp, c sharp′, f sharp′, b′, e″, a″.
Length, 70 cm.; of body, 35 cm.; width, 32.5 cm.; depth, 5.7 cm.

1078. THURINGIAN LUTE .... Germany
Flat cittern model. Six pairs of wire strings. Thirteen metal frets. It is understood that all the instruments in this group have frets, the number varying from ten to fourteen, occasionally more.
Length, 81 cm.; of body, 38 cm.; width, 27.5 cm.; depth, 5 cm.

1079. VIOLA D'ARAME .... Madeira
Flat cittern model. Six pairs of wire strings.
Length, 75 cm. Width, 26 cm. Depth, 7.5 cm.

1080. BANDURRIA .... France
Flat, oval body. Four pairs of wire strings.
Length, 57 cm. Width, 20.5 cm. Depth, 3.2 cm.

1081. BANDURRIA. Unusual shape. Ten wire strings........... France
Deep pear-shaped body. Five pairs of strings, two of over-spun silk, two of gut and one of wire.
Length, 63 cm. Width, 22 cm. Depth, 10 cm.

1082. CITTERN, or BANDURRIA .... Portugal
Cittern model. Six pairs of wire strings. Screw tuning mechanism.
Length, 69.5 cm. Width, 28 cm. Depth, 7 cm.
Signed—"Joas Miguel Andrade, Lisbon."

1083. CITTERN .... Portugal
Same structure as the preceding instrument, but larger.
Length, 86 cm. Width, 39 cm. Depth, 9 cm.
Signed—"L. A. Azevodo, Lisbon."

1084. BANDURRIA. Unusual shape. Ten wire strings........... Spain
Length, 63 cm. Width, 23 cm. Depth, 9 cm.

1085. MACHETE .... Madeira
Leaf-shaped body. Eleven wire strings.
Length, 76 cm. Width, 50.5 cm. Depth, 8 cm.
Signed—"Da Costa, Funchal."

1086. CITTERN .... England
Flat, nearly circular body. Six pairs of wire strings and four single ones.
Length, 80 cm. Width, 31.3 cm. Depth, 7.3 cm.
Signed—"Claget G. Gibson, 1763."

1087. CITTERN (Fr. *Cistre;* Ital. *Cetera;* Ger. *Cister*) .... England
Flat, pear-shaped body. Ornamental rose of brass, representing David with his harp. Four pairs of wire strings and two single strings. *Circa* 1800. Length, 70.5 cm. Width, 31.5 cm. Depth, 8 cm.
Signed—"Preston, London."

The Cittern enjoyed a great vogue in England during the sixteenth and seventeenth centuries, but after the Peninsular War it was supplanted by the Guitar. Allusions to it are frequent in English literature.

1088. CHITARRA BATTENTE (Fr. *Guitare toscana, Guitare en bateau*) .... Italy
Deep body decorated with inlaid scroll work. Five pairs of wire strings. Ten varieties exist, exemplifying modifications in stringing and, occasionally, in the manner of performance, as the *Chitarra coll'arco,* which is bowed.
Length, 70 cm. Width, 17.5 cm. Depth, 12.5 cm.

1089. CHITARRA BATTENTE .... Bohemia
Deep body, beautifully inlaid with ivory, as is also the neck. Six strings. Length, 81 cm. Width, 20 cm. Depth, 10 cm.
Signed—"Andreas Off, in Prag, 1658."

1090. CHITARRA BATTENTE .... Italy
Deep body, beautifully inlaid with mother-of-pearl. Five pairs of wire strings. Length, 90 cm. Width, 28 cm. Depth, 18 cm.
Nos. 1089 and 1090 are among the choicest treasures in the Collection.

1091. QUINTERNE. Flat pyriform body. Five pairs of wire strings. Reproduction of an instrument, signed—"Joachim Tielke, Hamburg, 1676," by Lyon and Healy, and presented by them to the University. Length, 76.5 cm.; of body, 37.5 cm.; width, 35.5 cm.; depth, 2.7 to 8 cm. .... Germany

1092. CETERA. Italian cittern .... Italy
The pear-shaped body is flat. The neck terminates in a carved head, representing Diana, and, on the back, two cherubs supporting a satyr's mask. From ornamental ivory peg-heads, 4 wire and 3 gut strings lead over 19 metal frets. A reproduction of an instrument made by Antonius Stradivarius, Cremona, Italy, in 1700, by Lyon and Healy, Chicago, and presented by them to the University, it exhibits the graceful form and delicate workmanship characteristic of the great Italian violin-maker. The *cetera* was used by the Italian *improvvisatori.*
Length, 96. cm.; of body, 48.5 cm.; width, 50.5 cm.; depth, 7 to 9.2 cm.

1093 MACHETE. Unusual form. Five gut strings............Madeira
Two constrictions in waist, the upper one of lesser diameter than the lower. The flat back and sides are made of a dark-brown indigenous wood.
Length, 74.5 cm. Widths, 17-10-7 cm. Depth, 6.3 cm.
Signed—"Da Costa, Funchal."

1094. MACHETE. Similar to No. 1093 ....Madeira
The name given by Da Costa to this and No. 1093 is *machete rajio.*
Length, 66 cm. Width, 14.8 cm. Depth, 6.9 cm.

1095. CAVACO. Body in form of a fish. Five gut strings........Madeira
Length, 67 cm. Width, 21 cm. Depth, 5 cm.
Signed—"Da Costa."

The Guitar (Fr. *Guitare;* Ital. *Chitarra;* Span. *Guitarra;* Ger. *Guitarre*) was derived from the Orient. Throughout the eighteenth century it dominated Europe. It was known by many names now obsolete (Fr. *Guiterne;* Ger. *Gittern, Chittern, Glythorn;* Span. *Vihuela*).

Structurally, it presents a flat back, sides with incurvations, and a neck with frets, over which run strings. While the usual number of strings is six, variations in this respect, as in the shape, are frequent. The usual tuning for six strings is e-a-d′-g′-b′-e″. By the use of the "Capo-tasto," or "Capo d' astro," a bar attached to the first fret, the tuning may be changed, making extreme keys much easier. There are many combinations with other types (mostly in form). See Nos. 1102 and 1103, and the Lyre-Guitars beginning with No. 1119. The Italian form is almost invariably strung with wire. The *Machete,* "Portuguese octave-guitar," of four strings, is the favorite instrument in Madeira. It has two tunings, d′-g-b-d″, or d-g-b-e″.

1096. MACHETE DE BRACO. (Port. *braco*—arm) ....Madeira
Shallow guitar model. Four gut strings. Seventeen brass frets.
Length, 49.5 cm. Width, 13.7 cm. Depth, 4.7 cm.

1097. GUITARRE .... Austria
Flat body with a false back over the usual one. Purfled sound-board and sound-hole. Six gut strings. Seventeen frets.
Length, 91 cm. Width, 33 cm. Depth, 8.2 cm.
Signed—"Joh. Gottfried Scherzer, Wien." It also carries the name of a former owner, "Eugene Petetin, Ancien Officier de Marine."

1098. CHITARRA .... Italy
Body of gourd. Sound-board inlaid with ivory and mother-of-pearl. In addition to the above the neck has tortoise-shell inlay. Six fine wire strings. Nine gut frets. It is frequently called the "Pessarola."
Length, 51 cm. Width, 10.5 cm. Depth, 6 cm.

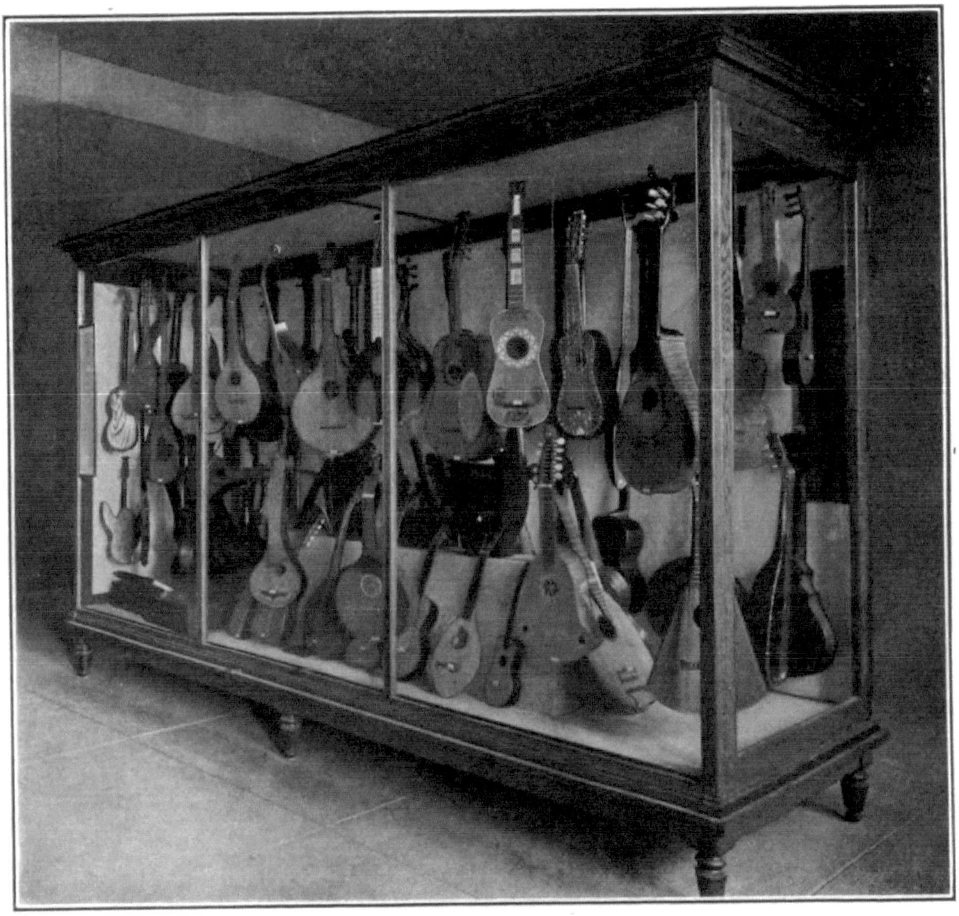

PLATE X.

CASE X. WEST SECTION. NOS. 1072 TO 1103 (LEFT TO RIGHT)

1099. BALALAIKA, or BAL'ALAJKA .... Russia

Deep body with rounded back. Triangular sound-board. Three gut strings. Fifteen metal frets. A genuine product of peasant industry. The instrument is of Tartar origin.

Length, 53.5 cm. Width, 37 cm. Depth, 11 cm.

The Russian novelist Gogol, in "Dead Souls" (1837-38), speaks of "pumpkins called calabashes, with which, in Russia, *balalaikas* are made, those light, two-stringed instruments, the ornament and solace of the susceptible youth of twenty, who walks along in his dandified way, winking at the white-bosomed, white-necked maidens who have assembled to listen to his soft music."

1100. UKULELE. (Flea). European model .... Hawaii

Guitar model. Machine head. Four gut strings. Eleven brass frets. "Taro-patch fiddle" is a name frequently applied to the instrument. The *ukulele* is not an idigenous product but was introduced by the Portuguese about 1877.

Length, 46.5 cm.; of body, 21.6 cm.; width, 15. cm.; depth, 5.4 cm.

1101. GUITAR. Five gut strings. Twelve brass frets........... Hawaii

Length, 68.2 cm. Width, 22 cm. Depth, 6.2 cm.

1102. LUTE-GUITAR (Fr. *Guitare-luth;* Ger. *Lautenguitarre*) . . . England

Deep, lute-shaped body. Broad finger-board, carrying twelve frets. Machine head. Eight strings.

Length, 76.7 cm. Width, 33 to 8.3 cm. Depth, 11.7 cm.

1103. GUITARE .... France

Flat, oval body. Machine head. No frets. Usual guitar stringing. Neck, head and sound-board inlaid with mother-of-pearl and glass prisms. Length, 87 cm. Width, 21.6 to 6.4 cm. Depth, 8.5 cm.

Signed—"E. Mediot, Paris, 1890."

1104. GUITARRE .... Germany

Pear-shaped body. Two sound-holes. Purfled sound-board. Usual stringing. Very old. Length, 86 cm. Width, 31 cm. Depth, 7 cm.

1105. CHITARRA .... Italy

The typical body is beautifully inlaid. An ivory plate on the neck shows the coat of arms of the noble family for which it was made. Original (in South Kensington Museum, London) by Antonius Stradivarius, Cremona, Italy, in 1680. Reproduced by Lyon and Healy, by whom it was presented to the University.

Length, 97. cm.; of body, 44 cm.; width, 26 cm.; depth, 7 cm.

1106. GUITARRE . . . . Germany
Circular body. Sound-board, representing a human face, the neck forming the nose. Purfled. Usual stringing. 1873.
Length, 82.5 cm. Width, 35.5 cm. Depth, 8.3 cm.
Signed—"A. Sprenger, Nürnberg."

1107. GUITARE . . . . France
Body with rounded shoulders and lower bouts. Purfling of ivory and ebony. Usual number of frets and strings.
Length, 94 cm. Width, 29 cm. Depth, 8 cm.

1108. CHITARRA . . . . Italy
Deep body with sunken sound-board. Usual number of frets and strings. Length, 82 cm. Width, 27 cm. Depth, 10.5 cm.
Signed—"Luigi Filano, Napoli, 1829."

1109. GUITARE . . . . France
Flat body with slight incurvations. Usual number of frets and strings. Three of the latter are of over-spun silk.
Length, 91.5 cm. Width, 25.5 cm. Depth, 8.5 cm.
Signed—"Fait par Pierre Louvet, Montmarts a la Veille Royal, à Paris, 1750."

1110. CHITARRA . . . . Italy
Shallow body. Sound-board. Inlaid with a floral design in mother-of-pearl. Usual number of frets and strings.
Length, 94 cm. Width, 29.5 cm. Depth, 7.5 cm.

1111. CITHER, or GUITARRE . . . . Germany
Deep, pear-shaped body. Sixteen frets. Usual guitar stringing.
Length, 82 cm.; of body, 38 cm.; width, 24 cm.; depth, 9 cm.
Signed—"fecit John Bullenheimer, Affenheim, 1846."

1112. GUITAR. Unusual construction . . . . Madeira
Usual guitar body, with second sound-board underneath the usual one. Usual frets and strings.
Length, 92.5 cm. Width, 29 cm. Depth, 8.5 cm.
Signed—"A. M. Da Costa, Funchal."

1113. GUITAR. Usual characteristics . . . . Philippine Islands
Length, 90 cm. Width, 29 cm. Depth, 9 cm.
(Theodore De Laguna.)

1114. CHITARRA . . . . Italy
Flat quadrangular body. Sound-board painted to represent a grid-iron. Twelve frets. Usual strings.
Length, 93 cm.; of body, 45 cm.; width, 28 cm.; depth, 5.8 cm.

1115. CHITARRA . . . . Italy
The body resembles the early Egyptian harp. Twenty metal frets. Usual guitar stringing.
Length, 75 cm.; of base, 32 cm. Depth of base, 12.5 cm.

1116. "GIBSON" GUITAR . . . . United States
A fine model of a strictly modern type. The workmanship is very beautiful. Usual frets and method of stringing.
Length, 98 cm. Width, 28.5 cm. Depth, 9.3 cm.
(Gibson Guitar and Mandolin Co. and the University Music House.)

1117. GUITARRE . . . . Germany
Pear-shaped body resting on a heavy base. Usual frets and strings. An instrument with a wonderful tone.
Height, 94 cm. Width, 32 cm. Depth, 9.3 cm.
Signed—"Tieffenbrunner, München."

1118. CHITARRA . . . . Italy
Body representing a gorged serpent. Elaborately inlaid. Twenty frets. In addition to the usual strings, the neck carries two open strings. Length, 82 cm. Width, 33 cm. Depth, 9 cm.

1119. LYRE-GUITAR. Lyre-shaped body. Incomplete . . . . Algiers
Length, 72 cm. Width, 32 cm. Depth, 8 cm.

1120. CHITARRA . . . . Italy
Broad body. Usual number of frets. Machine head. Besides the usual strings it carries three over-spun open strings.
Length, 95 cm. Width, 35 cm. Depth, 8.6 cm.
Signed—"O. Sebastiano, Genoa, 1868."

1121. LYRE-GUITAR . . . . Spain
Lyre-shaped body. Three sound-holes. Usual frets. Six pairs of gut strings and one of over-spun silk.
Length, 82.5 cm. Width, 35 cm. Depth, 16.2 cm.
Signed—"Q. Marin, Valencia."
To call this Spanish instrument a *Lira-guitarra* would not be illogical, and the name *Arpa-chitarra* for No. 1124, p. 164, might be justified, but as neither of these designations occur in the literature of the subject they may not be assumed.

1122. LYRE-GUITAR. Eighteenth century . . . . England
Body lacquered, and decorated in gilt. Usual stringing.
Length, 80.5 cm. Width, 40 cm. Depth, 10 cm.
Signed—"R. Warnum, London."

1123. LIRA-CHITARRA (Eng. *Lyre-guitar;* Fr. *Lyre-guitare*) ...... Italy
The body, of unusual shape, is finely inlaid. Three sound-holes. Twenty frets. Usual strings.
Length, 91.5 cm. Width, 40.5 cm. Depth, 7 cm.
Signed—"Gennaro, Naples, 1898."

1124. HARP-GUITAR (Eng., Fr. *Guitare-harpe;* Ger. *Guitarrenharfe*) Italy
In its general outline the body resembles the harp, hence its name. Nineteen frets. Five strings on finger-board and seven of over-spun silk. Length, 95 cm. Width, 41.5 cm. Depth, 9 cm.

1125. GUITAR .... England
Broad body with double neck. The larger carries the usual frets and strings, the smaller, four of over-spun silk. That this guitar carries a modest number of necks is shown by comparison with the *Guitare décacorde*, which has five.
Length, 94.5 cm. Width, 34.5 cm. Depth, 7 cm.

1126. GUITARRE .... Germany
Purfled body. Two necks, one bearing a finger-board with eighteen frets, and usual strings, the other carrying six open over-spun strings. The necks unite in a machine head.
Length, 100.5 cm. Width, 33.5 cm. Depth, 9 cm.

1127. GUITARE .... France
Typical body. Broad neck carrying, in addition to the usual frets and strings, five over-spun strings of silk.
Length, 91.5 cm. Width, 30 cm. Depth, 9 cm.
Signed—"Lacote, Luthier à Paris, Année 182."

1128. BIJUGA-CITHER, or ZWÖLFCHÖRIGE-CITHER .... Germany
Pear-shaped body. The neck ends in two peg-heads, the lower of which carries five strings, the upper eight. A revolving cylinder, with bridges, raising the pitch of different groups of strings, is placed at the base of the upper peg-box.
Length, 91 cm.; of body, 37.2 cm.; width, 33.5 cm.; depth, 9.3 cm.

1129. MANDOLINE-GUITAR .... United States
Guitar body with two necks of unequal length. The longer has the usual guitar stringing, but the strings are of wire, the lower three over-spun. The shorter has the usual mandoline stringing with four pairs of wire strings. An example of modern cross-breeding.
Length of guitar, 94.5 cm.; of mandoline, 76 cm. Width, 34.5 cm. Depth, 10 cm.
Signed—"Schwankowsky, Detroit."

1130. LIRA-CHITARRA . . . . Italy
The graceful body is purfled, and ornamented with scroll-work.
Length, 93 cm. Width, 37.5 cm. Depth, 9 cm.
Signed—"Geo. Battista, fecit, Napoli, 1807."
This instrument was purchased by Mr. Stearns in 1881 from an antiquarian in Prague, and became the foundation of the Collection.

1131. LYRE-GUITAR . . . . Egypt
Typical form of body. Cross bar and finger-board. Usual guitar stringing. Length, 86 cm. Width, 50 cm. Depth, 11 cm.
Signed—"Braziano Macchi."

1132. LIRA-CHITARRA (Ger. *Lyraguitarre*) . . . . Italy
Large lyre-shaped body, purfled and inlaid. Twenty-three frets, over which run the usual number of strings. At the left of finger-board run four open over-spun strings. Machine head.
Length, 95 cm. Width, 48 cm. Depth, 9.2 cm.
Signed—"Pietro Messori, Modena."

1133. GUITAR. Lyre-shaped body, beautifully decorated with a floral design, and also elaborately inlaid. The middle part, on which is a mirror, opens and reveals a jewel case. While this is not primarily a musical instrument, it is playable, and may properly serve as a reminder that many more important types have found a home in my lady's boudoir. In all probability this is an Italian product.
Height, 72.2 cm. Width, 42.2 cm. Depth, 5.1 cm.
On the floor, at the right, under No. 1077, a guitar case is displayed, also a set of one hundred photographs of early rosette sound-holes, from instruments in the possession of Sig. Franciolini, a rather imaginative instrument-maker in Florence—who, in all probability, is responsible for Nos. 1073-74.

CASE XI.

CLASS IV.

Section E. Continuation.

In point of seniority the Monochord can easily maintain itself. Not to go too far back, we know that it was used by Greek theoreticians to demonstrate the ratios of intervals. It was used for the same purpose in the Middle Ages. By the addition of frets to indicate the fundamentals of the Guidonian hexachords its usefulness was greatly increased. Eventually more strings were added, and when keys usurped the function of the frets, the combination of *clavis* and *chorda* suggested the name "Clavichord" as the designation of the first direct descendant of the type. It is also related to the Zither.

The Banjo can neither claim antiquity nor exalted musical value. Its origin is disputed; phonetic degeneration from *banjore*, or *bandore*, from the Javanese town *Ban Joemas*,[1] or from *bania*, a Senegambian lute,[2] being etymological surmises of the origin of the name. In its essentials it justifies the position assigned it, midway between the Guitar and Zither. In the present distribution, variants of the Lute, Guitar and Banjo are placed before the Monochord in order to emphasize the relationship of the latter to the Zither.

1134. LUTE-BANJO .... Canada
Pear-shaped body. The neck is removable allowing the use of either a lute or guitar neck. Five strings, of which the fifth runs from a peg set half-way up the neck on the bass side. This resembles the "chanterelle," or melody string of the banjo; hence its name.
Length, 90 cm.; of body, 35.5 cm.; width, 29.5 cm.; depth, 8.5 cm.
Signed—"J. L. Orme and Sons, Ottawa, Canada."

1135. GUITAR .... England
Body with pointed shoulders. Five strings, the fifth placed as in No. 1134. It might be called a "Guitar-Banjo."
Length, 87 cm. Width, 30 cm. Depth, 8.5 cm.

1136. BANJO-GUITAR .... United States
Unusual form, but otherwise similar to the two preceding instruments.
Length, 89 cm. Width, 29 cm. Depth, 7.5 cm.
Signed—"Hartmann Brothers and Reinhard, New York."

---

[1] Morris, p. 185.
[2] Engel, "Catalogue of Instruments in the South Kensington Museum," p. 151.

1137. BANJO .... England
Wooden hoop. Parchment head tightened by screw braces. Marquetry head and finger-board. No frets. Six gut and over-spun silk strings, the sixth being the chanterelle (Fr. *Corde d'un violon*, specifically the E string of the violin).
It will be noticed that the typical banjo body resembles the Tambourine, minus the "jingles."
Length, 92 cm. Width, 30 cm. Depth, 7 cm.

1138. BANJO .... United States
Black wooden hoop, surrounded by a second of German silver. An open-work plate of the same material covers the parchment head. Usual stringing. Seventeen frets.
Length, 92 cm. Width, 33 cm. Depth, 6.5 cm.

1139. ZITHER-BANJO .... England
Wooden hoop. Parchment head tightened by screws. These are enclosed in a shell of ebonized wood. Usual stringing. Nineteen frets.
Length, 81 cm. Diameter of head, 24 cm.; of shell, 28 cm.; depth, 8.5 cm.

1039A. BANJORINE. Five strings. Eighteen frets..........United States
This form differs from the ordinary banjo only in that it has a shorter neck.
Length, 69 cm.; of neck, 38 cm. Diameter, 31 cm. Depth, 5 cm.
(Albert A. Stanley.)

1039B. MANDOLIN-BANJO. Four pairs of strings. Usual frets. United States
Frequently and erroneously called by the name of the preceding instrument, this type, like the many hybrids of the day, enjoys a great vogue. It is tuned in fifths like the violin—g, d′, a′, e″.
Length, 56.6 cm.; of neck, 30.9 cm. Diameter, 25.7 cm. Depth, 6.4 cm.
(Allmendinger Music Shop.)

The banjo body has been utilized in many instruments quite unlike it in every respect. No. 2292 in the Crosby Brown Collection is a violin; No. 1073 in the Paris Collection (*Conservatoire*) is an instrument in size and stringing resembling a double-bass, while No. 1010, Case IX, Stearns Collection, is a harp with a typical banjo body.

1140-1141. MONOCHORDS. Native name unknown ....India
The oval bodies of cocoanut-shells are polished. Each carries a belly of wood with F-holes. The second specimen is somewhat the larger. Respective lengths, 63, 69.5 cm. Widths, 15, 10 cm. Depths, 5.5 to 6 cm.

1142. BANJO-MONOCHORD. Native name unknown .... Brazil
Body of the top of a large cocoanut, gilded. Parchment head and screw bracing. Length, 75 cm. Diameter of head, 12.5 cm. Depth, 7 cm.

1143. MONOCHORD .... Germany
Kite-shaped body of wood decorated with colored pictures in decalomania. Gut string. The work of a Bavarian peasant.
Length, 30 cm. Width, 20.3 cm. Depth, 3.9 cm.

1144. PSALMODIKON. Monochord .... Norway
Oblong body. One string running over a serrated strip of wood. A printed label defines the point at which the string must be "stopped" to produce a given tone. It gives a chromatic series from g to g sharp‴. The modern form has a violoncello-shaped body and from four to eight sympathetic strings.
Invented by Jos. Dillner (1785-1862).
Length, 80 cm. Width, 11 cm. Depth, 7 cm.
Signed—"K. Trahm."

1145. SCHEITHOLT. (Fr. *Buche*) .... Germany
Slightly tapering body. One melody, and three accompaniment strings. A primitive zither type. This specimen is very old.
Length, 78 cm. Width, 2.5 to 12.3 cm. Depth, 5.6 cm.

1146. BUCHE, or EPINETTE DES VOSGES .... France
A small type. Length, 59.5 cm. Width, 3.5 to 8 cm. Depth, 2.8 cm.

The Scheitholt was the immediate ancestor of the Zither (Gk. *Kithara;* Lat. *Cithara;* Ital. *Chitarra;* Span. *Guitarra;* Ang.-Sax. *Cytere;* Old Eng. *Cittern;* Ger. *Zitter*). We know the Zither as the instrument used by the peasants of the Styrian and Bavarian Alps. Its salient features are a shallow, flat, resonance box, over which run a variable number of strings. Some of these—the accompaniment strings—are "open," vibrating their entire length, while others are "stopped" by pressing the string against a "fret," allowing only a fractional part of the string to vibrate. Its fundamental weakness is a lack of resonance. Its resources have been increased by the addition of strings but, to quote a celebrated virtuoso, "The strings are so near apart," that the difficulty of performance is out of all proportion to the results obtained. In playing the Zither, which lies flat, the thumb, first, second, and third fingers of both hands are used. A partially opened ring is placed on the right thumb. There are three classes of Zithers, differing in pitch. The most important forms are the Mittenwalder and the Bavarian. The earliest example of the latter form is dated the seventeenth century. The tuning of the free strings is in fourths and fifths. The complications incidental to structure and performance are carefully and authoritatively treated by Maclean.[3]

[3] Monthly Mag. International Musical Society, 1909, Part II, p. 341.

1147. ZITHER. Seventeenth century . . . . Germany
Narrow body terminating in a carved head. Thirteen frets. Two pairs of melody strings, and eleven open strings, of which four are octaves. Three rosette sound-holes in sound-board, one of which is in a rounded projection on the side.
Length, 53.5 cm. Width, 24 cm. Depth, 4.2 cm.
Signed—"Josef Mayr, in Halle."

1148. ZITHER . . . . Austria
Body with one straight and one curved side. Twenty frets. Three stopped, and fourteen open strings.
Length, 56 cm. Width, 26 cm. Depth, 3.2 cm.
Signed—"Jos. Neuner, Passau."

1149. ZITHER. Eighteenth century . . . . Germany
Narrow body with rounded projection on one side. Fifteen frets. Two pairs of wire open strings. Fourteen fine strings.
Length, 50 cm. Width, 30.5 cm. Depth, 2.7 cm.

1150. ZITHER. Similar in form to No. 1147 . . . . Germany
Twenty-six frets. Fourteen open, and three stopped strings.
Length, 59 cm. Width, 21.3 cm. Depth, 3.5 cm.

1151. ZITHER. Pear-shaped body. Usual frets and strings . . . . . Germany
Length, 54 cm. Width, 28 cm. Depth, 5.2 cm.
Signed—"Franz Kreu, Munich."

1152. ZITHER. Similar to No. 1148 . . . . Germany
Length, 63.5 cm. Width, 30.5 cm. Depth, 3.7 cm.

1153. ZITHER . . . . Germany
Guitar-shaped body. Nineteen frets. Ten open, and four stopped strings. Length, 51 cm. Width, 31 cm. Depth, 5.1 cm.

1154. ZITHER . . . . Germany
Typical form. Twenty-nine frets. Twenty-five open, and five stopped strings. Tuning mechanism. Modern.
Length, 51 cm. Width, 30.5 cm. Depth, 2.7 cm.

1155. ZITHER. Seventeenth century . . . . Germany
Shallow body. Eighteen frets. Twelve open, and three stopped strings. Length, 57.2 cm. Width, 30.3 cm. Depth, 4.2 cm.

1156. ZITHER . . . . Germany
Round body with wide neck. Sixteen frets. Seven open, and three stopped strings. Erroneously said to date from the fifteenth century. Length, 51 cm. Width, 31 cm. Depth, 5.1 cm.

1157. ZITHER. Eighteenth century .... Germany
Guitar-shaped body. Nineteen frets. Ten open, and four stopped strings. Length, 51 cm. Width, 28.2 cm. Depth, 3.3 cm.

1158. ZITHER .... Germany
Typical body. Twenty-nine frets. Twenty-six open, and five stopped strings. Length, 53 cm. Width, 29 cm. Depth, 4 cm.

1159. ZITHER .... Germany
Pear-shaped body. Fifteen frets. Nine open, and three stopped strings. Length, 61.7 cm. Width, 29.7 cm. Depth, 6.2 cm.

1160. "REGENT" ZITHER (No. 3) .... United States
Flat body. Twenty-four wire strings arranged in three groups of chords. The pitches of the strings are given on a printed label. By attaching a strip of paper on which are printed certain directions, a tune may be played by plucking the strings in the order indicated.
Length, 38 cm. Width, 15.2 to 20.3 cm. Depth, 8 cm.

1161. "REGENT" ZITHER (No. 5) .... United States
Similar to the preceding instrument but of greater possibilities.
Length, 48 cm. Width, 32.2 cm. Depth, 8 cm.

1162. "AUTO HARP," "Miller's Akkord Zither" .... Germany
Twenty-four wire strings controlled by bars with felt dampers.
Length, 49 cm. Width, 10.1 to 28.4 cm. Depth, 7.8 cm.

1163. "SYRENE" .... Germany
Body of black wood. Thirty-seven wire strings. Over the strings a steel plate is placed through which project thirty-seven small points.
A perforated strip of cardboard is moved over these points, permitting only certain combinations to sound when a plectrum is drawn across the strings.
Length, 56.4 cm. Width, 40.4 cm. Depth, 8.5 cm.

1164. BECKER'S "SOLOPHONE" .... Germany
An instrument on the same principle as the preceding, excepting that it is manipulated by pistons.
Length, 44.8 cm. Width, 34.4 cm. Depth, 9 cm.

1165. "ARPANETTA" .... Germany
Flat body with curved peg-head. Thirty-six wire strings. When a perforated strip is drawn under the strings by rollers, brass plectra and felt dampers are set in operation defining the strings that can be made to sound.
Length, 63.4 cm. Width, 53 cm. Depth, 10.5 cm.

1166. KLAVIATURZITHER (Eng. *Zither Piano*) .... Germany
A trapezoidal body mounted on three legs. Tangents attached to the ends of the key-levers pluck the string as in the ordinary zither. The piano key-board has a compass of five octaves.
Length, 48 to 91 cm. Width, 96 cm. Depth, 20.5 cm. Height, 81 cm.
Signed—"Zavelberg and Kremer, D. R. P. No. 79381,
Köln. Pat. i, 10 Staaten."
As the key-mechanism normally does not belong to this type, its presence in this particular instrument does not place it in Class V. For convenience, Nos. 1330—a monochord, or violin—and 1346—a harp—are placed in Case XIV, but they are not legitimate key-board instruments.

1167. KANOON, QANON, or QANUN .... Turkey
Flat trapezoidal body of light colored wood, artistically inlaid. On the resonance box rest two bridges over which sixty-seven strings are drawn. Twenty-four are of over-spun wire, the remainder of gut. They are grouped in sets of two, three and four. Played with plectra. Length, 88.6 cm. Width, 5.2 to 36 cm. Depth, 7 cm.

Section F. Vibrating Strings actuated by Impact.

The Dulcimer and its kin hark back to the Assyrian *Azor*. At an early date it migrated to Arabia and Persia from whence it spread throughout the entire Orient. Known at a later date in the Caucasus as *Santir*, it is today, as the *Cimbalon*, the chief musical asset of the gypsy bands of Hungary and Transylvania. A perfected instrument of this type, called the *Panteleon*, gave Schröter the first hint of a keyed instrument that could produce *forte* and *piano*. As is well known he was forestalled in working out the principle by Cristofori, the Italian. The latter may have been incited by the instrument of this type called in Italy *Strumenti da porco*, later known in Germany as *Schweinskopf*. The present more euphonious German name is *Hackbrett*, a board on which butchers chop sausage meat.

1168. TAMBOURIN A CORDES, or TAMBOURIN DU BEARN. Also known as *Tambourin de Gascogne*..... Basque Province, France
Over the long resonance box run six gut strings. These are struck with a stick held in the left hand. The instrument rests in an upright position on the right arm. The right hand manipulates the finger-holes of the *Galoubet*, or *Churula* (Case VI, No. 493) which is always played at the same time This practice is called by the onomatopœic term *tutu-panpan* (Prov.).[4]
Length, 88.5 cm. Width, 17.5 to 11 cm. Depth, 6.7 cm.

---

[4] Mahillon, *Cat.*, Vol. III, p. 377.

In a chapel in the only ancient Gothic church in Rome, *Santa Maria sopra Minerva*, is a fresco by Filippino Lippi, painted in 1487 (restored), which shows a viol-shaped *tambourin du Bearn* and *schwegel*—a vertical flute corresponding to the *galoubet* or *Flûte des vielleurs*. (See Sachs, p. 146.)

1169. DULCIMER . . . . England
Body of mahogany. Seven groups of wire strings, four in each group, run over movable bridges. Struck with beaters of whale bone, the ends of which are bent into a loop and padded with chamois skin.
Length, 33 to 77 cm. Width, 30 cm. Depth, 7 cm.

1170. YANG K'IN, "Foreign kin" . . . . China
Body of enamelled wood with curved outlines. Fourteen sets of strings, of four each, are drawn over the sound-board. Carved ivory rosette sound-holes. Struck with thin strips of bamboo and a brass hammer. Length, 74.4 cm. Width, 29.5 cm. Depth, 5 cm.

1171. KANUNA . . . . India
Twenty-two brass wire strings are stretched over the resonance chamber or body. Played with hammers. A hinged door opens into the interior, which is a receptacle for music, the hammers, or both.
Length, 95 to 80 cm. Width, 46 cm. Depth, 17 cm.
A more elaborate form is called the *svaramandala*,[5] and a smaller type with fewer strings is known as the *khudra katayana-vina*.

1172. TRIPLE DULCIMER . . . . United States
Trapezoidal body resting on three piano legs. As there are three independent sets of strings, three can perform at the same time on this instrument, which has been called by its inventor—one Mackenzie—the "Piano Harp."
Length, 183.5 to 67.8 cm. Width, 42 to 57.8 cm. Height, 65 cm.

1173. YANG K'IN . . . . China
Body of wood. Fourteen pairs of fine steel wire strings run over two metal bridges. Played with two curved wooden mallets and the usual brass hammer.
Length, 71 to 42 cm. Width, 26.3 cm. Depth, 3.7 cm.
(B-S.)

1174. YANG-K'IN . . . . China
Similar to the preceding instrument but with wooden bridges. Played with two delicately balanced bamboo hammers, and a combination tuning-key and hammer of brass. Carried in a wooden case.
Length, 70 to 42.5 cm. Width, 25 cm. Depth, 4.1 cm.
(B-S.)
The *san-gen-da-kin*, with forty-two wire strings, and two bridges (Crosby Brown Collection, No. 2006), and the *san-den-kin*, with three silk strings, represent the type in Japan.

---

[5] Day, pp. 133, 134.

1175. YANG-KÖM . . . . Corea
Body of *odang* wood. Fourteen groups of four fine wire strings each. This is also carried in a case, the lid of which bears an inscription in Chinese characters. The instrument, which is extremely light, is supported by the tip of the left thumb, while the fore finger is inserted in a hole in the base. The strings are struck by a long, thin strip of bamboo held in the right hand. It is a favorite instrument of the educated classes, used both for solo work and as an accompaniment for the voice.
Length, 64 to 44 cm. Width, 16.6 cm. Depth, 3.1 cm.
Collected by a Mr. Cooper, of Chemnepo, Corea.

1176. SALTERIO . . . . Italy
Body decorated with gilt carving and marbled sides. Two carved roses in sound-holes. Over the sound-board run ninety-one strings of brass wire divided into sixteen groups of four each, and nine groups of three each. Three movable gilded wooden bridges.
A most artistic eighteenth-century representative of the type.
Length, 33 to 77 cm. Width, 30 cm. Depth, 7 cm.

To recapitulate: The real Harp has free strings, one to each tone. In the couched form the strings run over the resonance box. The Lyre in its essentials resembles the harp, but varies in form. The Tamboura type has wire strings and frets. The Lute has a pear-shaped body with a vaulted back and gut strings. The Tanbourica has the lute body with wire strings. The Cittern has a flat body and wire strings. The Guitar has a flat back with incurving sides, a fretted neck, with gut and over-spun silk strings. The last four types mentioned have large sound-holes, as the strings are plucked and do not run free. All have fretted necks. The Banjo has a round body, a parchment head, gut and over-spun strings, of which one, the "chanterelle," runs from a peg inserted at a point half-way up the side of the neck, which carries frets. The Monochord, as its name implies, has but one string. In shape it is variable and by no means restricted to the early oblong form. The Zither has a flat body, wire strings, some of which run over a fretted flat finger-board, and is played with a plectrum. In these modern days it has responded to the call for mechanical control, and the elimination of musical knowledge. The Dulcimer has wire strings which run over a resonance body and are responsive to the blows of a hammer or hammers. In all these types, including those displayed in Case XII, Nos. 1177 to 1222, the many variants display affinities, while the caprice of makers has interjected puzzling problems in classification. The geographical distribution of these types is world-wide; consequently they are, in their ethnological suggestion, equally inclusive.

CASE XII.

Class IV.

Oriental Types.

Sections A-D-E. Vibrating Plucked Strings.

With a few exceptions, the instruments in this Case come from the Orient. Many of them are of distinct beauty and all are of great interest.

1177. Gopi-yantra . . . . India

Body of calabash shell. A bamboo rod, split in the middle, is attached to the body. From a peg on one side a single string runs to the bottom of the instrument.

Height, 88 cm. Width of body, 13 cm.; depth, 20 cm.

1178. Ananda-lahari . . . . Bengal, India

Body of bamboo. Parchment secured to bottom. One string runs from this to the end of a rod standing at an angle.

Height, 71 cm. Depth of body, 13 cm.; diameter, 18 to 12 cm.

1179. Eka-Tantrika, or Eka-tara . . . . India

Body of gourd with a head of rawhide. One string of fibre.

Height, 77 cm. Depth of body, 17 cm.; diameter, 17 cm.

1180. Eka-tara. Similar to the preceding . . . . Deccan, India

Eka-tara means "the one-stringed." Used by beggars.

Length, 94.5 cm. Depth of body, 12.5 cm.; diameter, 21 cm.

1181. Yektar, or Tuntuni . . . . India

Body of wood, covered with red cloth. Parchment head, or bottom, tightened by rings which engage cords. One string attached to a ring. The instrument is held under one arm, the string is drawn taut by one hand, and plucked by the other.

Height, 57 cm. Depth of body, 13.5 cm.; diameter, 12 cm.

1182. Tonkari, or Mukko. Ainu Psaltery . . . . Japan

Long, narrow, sword-shaped body of wood, stained black. Five strings, giving a pentatonic series, run over two low bridges to long tuning-pegs in sides of sword-handle.

Length, 172.2 cm. Width, 8 cm. Thickness, 3.5 cm.

1183. Blikan . . . . Borneo

This resembles the *blikan* of Borneo in every respect but one, viz.: the body tapers to lower end instead of being cut off square. It has the same stringing and ornamental string-fastener. The difference between the length of this specimen—148 cm.—and 136 cm.—the length of the one in the Metropolitan Museum of Art, New York[1]

[1] Morris, p. 16.

—represents the tapering end. The greatest width is the same—14.2 cm. In view of the frequency with which variants of such instruments occur, the name *blikan* is given with considerable conviction, but with a full sense of the possible error involved.

1184. BLIKAN. Similar to No. 1183, but smaller . . . . Borneo
Length, 98.5 cm. Width, 14.2 cm. Depth, 5 cm.

1185. STRINGED INSTRUMENT . . . . Java
Long boat-shaped body carved from a single block of wood. Five frets. Two wire strings. Sometimes called *viola-da-kavan*, but without authority.
Length, 77 cm. Greatest width, 9 cm. Depth, 7 cm.
No. 1491 in the Crosby Brown Collection (Morris, p. 6) is a specimen (also given no name) considerably larger (97.9 cm. long and 10.4 cm. wide) and, unlike this, painted in red and green.

1186. HERRAUU. Zeze type. One string. Three rude frets. . Madagascar
Gourd resonator, decorated in incised lines and floral designs.
Length, 61 cm. Width, 3.1 cm. Dimensions of gourd, 9.5 by 12 cm.

1187. GUITAR. Two strings. Gourd resonator . . . . Source unknown
This resembles the unknown instrument listed as No. 959, in Case IX. It has wire strings running over two tubes on each of which are incised frets, in two groups of four each.
Length, 60 cm. Depth of gourd, 15.2 cm.; diameter, 16 cm.

1188. GUENBRI . . . . Sahara, Africa
Oblong box with belly of rawhide. Three strings, tightened by pushing them up the neck. Decorated with leather fringes carrying cowrie-shells. A very rude and inchoate specimen.
Length, 90 cm.; of body, 46 cm.; width, 21 cm.; depth, 10 cm.

1189. GUENBRI . . . . Soudan, N. E. Africa
Oblong box covered with brocade. Painted parchment belly. Two gut strings. Other names for the *guenbri* are: *gnbri, ginbri, gimbrede, gunibri, ganibri,* and possibly still others.
Length, 53 cm.; of body, 28 cm.; width, 15 cm.; depth, 16.5 cm.

1190. GNBRI . . . . Soudan, N. E. Africa
An elongated body covered with parchment at the lower end. From the bamboo neck extend two strings over a bridge. Played with a plectrum. This closely resembles the *mijue mijue* of Sumatra (Morris, p. 14) excepting that the long pointed end is absent. This is an example of the frequently perplexing, but always interesting points of contact between types representing widely separated countries.
Length, 58.1 cm.; of body, 18 cm.; width, 9 cm.; depth, 5 cm.

1191. GINBRI . . . . Soudan, N. E. Africa
Body formed from a section of gourd with skin drawn over the front. From the neck of wood run two strings.
Length, 42 cm.; of body, 18 cm.; width, 9 cm.; depth, 7 cm.

1192. GUENBRI . . . . Algeria
Body of the handsomely marked shell of a land tortoise. Belly of parchment decorated with native characters in red. Two gut strings run from pegs in neck over a bridge to a peg at the bottom of the body.
Length, 44.5 cm.; of body, 17 cm.; width, 12 cm.; depth, 6.5 cm.

1193. GUNIBRI. Frequently called *guniberry*. . . . . Soudan, N. E. Africa
An elongated pear-shaped body over the front of which a skin—the forehead of an ox—is drawn. Rudely carved peg-head. A small mirror and a string of wooden beads serve for decoration.
Length, 65.9 cm.; of body, 35.5 cm.; width, 12.3 cm.; depth, 7.6 cm.

1194. LOKANGA. Two strings. Zese type . . . . Madagascar
Body a straight tube of reed, to which a large gourd resonator is attached. Two fibre strings.
In playing, the gourd is pressed against the breast. This practice is a common one, for thereby the resonance is increased.
Length, 58.6 cm. Width, 2.5 cm. Diameter of gourd, 19.4 cm.
The Swahili call the three strings of the *zeze*, *kifumwali*, *utembwe*, and *umondo*.[2] In Mozambique this instrument is called *yatta-yatta*.[3] It is known under many an alias in the widely distributed sections in which its note is heard.

1195. JANTAR. Two strings. Resonator in two sections . . . . India
The body ends in a rude violin scroll and peg-box. The strings are tightened by screw-pegs. The resonator consists of two sections of gourd, one superimposed on the other. It exhibits considerable constructive skill.
Length, 62 cm. Width, 3 cm. Diameter of gourds, 9 and 17 cm.

1196. GUENBRI . . . . North Africa
The back of a turtle forms the body. Parchment belly. Two gut strings.
Length, 84 cm.; of body, 18 cm.; width, 16 cm.; depth, 10.2 cm.

---

[2] Sachs, p. 430.
[3] Sachs, p. 426.

PLATE XI.

CASE XII. WEST SECTION. NOS. 1180 TO 1227 (LEFT TO RIGHT)

1197. CAMBREH* . . . . Sierra Leone, Africa
Long narrow body carved from a single block of *bileke* wood. Head of parchment. Four strings of horse-hair. Played with a plectrum, *colondee*, the tooth of a native rodent, *agonto*.
Length, 71 cm.; of body, 38.5 cm.; width, 10 cm.; depth, 7 cm.

1198. CAMBREH . . . . Haussa Tribe, W. Africa
Body of palm-wood. Belly of parchment. Three strings of horse-hair, fastened to leather bands about the neck, the primitive tuning device. Length, 54 cm. Width, 10 cm. Depth, 8 cm.

1199. GUITAR . . . . Egypt
Body of rude construction. Parchment belly. Five gut strings, four of which are grouped in pairs. Played with a bone plectrum.
Length, 68.5 cm. Width, 12 cm. Depth, 7 cm.

1200. GUITAR. Native name unknown . . . . Somali-land, Africa
Body, neck, and head, of one piece. Parchment belly. Finger-board ornamented with rude carvings; the body with a rosette sound-hole, and a mirror. Six gut strings, in groups of two each.
Length, 65.9 cm. Width, 10 cm. Depth, 6.4 cm.

1201. GUITAR . . . . Arabia
Carved from a single block of hard brown wood. Parchment belly. Elaborately constructed finger-board. Carved head. Six strings of gut. Rosette sound-hole. The body of this instrument resembles an elongated *rebab*, but it does not present the characteristics of any of the Arabian bowed instruments. It can safely be included in the designation given above.
Length, 63 cm. Width, 11 cm. Depth, 6 cm.

1202. STRINGED INSTRUMENT. Tanbur type . . . . Slavic
Elaborately decorated body. Circular sound-hole cut in centre of the back. Parchment belly. Inlaid finger-board. Four wire strings.
Length, 106.5 cm.; of body, 34 cm.; diameter, 28 cm.; depth, 11.5 cm.

1203. GUITAR. Native name unknown . . . . China
The entire shell of a large turtle forms the body. Six strings. Eleven frets. The peg-end of the finger-board bends backwards and terminates in a typical Chinese scroll (reversed). The fact that neither Mahillon, Moule, Sachs nor Van Aalst mentions such an instrument is significant. It suggests European influence.
Length, 101 cm.; of body, 38 cm.; width 33 cm.; depth, 31 cm.

---

* Mahillon (*Cat.* II, p. 174) gives an illustration of a native playing an instrument identical with this. He calls it the *halam*, "an instrument resembling the *cambreh*," but gives no further information save its source, Senegal. Sachs (p. 76) gives the alternative name, *chalam*, and calls it a "stringed instrument."

1204. TA'KHE, (Lizard) .... Siam and Cambodia

Body of dark red wood resting on six short legs. Three strings pass over a group of frets. Played with an ivory plectrum held in the right hand while the left stops the strings.

This is a variant of the *megyoung*, Case IX, No. 990.

Length, 124 cm. Width of body, 11 to 21 cm.; depth, 12 cm. Height, 19 cm.

1205. DOMRA[4] .... Russia

Oval, bowl-shaped body. Leather belly. Carved head. Three strings of wire. Played with a wooden plectrum, *schepochka.*

Length, 91 cm.; of body, 23.5 cm.; diameter, 24 cm.; depth, 9.5 cm.

1206. STRINGED INSTRUMENT. Tanbur type................ Slavic

This instrument, like No. 1202, refuses to be placed. No one among the many authorities consulted has been able to give more specific information than that contained in the title. Both instruments are of unusually fine construction, of sonorous tone, of unmistakable type and, in a general way, their provenance is quite certain, but as they do not correspond in details to anything in the literature of the subject—the nearest approach being No. 769, Mahillon II, 114-5—the titles chosen will have to stand for the present at least, for "while there's life there's hope."

Length, 19 cm.; of body, 30.5 cm.; diameter, 26.5 cm.; depth, 8 cm.

1207. THARI .... Caucasus

Body carved from a single block of wood. Belly of fine parchment. Sixteen gut frets. Five strings.

Length, 83 cm.; of body, 30 cm.; width, 20 cm.; depth, 18 cm.

1208. TAR .... Shiraz, Persia

Body similar in form to preceding. The entire body, neck, and peg-box, are exquisitely inlaid with minute bits of metal, wood, and ivory in geometrical patterns. Inlaid finger-board. Parchment belly. Five fine wire strings.

Length, 91 cm.; of body, 35 cm.; width, 23 cm.; depth, 18 cm.

---

[4] With only partial assurance of its correctness, the name *domra* is assigned for the following reasons: It corresponds to the description given by Sachs (p. 114); it has the peculiar wooden plectrum; it has everything in common with Slavic and Balkan types; no authority consulted could suggest either name or source, other than one of those just given; and, finally, Mr. Stearns' correspondence shows that in 1900 he was negotiating for specimens of the instrument, although there is nothing to indicate that the negotiations were successful. The Turkish-Albanian *yonghar* and the Georgian *chonguri,* each with three strings, and the *changura* (*kontrashica*), with four strings, might be suggested, but their identification is incomplete in essential details. Not one of these instruments is listed in any catalogue, nor is the *domra.*

1209. YUEH CH'IN, or YUE K'IN. "Moon-guitar" ....China
Flat, circular body with neck and rim of *shitan* wood. Eleven frets. Two pairs of waxed silk strings. Wire snare within body. This is not for noise merely, but, as it has a fixed pitch, it aids the musician in his tuning.
Length, 62 cm.; diameter of body, 35.1 cm.; depth, 3.9 cm.
(B-S.)

1210. YUEH CH'IN. Similar to No. 1209, but 3 cm. shorter......China
The body of the *yueh ch'in* is of *wu t'ung* wood and the connecting rim of boxwood.

1211. GEKKIN ....China, and Japan
The peg-head is carved and bent forward as in the typical *gekkin*, but the face of the body lacks the usual decorations.
Length, 62 cm. Diameter of body, 31.6 cm.; depth, 3.8 cm.
(B-S.)

1212. CAI DAN NGNYET .... Anam
Flat, circular body, with neck and rim of *shitan* wood. Eleven strings. This has a much shorter neck than No. 1217, which is a typical specimen. Possibly it would be more discreet to simply call this a "moon-guitar" but, as it is from Anam and the Anamese *ngnyet* means "moon," the risk is assumed.
Length, 56 cm. Diameter of body, 34.5 cm.; depth, 3.6 cm.

1213. MOON GUITAR .... Japan
Peculiar proportions. Decorated with carved wooden ornaments, and a trefoil of fish-skin under the strings. Fourteen frets. Two pairs of silken strings. The body also contains a wire snare.
This instrument has the round body and decoration of the *gekkin*, but not the short neck; it has the long neck of the *genkwan*[5] but not the octagonal body. The number of frets, and certain of the measurements do not coincide with either.
Length, 94 cm. Diameter of body, 2.5 cm.; depth, 3 cm.

1214. PEPA, or P'IP'A .... China
Oval body, with sound-board of *wu t'ung* wood. Carved head terminating with a floral design in etched mother-of-pearl. On sound-board an oblong gilded plaque carries an inscription in Chinese characters.
Length, 97 cm. Width, of body, 3 to 23.6 cm.; depth, 6 cm.

1215. BUGAKU-BIWA .... Japan
Shallow elongated body of a very heavy wood (the instrument weighs 6½ lbs.). Four frets. Four strings.
Length, 99 cm.; of body, 60 cm.; width, 29 cm.; depth, 5 cm.

---

[5] Piggott, p. 171.

1216. SATSUMA-BIWA . . . . Japan
Flat oval body decorated with two metal crescents. Four strings. The neck can be removed in order that the instrument may be packed in small compass.
Length, 102 cm.; of body 40.5 cm.; width, 18.7 cm.; depth, 6.2 cm.
Piggott (pp. 168-9) gives full measurements of these forms of the *biwa*.

1217. CAI DAN NGNYET. An unusually beautiful specimen . . . . Anam
Typical body. Neck, finger-board, and head elaborately inlaid with a floral design in etched mother-of-pearl. On sound-board an oblong gilded plaque carries an inscription in Chinese characters.
Length, 101.4 cm. Diameter of body, 38.8 cm.; depth, 9.8 cm.

1218. MOON-GUITAR . . . . China
Typical body. The rim and long neck are of *shitan* wood. Peg-box and tail-piece mounted with ivory. Eight frets. Two pairs of gut strings. The long neck indicates a variant.
Length, 97.2 cm. Diameter of body, 38 cm.; depth, 7 cm.

1219. SAN HSIEN, or HSIEN TZÖ. (Name in Pekin) . . . . China
Oval body of wood. Back and belly of python-skin. Three strings pass over a bridge on belly. A wedge-shaped block of ivory is tied to the finger board, and by changing its position the tuning of the strings is made more accurate. Played with plectrum of tortoise-shell or with the fingers.
Length, 89.5 cm.; of body, 16.4 cm.; diameter, 15 cm.; depth, 7 cm.

1220. CAI TAM. An exact replica of No. 1219 . . . . Anam

1221. KRA-CHAPEE, or KA:CHABPI . . . . Siam
Flat circular body. Long neck of hard wood, with broad head curving backwards. Three strings, two of gut and one of wire.
Length, 168 cm.; of body, 38 cm.; diameter, 34 cm.; depth, 6 cm.

1222. SAMISEN . . . . Japan
Rectangular body, decorated in gilt and lacquer. Front and back of parchment (cat-skin). Three fine strings of waxed silk. Played with a plectrum, *bachi*, or *batsi*—24.6 cm. long—made of *shitan* wood edged with ivory. Two *bachi* are placed on the floor directly underneath.
Length, 97 cm.; of body, 21 cm.; width, 19.5 cm.; depth, 24.6 cm.

The modern Japanese theater orchestra combines two *samisens*, one flute, three drums—*uta-daiko*, *o-tsuzumi*, *ko-tsuzumi*—and two reciters. Ordinarily it is called the *hyashi-kati*, "the accompaniment party," but when in full dress it becomes the *dega-tari*, "the orchestra which appears." A dance orchestra, *shita-kata*, has no reciters, and the *o-tsuzumi* and *ko-tsuzumi* are played by one person.*

* Piggott, p. 30. On pages 32 and 34 he gives illustrations of these orchestras.

1222A. GUITAR. Native name unknown .... Nicaragua
Body of hard wood. Four gut strings. Thirteen gut frets.
Length, 40 cm.; of body, 23.3 cm.; width, 9.8 cm.; depth, 4.5 cm.
(Henry Kraemer.)

The instruments based on the principle of the plucked string, and included in the series from 950 to 1222, cover a wide geographical range, and date back to an antiquity so remote as to appall any but an Oriental mind. The Japanese challenge our credulity by pointing to the semi-mythical *sage-koto* (3468 B. C.) used by the Emperor's concubines, and to the more modern *hitzu no koto*, dating from 2000 B. C.

While this type has been, and still is, a favorite, its musical possibilities are restricted when compared to those inhering in the relatively modern bowed instruments, for the secret of the wonderful resources of the violin-type lies in the fact that the tone is produced by the continuous friction of a bow on the string, rather than by intermittent plucking. The tone produced by the latter process is neither resonant nor sustained.

The bow was discovered by the Arabians, and was carried by the Moors to Spain. Through its discovery the range of musical expression was greatly extended. Almost invariably bowed instruments have a "true" finger-board, making finer distinctions of pitch than are possible with frets. The bridge over which the strings are drawn is also a most important factor. Occasionally, in primitive and certain Oriental types, the bridge is missing. In the more important East Indian types sympathetic strings are used.

Section G. Vibrating Strings running over Bridge and "True" Finger Board, actuated by the Friction of a Bow. (Primitive and Oriental.)

1223. FIDDLE .... Alaska
Long narrow body of drift-wood. One string of whale bone. Rude bow. Length, 37.5 cm. Width, 5.7 cm. Depth, 2.3 cm.

1224. FIDDLE. Similar to No. 1223 ...... Cape Prince of Wales, Alaska

1225. FIDDLE. Native name unknown .... Madagascar
The body is formed from half of a large cocoanut-shell, over the open end of which is cemented a belly of bladder. Finger-board of a bamboo joint. Thin wire strings run over a bridge to rude tuning-pegs in the neck.
Length, 46.5 cm. Diameter of body, 14.5 cm. Length of bow, 32 cm.

1226. FIDDLE .... Philippine Islands
Body from a section of bamboo. Four gut strings run over a high bridge. A rude bow of bamboo and horse-hair.
Length, 71.7 cm. Diameter of body, 6.4 cm.

1227. TZIT-IDOATL.[6] "Music wood." Apache fiddle ...... New Mexico
Body formed from a section of the Mexican Agave (*Agave Mexicana*), from which the pith has been removed. Decorated. One string. Bow with horse-hair strings.
Length, 48.1 cm. Diameter, 10.2 to 8.5 cm.

1228. GOGE, pl. *goguna* .... Soudan, N. E. Africa
Bowl-shaped body covered on the back with red velvet, on which are arranged rows of cowrie-shells and strips of leather. One heavy string of loose horse-hair running over bridge of unusual proportions.
Length, 48 cm. Diameter of body, 27 cm.; depth, 11.3 cm.

1229. REBAB. Rude *Rebab esh sha'ir* .... West Africa
Calabash body over which a piece of raw parchment is tightly drawn. One string. Rude bow.
Length, 54.2 cm. Diameter of body, 10.8 cm.; depth, 7.6 cm.

1230. REBAB ESH SHA'IR .... Soudan
Body of calabash covered with skin. One string of white horse-hair. Rude bow. Length, 82 cm. Width of belly, 14 cm.; depth, 11 cm.

1231. REBAB ESH SHA'IR .... Soudan
Body of wood decorated with bits of brass and cowrie shells. Parchment belly. One string.
Length, 50.7 cm. Diameter of body, 12.3 cm.; depth, 7.6 cm.

1232. KEMANGEH A GOUZ. A very small example .... Egypt
Body of a half cocoanut with parchment belly. Two strings. Rude bow. An iron rod runs through the instrument, forming a rest.
Length, 44 cm. Width of body, 6.4 cm.; depth, 6 cm.

1233. KEMANGEH A GOUZ. Similar to No. 1232 .... Soudan
This has a long iron rest, projecting from the bottom.
Length, 81.5 cm.; of rod, 30.4 cm. Width of body, 30.4 cm.; depth, 7.7 cm.

1234. REBAB .... India
Body of wood decorated with bits of brass and cowrie-shells. Parchment belly. One string.
Length, 50 cm.; of body, 14.5 cm.; width, 11 cm.; depth, 7 cm.
Rebab is a generic name for any bowed instrument in the Moslem countries. The word is derived from the Persian *revave*, which means "sorrowful toned."

1235. KEMANGEH .... Egypt
Rude guitar model, without frets. Inlaid finger-board. Four strings.
Length, 70 cm.; of body, 30 cm.; width, 18 cm.; depth, 5.2 cm.

---

[6] Morris, p. 105.

1236. KEMANGEH . . . . Soudan
Body of calabash shell, with wooden belly. Inlaid neck and head. Three gut strings. A cross between the Turkish and Egyptian types. Length, 56 cm.; body, 15 cm.; width, 11 cm.; depth, 6.5.

1237. KEMANGEH . . . . Turkey
Body, head, and neck of one piece. Wooden belly. Three gut strings. Length, 44 cm. Width, 14.3 cm. Depth, 5 cm.

1238. KEMANGEH . . . . Turkey
Similar to the preceding instrument, but inlaid with ivory and ebony. Length, 42 cm. Width, 14.3 cm. Depth, 5 cm.

1239. REBAB ESH SHA'IR, or BOOGA . . . . Egypt
Body in form of an inverted keystone. Belly of rawhide. One horse-hair string. Iron rod, as in No. 1235.
Length, 79 cm.; body, 19 cm.; width, 13.5 to 10 cm.; depth, 5.3 cm.

1240. REBAB EL-MUGHANNI . . . . Egypt
Wooden body with fret-work back. Parchment belly. Inlaid neck and head. Two strings. This is the "singer's *rebab*."
Length, 66 cm.; of body, 16 cm.; width, 10 cm.; depth, 5.8 cm.

1241. REBAB EL-MUGHANNI . . . . Egypt
Keystone-shaped body with inlaid neck and ivory tuning-pegs. Two strings.
Length, 88.5 cm.; of body, 27 cm.; width, 26 to 18 cm.; depth, 6 cm.

1242. REBAB ESH SHA'IR. "The poet's *rebab*" . . . . Egypt
Length, 71.1 cm.; of body, 26.6 cm.; width, 7 to 12.7 cm.
When used to accompany the Abu-Said Romance the name *Abu-Said Fiddle* is frequently employed.

1243. REBAB . . . . Tunis, North Africa
Elongated body. Parchment belly. Ornate sound-holes. Sides inlaid. Two gut strings.
Length, 62 cm. Width, 11 cm. Depth, 5 cm.

This instrument is a fine specimen of the type introduced into Spain by the Moors. It is easy to see that its musical value was not very great. However, that in it inhered great potentialities, is proven by the evolution of the most perfect of our modern instruments from so incomplete a beginning.

1244. KOKYU, or KOKIU . . . . Japan
The body is of red wood with front and back of cat-skin. Structurally it is a bowed *samisen*, somewhat smaller than the typical plucked form. Three silk strings run over a bridge to characteristic tuning-pegs in the neck.
Length, 66 cm.; of body, 15.3 cm.; width, 14 cm.; depth, 7.2 cm.
Piggott (page 177) gives detailed measurements of the *kokyu*, with four strings, which is the usual number.

1245. REBAB . . . . Sumatra
This and the following specimen indicate that the vogue of the *rebab* is not restricted to Persia and Arabia or contiguous countries. The shallow body of wood is in the shape of an elongated pear and carries a long neck. The body is decorated with a carved band. Two strings.
Length, 78 cm.; of body, 28.5 cm.; width, 11.1 cm.; depth, 7 cm.

1246. REBAB . . . . Java
Round body with head of skin, *batok;* a foot, *lemahan;* neck, *watangan;* long tuning-pegs, *manoi;* and thin strings.[7]
Elaborately decorated with mother-of-pearl inlay.
Length, 75 cm. Width, 11.5 cm. Depth, 9 cm.

1247. HAGGUM, HAI-KÖM, or HAING-KÖM . . . . .Corea
Barrel-shaped body of bamboo. Parchment belly. Neck of *shitan* wood. Two strings run over a low bamboo bridge. Typical bow.
Length, 62 cm. Diameter of body, 8.8 cm.; depth, 7.5 cm.
(B-S.)

1248. KEIKIN . . . . China
Four strings run through an ivory ring reducing the vibrating length to 27 cm. The hairs of the bow (74 cm. in length) are intertwined in the strings.
Length, 73 cm. Diameter of body, 8 cm.; depth, 11 cm.
(B-S.)

1249. KO-KIN, or GIRINE . . . . .Japan
Of the same general type as the preceding instrument, but smaller. The body and neck are of hard, dark-brown wood. Two strings.
Length, 45 cm. Diameter of body, 5 cm.; depth, 14 cm.

1250. KO-KIN. In every respect similar to No. 1249 . . . . .Japan

1251. CAI NHI, or DOUCO . . . . .Anam
The entire body and tuning-pegs are lacquered in black and gold. The head is of *kiri* wood, the neck of *shitan* wood. Two strings.
Length, 57.5 cm. Diameter of body, 8 cm.; depth, 8.5 cm.

1252. CAI NHI. A replica of the preceding instrument. . . . . .Anam
Length, 54.5 cm. Diameter of body, 8.5 cm.; depth, 8.5 cm.

1253. DOUCO. Similar to No. 1251, but with snake-skin head. . . .Anam

[7] Sachs, p. 317.

PLATE XII.

CASE XII. EAST SECTION. NOS. 1215 TO 1269 (LEFT TO RIGHT)

1254. CAI NHI . . . . Anam
This is the most beautiful of the group. The neck and tuning-pegs are of ebony, inlaid in a floral design in etched mother-of-pearl. The bow, of bamboo, is strung with white horsehair.
Length, 171 cm. Depth, 12.1 cm. Diameter of body, 5.2 cm.

1255. SHARODE. Unusual form . . . . India
Carved from a single block of wood. Parchment belly. Four gut strings.
The body resembles the *rudra-vina*, but the neck is much smaller. The stringing resembles the *sharode*. Nine sympathetic strings run from pegs on the side over the same bridge as the melody strings.
Length, 82.6 cm.; of body, 19 cm.; width, 24 cm.; depth, 11 cm.

1256. SARINDA, SAROH, or CHIHIKONG . . . . India
The body, with rounded back and deep incurvations on the sides, is carved from a single block of wood. A parchment belly covers the lower end only. Three gut strings fastened to a projection at the base run over a bridge resting on the parchment to tuning-pegs in peg-box. The neck is very short.
Length, 54.5 cm.; of body, 32 cm.; width, 16.8 cm.; depth, 3 cm.

1257. SARINDA . . . . India
Body of gourd with super-imposed carvings of wood. Lower part of strings running over a high bridge of ivory. Five sympathetic strings.
Length, 61.5 cm.; of body, 42 cm.; width, 22 cm.; depth, 17.5 cm.

1258. SARINDA . . . . India
Body of gourd with super-imposed carvings of wood. Lower part of the front covered with parchment. Three strings of wire and one of gut. Thirteen sympathetic strings.
Length, 63 cm.; of body, 40 cm.; width, 27 cm.; depth, 19 cm.

1259. CHIKARA . . . . India
Pear-shaped body of gourd. Neck and scroll of European type. Wooden belly with violin sound-holes. Four bowed gut strings. Seven sympathetic strings. The native name of the bow is *sargi*.[8]
Length, 54.5 cm. Width, 19 cm. Depth, 15 cm.

1260. CHIKARA . . . . India
Pear-shaped body with deeply incurving sides to admit of the free use of the bow. Parchment belly. Three bowed gut strings. Five sympathetic strings.
Length, 56 cm. Width, 14.5 cm. Depth, 10 cm.

---

[8] Sachs, p. 101.

1261. CHIKARA . . . . India
An elaborately decorated example. Four bowed gut strings. Nine sympathetic strings.
Length, 54 cm. Width, 11 cm. Depth, 8 cm.

1262. TAUS, or TAYUC. "Peacock-vina" . . . . India
The wooden body is carved and painted to resemble a peacock. Belly of painted parchment. Four wire strings. Fifteen sympathetic strings. It may be played with a bow (carried in a receptacle in body), or plucked. The *taus* is also called *mohur*, and *mayuri*.
Length, 114 cm.; of body, 29 cm.; depth, 19 cm.; width, 18 cm.

1263. ESRAR . . . . India
Body with deeply incurving sides. Parchment belly. Five melody strings. Fifteen sympathetic strings.
Length, 116.7 cm.; of body, 25 cm.; width, 20 cm.; depth, 15 cm.

1264. SUR-SANGA . . . . India
Violin-shaped body. Parchment belly. Seventeen frets. Four wire strings. The *sur-sanga* is an *esrar* with no sympathetic strings. It may be played with a bow, or plucked.
Length, 124 cm.; of body, 37 cm.; width, 22 cm.; depth, 7 cm.

1265. SARANGI . . . . India
Body in shape of an inverted key-stone. Three heavy gut strings (bowed) and one of copper wire. Twenty-four sympathetic strings. The body has an incurvation in the right side, and a rounded back.
Length, 58 cm.; of body, 23 cm.; width, 16 to 24 cm.; depth, 16.5.

1266. SARANGI, or SARUNGI . . . . India
Similar to preceding example but with eleven sympathetic strings only.
Length, 52.3 cm.; of body, 23.5 cm.; width, 12 to 14 cm.; depth, 11.5 cm.

1267. SHARODE, or CARADIYA-VINA . . . . India
Body of painted wood with parchment belly. Peg-box represents a bird's head. Five gut strings.
Length, 91.2 cm.; of body, 27.9 cm.; width, 22 cm.
Sharode is the Arabian name for a bass string. According to Sachs, quoting from *Mefatih ol ulum*, it resembles an instrument devised (912 A. D.) by the philosopher, Ibn Achwas es-Saadi, of Bagdad.[9]

[9] Sachs, p. 369.

1268. SHARODE . . . . India
Hard wood body with deeply incurving sides. Six gut strings. Eight sympathetic strings.
Length, 98.9 cm. Width, 24 cm. Depth, 20.3 cm.

1269. RUDRA-VINA. "Vina of the god Rudra" . . . . .India
Beautifully decorated body of wood. Inlaid neck and finger-board. Five gut strings.
Length, 76 cm. Width, 25.5 cm. Depth, 13 cm.

It will be noticed that all the East Indian instruments in this, as in Case IX, are exceedingly beautiful, both in form and decoration. The quality of tone is of peculiar sweetness. The extensive use of sympathetic strings (of very fine wire) is a notable feature of most East Indian types.

How far sympathetic strings affect the tone of an instrument very largely depends on the imagination of the hearer, although not entirely.

A half-century ago, Blüthner, a celebrated maker of Leipzig, introduced sympathetic strings in his Grands, but they were found to be of no value.

CASE XIII.

CLASS IV.

Section G. Continued (European).

1270. CRWTH (crooth), or CROWD .... Wales

This instrument is held by many Anglo-Saxons to be the most ancient bowed instrument. It was mentioned by Venantius Fortunatus Bishop of Poitiers, *circa* 609; pictured in mediaeval M. S. S. and maintained itself in Wales until the beginning of the last century. A square body, with a curved projection from the top, carries four strings, running over a bridge and true finger board, and two free strings on the right side (as held in playing). The first are played with a bow, the second are manipulated with the thumb of the left hand. There were two systems of tuning—g-g′ (free strings)-c′-c″-d′-d″ (bowed) or a-a′; e-e″; b′-b″. This is a reproduction, as originals cannot be obtained.

Length, 55 cm. Width, 19.7 to 15.6 cm. Depth, 3 to 2 cm.

1271. TRUMSCHEIT (Eng. *Trumpet Marine;* Fr. *Trompette marine;* Ital. *Tromba marina*)[1] .... Germany

Long tapering body with flat sides. Two circular sound-holes in belly. When the single thick gut string is correctly bowed, an harmonic of trumpet tone-quality is produced. The assumption that the name came from its use at sea has no evidence in its support.

More probable is the explanation given by Galpin (p. 98), that it was named after Marin, a celebrated trumpeter of the century (the 15th) in which the shaking bridge was introduced. This trembling or shaking bridge seems to be responsible for the trumpet-toned harmonics, but how this effect is produced is a question which still remains unanswered. This example is of the seventeenth century.

Length, 167 cm. Width of base, 22 cm.; depth, 10.5 cm.

1272. TRUMSCHEIT. Seventeenth century .... Germany

Similar to the preceding, but without sound-holes.

Length, 165 cm. Width of base, 22 cm.; depth, 12.5 cm.

---

[1] The name *Tromba Mariana,* "The Virgin's Trumpet" (Ger. *Nonnengeige*), based on its use by nuns for playing trumpet parts and quite generally accepted, is questioned by Galpin, p. 98.

PLATE XIII.

CASE XIII. WEST SECTION. NOS. 1270 TO 1293 (LEFT TO RIGHT)

(A part of Case IX. is shown with Nos. 905 to 920, on the top)

1273. TROMBA MARINA. Seventeenth century . . . . Italy
Body with rounded back, elaborately inlaid. The peg-box terminates in a carving of a satyr's head.
Length, 124 cm. Width of base, 15.5 cm.; depth, 9 cm.

1274. TRUMSCHEIT. Seventeenth century . . . . Germany
Peg-box terminates in a carving of a lion's head. On front of neck the following notes are marked in ink on a small piece of paper; G-F-G-C-D-E-F-G-H-(The German B natural) and C.
Length, 206 cm. Width of base, 41 cm.; depth, 20 cm.

The Violin (Fr. *Violon;* It. *Violino;* Ger. *Violine*), the most important of the bowed instruments, was evolved from an early type. The word "Fiddle" is derived from the Low Latin *Fidula,* a contraction of *Fidicula.* The Geige was an instrument with a penetrating, raucous tone. The Viol, which it superseded, had a very sweet and mellow quality of tone, but lacked resonance. So, following the principle of survival in musical instruments, i. e., "The Survival of the Loudest," it disappeared. Its only representative in the modern orchestra is the Contrabass. The structure of the Violin seemingly violates all scientific principles, but through the work of generations of inspired makers it has reached perfection. It consists of a back and belly, one of maple, the other of pine, connected structurally by a rim with incurving sides, and brought into sympathetic vibration with each other by the sound-post, which is so adjusted as to properly relate the vibrating parts. It has a bridge over which run four strings tuned to g-d′-a′-e″. The "fourth" string (g) is overspun. It has a neck with a "true" finger-board. The bow is a very important factor and the celebrated bow makers, like Tourte, have brought it to the same state of perfection as the instrument itself.

1275. FIDDLE . . . . Chile
Body of stained wood. Three gut strings.
Length, 27 cm.; of body, 27.; width, 16 cm.; depth, 5 cm.
This rude specimen, with but three strings (gut), came into Mr. Stearns' possession with the name *robel,* or *rovel* indicated. No data can be found to show whether either is correct. In Brazil there is a dancing-master's fiddle called *rabeljo,*[2] evidently a name derived from the Spanish *rabel* (rebec), or rather its diminutive *rabelillo.*[3]

1276. VIOLINO . . . . Italy
Typical structure. Back inlaid with a representation of a mediaeval chateau.
Length, 63 cm. Width, 21.3 cm. Depth, 6 cm.
Signed—"Paolo Maggini, fecit in Brescia, 1608."

---

[2] Morris, p. 244.
[3] Sachs, p. 313.

1277. VIOLINO .... Italy
This differs from the usual type in that the strings are tightened by a metal device. A similar device in use on other bowed instruments may have suggested its application, but whether by the maker whose name appears below, or by some other, is an open question.
Length, 61 cm. Width, 20.7 cm. Depth, 6.2 cm.
Signed—"Nicolaus Amatus, Cremonen. Hieronyme filius antonii nepos, fecit, 1670."

1278. VIOLON. Typical model .... France
The name "Hopf" appears on the back.
Length, 48 cm. Width, 16 cm. Depth, 4.5 cm.

1279. VIOLIN. Typical model, but with moulded back......... England
Length, 60.5 cm. Width, 20.5 cm. Depth, 5.8 cm.

1280. VIOLON. Typical model and average dimensions......... France

1281. VIOLON. Typical form, but with pointed bouts........... France
Length, 60.5 cm. Width, 20.2 cm. Depth, 5.8 cm.

1282. VIOLINE. Bowed-zither form. Usual stringing......... Germany
The body somewhat resembles the Streichzither in form, but has the violin stringing.
The peg-box terminates in a carved lion's head.
Length, 62 cm. Width, 22 cm. Depth, 5.2 cm.
Signed—"Streich-Melodie, J. W. Sett."

1283. VIOLON .... France
Moulded full back. Peg-box terminating in the carved head of a lioness.
Length, 60.5 cm. Width, 20.5 cm. Depth, 5.5 cm.

1284. VIOLIN. Typical form .... United States
This violin was made by Mr. N. W. House, of Ann Arbor, from wood taken from a table used by the first settlers of the city, and presented by him to the University.
Length, 60 cm. Width, 26 cm. Depth, 5.2 cm.

1285. VIOLON CHANOT .... France
Length, 60.5 cm. Width, 20.5 cm. Depth, 5.5 cm.
This form was held by M. Chanot, a distinguished French scientist, to be more in accordance with principles of acoustics than the regular shape. It has had no vogue whatever.

1286. VIOLA .... England
Somewhat larger than the Violin, but of the same form. The stringing is c-g-d′-a′.
Length, 66 cm. Width, 23 cm. Depth, 6.8 cm.

1287. TENOR-VIOLA DA BRACCIO .... Italy
Peculiarly shaped sound-holes. Reddish-yellow varnish.
Length, 71 cm. Width, 29.8 cm. Depth, 8 cm.

1288. QUINTON. Eighteenth century .... England
Body with sloping shoulders. Five strings. This instrument belongs to the viol family and generally has the flat back characteristic of that type.
The stringing of the Treble Quinton is g-d′-a′-d″-g″; of the Tenor, c-g-d′-g′-c″.
Length, 62.5 cm. Width, 21 cm. Depth, 5.8 cm.

1289. ARMGEIGE (Eng. *Arm viol;* Ital. *Viola da braccio*). Early date .... Germany
Deep model. Flame sound-holes instead of the F-holes seen in the violin family. *Viola da mano* is a sixteenth-century Italian name.
Length, 73 cm. Width, 24.5 cm. Depth, 7.4 cm.

1290. VIOLA DA BRACCIO. Eighteenth century................. Italy
Deep model with exaggerated outline. Flat back in four sections. Peg-box terminates in a carving representing a blindfolded female head. The label is illegible, but on the bridge is inscribed—"B. Kirsch. Nürnberg." In all probability, this is the name of a former owner. Length, 76 cm. Width, 28.3 cm. Depth, 5.5 cm.

1291. VIOLA DA BRACCIO. Sixteenth, or seventeenth century .... Italy
Narrow model. Six strings, arranged in the usual way, run over the finger-board and two bass strings run free at the side.
Length, 73.5 cm. Width, 24.3 cm. Depth, 6.5 cm.
Signed—"Gaspero da Salo, da Brescia."

1292. VIOLA. Sixteenth century. Unusually broad base.......... Italy
Length, 63 cm. Width, 36 cm. Depth, 9 cm.
Signed—"Gio. Maria del Bussetto, fece in Cremona, 1546." .....

1293. VIOLA DA BRACCIO .... Italy
Deep model with moulded back. Peg-box of unusual shape. Seven gut strings, the lower of which are overstrung.
Length, 76 cm. Width, 23.5 cm. Depth, 7.5 cm.
Signed—"Joanes Marcus," but bearing no date.

1294. VIOLA D'AMORE (Ger. *Liebesgeige*). Eighteenth century..... Italy
Narrow model. Ebony and ivory inlay. Six gut strings, played with the bow, and six sympathetic strings of fine wire.
Length, 78 cm. Width, 23 cm. Depth, 6 cm.

1295. VIOLA D'AMORE. Eighteenth century .... Italy
Narrow model. Tail-piece and finger-board inlaid with mother-of-pearl, tortoise-shell, ivory, and ebony. Seven bowed, and seven sympathetic strings.
Length, 80 cm. Width, 21.5 cm. Depth, 8.3 cm.

1296. LYRA VIOL, or VIOLA BASTARDA. Eighteenth century..... France
Deep model. Inlay of mother-of-pearl. Seven gut strings, and seven sympathetic strings of wire.
Length, 93 cm. Width, 33 cm. Depth, 9 cm.
Signed—"Louis Guerssan, près la comedie Francaise, in Paris, 1737."

1296A. VIOLA D'AMORE .... Italy, or France
This beautiful instrument, of the seventeenth century, exhibits the rare workmanship characteristic of early Italian and French makers, and is the choicest example of its type in the Collection. The top of the body—with C sound-holes—is purfled with ivory and ebony inlay, and the back carries a representation of a shepherdess surrounded with scroll-work designs. The curved peg-box ends in a carving of a man's head. Six bowed strings run over a finger-board of ebony, inlaid with boxwood in an artistic design, to a tail-piece of like material and decoration. Six sympathetic strings occupy their usual positions.
Length, 83 cm.; of body, 38 cm.; width, lower part, 25.4 cm.; upper part, 20 cm.; at waist, 13 cm.; depth, 5.8 cm.
(Albert Lockwood.)

1297. MINIATURE VIOLIN. Eighteenth century .... England
Probably this was used for the same purpose as the succeeding instruments. Length, 46.7 cm. Width, 12 cm. Depth, 4 cm.

1298. TASCHENGEIGE (Eng. *Kit;* Fr. *Pochette;* It. *Poccetta*) .. Germany
This miniature violin was used by teachers of dancing, who joyfully pursued their avocation by its aid. The name suggests the case—an overcoat pocket.
Length, 39.5 cm. Width, 3.3 cm. Depth, 2.3 cm.

1299. TANZMEISTERGEIGE. Seventeenth century .... Germany
Length, 59.5 cm. Width, 4.8 cm. Depth, 3.5 cm.

1300. KIT. Eighteenth century .... England
Length, 59 cm. Width, 6.4 cm. Depth, 5.8 cm.

1301. POCHETTE. Seventeenth century .... France
Length, 60 cm. Width, 6.5 cm. Depth, 5.7 cm.

1302. TASCHENGEIGE. Eighteenth century .... Germany
Length, 39.4 cm. Width, 3.2 cm. Depth, 3.3 cm.

PLATE XIV.

CASE XIII. EAST SECTION. NOS. 1294 TO 1329 (LEFT TO RIGHT)

1303-4. TANZMEISTERGEIGEN. Eighteenth century ....Germany
Lengths, 41.8-47 cm. Widths, 4.3-12 cm. Depths, 5-4.8 cm.

1305. POCHETTE. Boat-shaped body. Flame sound-holes ......France
This example dates from the seventeenth century and has the typical sound-holes of the period.
Length, 42.5 cm. Width, 4.5 cm. Depth, 3.5 cm.

1306. STIEFELKNECHTGEIGE. "Boot-jack violin" ....Germany
Length, 53.3 cm. Width, 12 cm. Depth, 3 cm.

1307. FOLDING VIOLON. Nineteenth century ....France
The neck, body, and finger-board are detachable and can be packed in a box. The bow folds on itself.
Length, 58.7 cm. Width, 11 cm. Depth, 6.2 cm.
Signed—"J. Grandjon, Paris."

1308. STOCKGEIGE (Eng. *Cane Violin;* Fr. *Canne-violon*) .....Germany
One side of this walking-stick is detachable, and reveals a violin with the usual stringing. The bow is carried in a German silver scabbard.
Length of cane, 91 cm. Greatest diameter, 4.4 cm.
Signed—"Moritz Glasel—Mark-neu-Kirchen I. S."

1309. PORCELAIN VIOLIN........Source unknown, probably Germany
Typical form. Violins have also been constructed from steel, clay, and various non-sonorous substances. They have no musical value.
Length, 58.7 cm. Width, 21 cm. Depth, 4.2 cm.

1310. MUTE VIOLIN. (Fr. *Violon sordine;* It. *Violino sordino;* Ger. *Stumme Violine*) .... England
This specimen has the belly, finger-board, neck, tail-piece, and usual stringing, but the back and sides are missing.
Length, 53.2 cm. Width, 32 cm.

1311. VIOLINO SORDINO. More incomplete than No. 1310........Italy
Like the preceding example this is designed for practice only.
Length, 60.5 cm. Width, 13 cm. Thickness, 3.7 cm.

1312. BASS-VIOLA DA BRACCIO. Eighteenth century ....Germany
The size and stringing—F, c, g, d′—correspond to the characteristics of the above named instrument. It has also a decided structural resemblance to a very small violoncello.
Length, 81 cm. Width, 29 cm. Depth, 11.3 cm.
Signed—"Johann Georg Hasert, à Eisenach, 1745."

1313. VIOLONCELLO. Eighteenth century . . . . England
Deep model. 'Cello stringing—C-G-d-a. Of the four strings the two lower are wound. The same tuning is found on the *Bass Viola da braccio*. Length, 100 cm. Width, 33 cm. Depth, 14 cm.
Signed—"Fred. Hintz, Fecit, London, 1763."

1314. KNIEGEIGE (Ital. *Viola da gamba*) . . . . Germany
The *viola da gamba* has the flat back of the viol family. It carries six strings, four of gut and two of overspun silk. A rest of black wood is inserted in the base of the instrument.
Length, 135 cm. Width, 37 cm. Depth, 15 cm.

1315. VIOLONCELLO. Late eighteenth century . . . . Germany
In every respect a worthy example of its type.
Length, 135 cm. Width, 49 cm. Depth, 17 cm.
Signed—"Andreas Kembler, Lauten und Geigenmacher in Dillingen, 1772."

1316. BASS FIDDLE, or Violoncello . . . . Probably of Asiatic origin
Body of a long, narrow gourd. The head resembles the type found on Chinese and Japanese guitars. The neck, finger-board and peg-box are of the European type. It carries four strings arranged in the usual manner. The bridge is distinctly Oriental.
Length, 153.1 cm.; of body, 62.9 cm. Diameter, 17 to 10.3 cm.

1317. HALBBASS (Eng. *Half-bass;* Ital. *Basso di camera*) . . . . Germany
Viol-shaped body. Four strings tuned by a screw mechanism. Tuning—C-G-d-a. This instrument was carried by a strap over the neck of the performer and was used in out-of-doors processions.
Suggestions of the convivial environment in which its note was also heard are conveyed by its popular designation—*Bierbass*—although this term was given it on account of its weak and characterless tone-quality.
Length, 136.8 cm. Width, 44.2 cm. Depth, 20 cm.

1318. RABECAO (Port. for Eng. *Double Bass;* Fr. *Contrebasse;* Ital. *Contra-basso, Violone grosso;* Ger. *Kontrabass*). Typical model . . . . Funchal, Madeira
Body of *noguera* wood. Three strings, tuned by cogwheels with thumb-pieces at the back. The tuning is the Italian—G-d-a, the tones sounding an octave lower than the notation. Modern instruments have four strings (E-A-d-g). Many older players prefer the three-stringed type on account of its (to them) greater sonority.
Length, 191 cm. Width, 66.5 cm. Depth, 25 cm.

At the side of No. 1318 a violin case of the seventeenth century, carved from two pieces of wood, is displayed. Its length is, 80.3 cm.; width, 23.7 cm. and depth, 14 cm.

Sub-section I. Bowed wire strings.

1319. STREICHZITHER. (Eng. *Psaltery-viol*) . . . . Germany
Kite-shaped body with two wire strings.
Length, 45.6 cm. Width, 21.4 to 3.8 cm. Depth, 3.3 cm.
This type combines the form of the violin—frequently with exaggerated details—with the wire strings and frets of the zither. The strings are bowed and, in their position, reverse the usual order. The German form is said to have been invented in 1823, but the English instrument was in existence in the seventeenth century. It cannot be said, that either the *Streichzither*, or any one of its variants has greatly extended the frontiers of the realm of music.
In Jacobi Bessoni's "Theatrvm instrvmentorvm" (1582) Fig. XXIX shows an instrument with viol body, fretted neck, and wire strings. It was played with a bow and may be looked upon as the founder of the family to which Nos. 1319-1327 belong.
Of the following examples, Nos. 1319, 1320, 1326, and 1327 have 25.27, 30, and 25 frets respectively.

1320. STREICHZITHER. Nineteenth century . . . . Germany
Leaf-shaped body, with four wire strings.
Length, 51 cm. Width, 15.2 cm. Depth, 3.3 cm.
Signed—"Georg Tiefenbrunner, Munich."

1321. PHILOMELE, or STAHLGEIGE. Nineteenth century . . . . . . Germany
In form resembling the *Diskant-viola da gamba.* (Ital. *Violetta piccola*). It carries four wire strings.
Length, 53.8 cm. Width, 20.7 cm. Depth, 3.8 cm.

1322. PHILOMELE. Similar to No. 1321, with sloping shoulders. Germany
This type was developed in Germany about the middle of the last century. Length, 54.8 cm. Width, 20 cm. Depth, 3.8 cm.

1323. VIOL-CITHER. Nineteenth century . . . . Germany
Length, 53.2 cm. Width, 23.9 cm. Depth, 3.8 cm.

1324. SULTANA, or CITHER-VIOL . . . . Ireland
Viol-shaped body, with sloping shoulders. Ivory inlay. Six strings, two lower of wire and the others of gut. It was often strung entirely with wire and had a fretted finger-board.
Length, 67 cm. Width, 23.2 cm. Depth, 6.7 cm.
Signed—"Perry, Dublin."

1325. STREICHMELODION, or BREITOLINE . . . . Germany
Finger-board with brass frets and mother-of-pearl inlay. Four metal strings. Played with a plectrum or a bow. The second name given refers to its invention by Leopold Breit, of Brünn, in 1856.
Length, 60.4 cm. Width, 20 to 30 cm. Depth, 5 cm.
Signed—"J. Haslwanter, Munich."

1326. STREICHZITHER. Nineteenth century . . . . Germany
Four strings, tuned by ivory thumb-pieces at side of head. The head terminates in an upturned trumpet bell. Fretted and inlaid finger-head. Length, 74.6 cm. Width, 18.8 to 27.8 cm. Depth, 3.8 cm.

1327. PHILOMELE . . . . Germany
Body with sloping shoulders. Flame-shaped sound-holes. Four strings. Peg-box terminates in a carved representation of a lion's head.
Length, 58 cm. Width, 22.8 cm. Depth, 3.8 cm.

Section H. Vibrating Strings actuated by the Friction of a Resined Wheel, and controlled by Slides, operated by Keys.

1328. PETIT-VIELLE. (Early Fr. *Vielle à roue;* Eng. *Hurdy Gurdy;* Ital. *Ghironda;* Ger. *Drehleier*) . . . . France
Length, 41.5 cm. Width, 17.2 cm. Depth, 6.3 cm.

1329. VIELLE . . . . France
Wooden body. Six strings. Resined wheel and keys. The body of this instrument is beautifully inlaid. Six strings are "stopped" by slides, and there are two pairs of drone strings.
Length, 74 cm. Width, 30 cm. Depth, 15 cm.
Signed—"Pouget Père et Fils, à Ardentes près Chateau roux."

The "Vielle" is one of the earliest types of European instruments. Its construction was the subject of a tract by Odo of Cluny—died 942—(*Oddonis quomodo organistrum construatur*—Gerbert, Script. I. 303). From the tenth to the twelfth century it was known as the "Organistrum." The present name first occurs in the fifteenth century. Although many great composers, including Haydn, have written music for it, few take it seriously now-a-days. Many will be surprised to learn that under its early name it was held in great esteem in the Church, from which it was banished by the introduction of small organs and condemned thereafter to lead a vagrant life.[4]

Early pictures show the *organistrum* played by two persons, one manipulating the slides, or keys, while the other turns the wheel. When, in the fifteenth century, the stringed instrument then known as the *vielle* was given the name *viole*, or *viola*, the qualifying *à roue* was no longer necessary as the two types were sufficiently differentiated. There is a little direct evidenec to support the asumption that either the *galoubet* or the *schwegel* was used in connection with the *vielle* (*viole*), but it is difficult to account for the term *flûte des vielleurs* otherwise.

[4] Galpin, p. 104.

CASE XIV.

CLASS V. INSTRUMENTS WITH VIBRATING STRINGS, REEDS, OR COLUMNS OF AIR, CONTROLLED BY A KEY-BOARD MECHANISM.

1330. VIOLON-AVEC-CLAVIER. (*Violon monocorde à clavecin*) . . . France
Lozenge-shaped body, mounted on legs. C-shaped sound-holes. One string of several twisted strands of steel wire passes from a peg at one end over the resonance body, and under a box containing a key-mechanism by which the string is "stopped." Compass—f to c‴.
Length, 121 cm.; of body, 49 cm.; width, 26 cm. Height, 62 cm.

Section A. Vibrating Strings actuated by Impact, through a directly-acting Lever Key-Action.

The Clavichord (Ital. *Clavicordo;* Ger. *Klavichord*), is first indisputably mentioned in the *Minneregeln* of Eberhard Cersne (1404),[1] although in a letter of John I. of Aragon, dated 1387, he asks Berthomen de Castre to send him an *exaquir*, which, in a later letter (1388) is described as an *isturment semblant d'orguens, qui sona ab cordes.*[2] As in 1400, key-board instruments of this type were in use, it is fair to assume that they developed a century earlier. To carry its invention back to Guido (d. 1050?)[3] is to enter the realm of fancy rather than of fact. In its earliest form it had no legs but was placed on a table. From the first its structural characteristics were fixed. Wire strings, stretched over a sound-board, were made to vibrate by brass tangents at the back end of key-levers. There were two types. In the older, the *gebunden* (fretted), each string was made to produce more than one tone, as the string was struck at different points. In the later, *bundfrei* (fret-free), each tone had its own string. The clavichord was the prime favorite, even after the pianoforte had been introduced, as it was more completely under the control of the performer, who could, by pressure, change the pitch while the string was vibrating, thus producing a wavy effect called the *bebung.*

Gottfried Silbermann (1683-1753) invented a clavichord in which strings of double length were struck in the middle by tangents, yielding the reduplicated octave of the entire string. He named it the *Cembal d' Amour.*

---

[1] Ambros, *Gesch. d. Musik,* I Auf. II, p. 507.
[2] Vander Straeten, *La Mus. aux Pays-Bas.* VII, p. 40.
[3] Athanasius Kircher—*Musurgia univ.,* p. 215—is responsible for this impossible supposition.

1331. KLAVICHORD. Eighteenth century .... Germany
Oblong case of mahogany. Black naturals and white sharps. Compass of six octaves from F to f'''. *Gebunden* type. Fifty-three unison pairs of wire strings. Tuned according to the "pure" system. It has black naturals and white sharp keys. This is not definitive of a very early date, as is generally held, for originally the naturals were made of boxwood and the sharps of ebony.[4] Bi-cord stringing was common, for Virdung, in *Musica getuscht* (1511) says: *gmainlich macht man drey saiten vff eine kor*,[5] a statement enforced by Praetorius (1618).[6]
Length, 152 cm. Width, 50 cm. Depth, 15 cm. Height, 75.5 cm.

Section B. Vibrating Strings actuated by Plucking, through an indirectly-acting Key-board Mechanism.

The Harpsichord (Fr. *Clavecin;* Ital. *Cembalo, Clavicembalo, Gravicembalo, Harpsicordo;* Ger. *Klavizimbel, Kielflügel*) is derived from the Dulcimer. The tone is produced by plucking the strings by quill plectra, forming a part of a very complicated key--mechanism. The tone lacks the ethereal quality of the clavichord, but has more power. As the harpischord was placed against a wall, the back of the case was generally unfinished.

In the attempt to make pure tuning possible, many complicated extensions of the harpischord were made at an early date.

In 1561, Nic. Vincentio devised the *Arcicembalo*, with six rows of keys, making thirty-one divisions of the octave possible. It was simplified by Gio. Batt. Doni in 1640, by reducing the number of key-boards to three. The diatonic, chromatic, and enharmonic *genera* (Gk.) could be displayed on this instrument.[7]

The *Universalklavizimbel*, invented by Karl Luyton of Vienna, appeared in 1580. With eighteen keys to the octave, enharmonics were possible.[8]

In 1600, Francisco Nigetti constructed the *Proteus cembalo onnisono*, with five rows of keys and each tone divided into five parts.[9] The *Sambuca lincea, Instrumentum perfectum*, by Fabio Colonna, *circa* 1618, had bi-cord stringing, eight rows of keys, and, incidentally, was seven and one-half feet in length.[10]

Coming down to modern times we have the "Sequential key-board" in which the white and black keys come in regular succession. C was always on

---

[4] Zarlino, *Inst. harmon,* II, p. 46, suggested that this practice naturally grew out of the meaning of the word "chromatic."
The historical development of the instrument is treated by Carl Krebs in *Die besaiteten Klavierinstrumente bis zum Anfang des 17 Jahrhunderts,* in *Vierteljahrschrift f. Musikwissenschaft,* 1892, pp. 91-126. The citations given above are also included in this monograph.
[5] *Musica getuscht* (1511), p. 38.
[6] *Syntagma musicum* (1618), p. 74.
[7] Sachs, p. 19.
[8] Praetorius, *Syn. Mus.,* p. 75, *seq.*
[9] Sachs, p. 306.
[10] Sachs, p. 330.

a black key, and but one fingering was necessary for all major scales. It was invented in 1843 by W. A. B. Lunn, of England, who masqueraded under the name of Wallbridge.[11]

This incomplete record predicates future attempts to solve this problem, but future historians will probably soon class them in the large company of the obsolete.

1332. HARPSICORDO, or GRAVICEMBALO .... Italy

A rare specimen of an early form. Shape of modern "grand." Elaborately painted decoration, both on inside and outside of body. Carved and gilded legs. Compass four and one-half octaves, from BB flat. Black sharps, and naturals of ordinary wood.

Length, 248 cm. Width, 92 cm. Depth, 24.1 cm. Height, 95 cm.

Signed—"Joannis Baptista Guisti, Lucensis, faciebat anno 1693."

1333. GRAVICEMBALO .... Italy

On the hinged fall-board is a picture of three monks, one playing a *Zink*, another a violin, while the third is singing from a book held in his hands. On the inside of fall-board appear several measures of music, also a Latin inscription, *Corda mulcet tristia.* "It sooths sad hearts."

Black sharps. Compass:—Three octaves and eight notes from E.

Length, 178 cm. Width, 72 cm. Depth, 26.7 cm. Height, 87.5 cm.

Signed—"Christoforus Rigunini. Firenze, A. D. 1602."

The Spinet (Fr. *Epinette;* Ital. *Spinetta;* Ger. *Spinett*) existed in various forms. It was generally placed in a case, from which it was removed when needed. In essentials it resembles the harpsichord, but has one string only. "Virginal" is another name, but not suggested by the fact that Elisabeth, the "Virgin Queen," played it almost exclusively.* The name occurs in early literature, and that the instrument was thus known in the time of Henry VII (1456-1509) is shown by the following lines, of that period, taken from a manuscript in the British Museum (18. & 11.).

"A slac strynge in a Virgynall soundethe not aright;
It dothe abyde no wrastinge, it is so louse and light.
The sownde borde crasede forsith the instrument
Throw mysgovernaunce do make notis whiche was not intente.[12]

Speaking of the wife of an old English squire, an early record says, "She plays on the Espinetto and Organs and Gittar and danceth very well."[13]

---

[11] Sachs, p. 343.

* On page 54 of *Musica instrumentalis deudsch* (1528), Agricola gives a cut of the Virginal under that name.

[12] Galpin, p. 113. On page XVIII he gives the exact title, "The Proverbis in the Garet at the New Lodge in the Parke of Leckingfelde." The lines given are quoted by Krebs, but incorrectly, as he kindly corrected the old spelling, as he did Virdung's grammar.

[13] P. H. Ditchfield, "The old English County Squire," p. 166.

In the "Diary of Martin Thomas Dallam"[14] we find: "Comminge to Graves-ende, I wente aborde our shipp called the Heckter, and thar placed my chiste, my beddinge and a pare of virginals,[15] which the merchantes did allow me to carrie for my exercise by the waye."

1334. SPINETTA. Eighteenth century .... Italy

The instrument proper lifts out of the beautifully decorated case. An artistically cut rose ornaments the sounding board. Compass: three octaves and one note. Quill plectra. One string to each note. This beautiful instrument was at one time erroneously attributed to the celebrated maker, Hans Rücker, of Antwerp.

Compass:—Three octaves and four notes from e.

It corresponds to the Italian *Spinettino*, an "octave (or fifth) spinet."

Length, 98.5 cm. Width, 40 cm. Depth, 28 cm. Height, 94 cm.

1335. SPINETTA. Sixteenth century .... Italy

Heptagonal body removable from its case. Projecting key-board. Compass of four octaves and one note from E. Fret-board of carved, open scroll work. Carved rose in sounding-board.

Length, 150.2 cm. Width, 49.6 cm. Depth, 23 cm.

Signed—"Ferandi de Rosos, Meliolanensis, M.D. LXXX."

1336. HARPSICORDO, or CLAVICEMBALO .... Italy

Case elaborately decorated, both inside and out. Spindle legs. Three manuals. The sharp keys are inlaid with two thin strips of ivory. Compass of four octaves and one note from E. One of the finest examples of the type in existence.

That this instrument is by Christofori has been contested, but there is sufficient evidence in support of the assumption that it is a product of his skill.[16]

Length, 215 cm. Width, 134 cm. Depth, 16 cm. Height, 97.8 cm.

---

[14] "Early Voyages and Travels to the Levant," Hak. Soc., 1893, p. 4. Thomas Dallam was the father of a celebrated family of English organ builders. He built the organ in King's College, Cambridge, in 1605-6, and in 1613, the early instrument in Worcester Cathedral.

[15] Abdy Williams (quoted by Galpin, p. 227), states that "owing to the use of the singular number *organum* (the Greek and Latin name for any kind of a machine) by mediaeval musicians to denote a special method of singing, the plural *organa* had to be employed for the instrument." The term "pare, or payre of" instead of referring to two instruments came to be used as the equivalent of *organa*.

[16] Regarding this instrument Mr. A. J. Hipkins—whose authority is final—wrote to Mr. Stearns as follows:—"London, 22 Aug., 1901, Dear Mr. Stearns:—I cannot express to you how much I am obliged by the very complete information you have favored me with respecting your splendid Cristofori harpsichord. It is indeed a treasure and the University of Michigan, which benefits so largely by your generosity, has in that priceless specimen a remarkable historical and artistic possession."

PLATE XV.

CASE XIV. WEST SECTION. NOS. 1336 TO 1339 (LEFT TO RIGHT)

1337. SPINETTINO (Fifth, or Octave-Spinet) . . . . Italy
This instrument rests in a painted case. The inside of fall-board carries a painting of a bird on a slender branch. Compass of three octaves and eight notes from e.
Length, 67 cm. Width, 45.8 cm. Depth, 16 cm.

Section C. Vibrating Strings actuated by Impact, through an indirectly-acting Key-board Mechanism.

As, in viewing the arrangement of the display pipes in an organ, we may see in the graduated sequence in which they stand a rehabilitation of the "Pipes o' Pan," so, in a modern grand pianoforte, the contour of the plate carrying the strings discovers a striking resemblance to the early harp.

As has been stated elsewhere, the Assyrian *azor* was the first stringed instrument in which the vibration of the tone-producing means was incited by impact. It may, therefore, be considered the earliest application of the fundamental principle underlying the pianoforte.

The two essential factors in all key-board instruments—(1) the means of tone-production and, (2) the controlling mechanism, will now be considered.

In the development of the first factor, omitting reference to the earliest stages, we find in the clavichord, harpsichord and clavitherium, the arrangement of the strings which has been perpetuated in modern instruments, and, in the order given, they display the forms known to us as the "square," "grand" and "upright." At this point it must be stated that in a few years the first will take its place in the ranks of the obsolete. A fundamental structural weakness—the lack of resistance to the "pull" of the strings—was removed, in 1825, by Alpheus Babcock, an American, who invented the cast-iron frame. This was applied to the "square," at that time the favorite form. Later (1844) Jonas Chickering, of Boston, produced a perfected cast-iron frame, also for a "square," but soon after (1851) applied the same invention to the "grand." In the first pianofortes single strings were used, largely on account of the structural weakness mentioned, but with the introduction of the iron frame it was possible to increase the musical resources of the instrument by the adoption of bi-cord, and triple stringing, i. e., two, or three, unisons to a tone, through all but the highest and lowest octaves. Another advance was made through the invention of over-stringing by Boehm, in 1835, and double over-stringing by Steinway & Sons, in 1859. The compass of the instrument was gradually extended until it has now reached 7 1/3 octaves.

The evolution of the second and most important factor dates from 1709, when Bartolomeo Christofori (1653-1731) invented the form of action containing the fundamental principles of our modern mechanism. This has been contested in certain quarters, but in vain, for his priority rests on uncontrovertible evidence.

In this, the earliest form of action, through an ingenious and delicately poised system of levers and hoppers, the blow on the keys is transmitted to a hammer which strikes the string and falls back. By a device called the "escapement" the hammer immediately resumes its position in readiness for another impact. Dampers of felt fall on the strings and silence the tone. This latter mechanism is now controlled by a foot pedal. Another pedal shifts the key-board (in the "grand") allowing the hammers to strike but one string.

The introduction of the prolongation pedal (Fr. *pedale de prolongement*) by Debain of Paris (1860) and Montal in 1862 was of great artistic import. It was simplified and greatly improved by Steinway of New York in 1874.[17] Many attempts to correct an obvious defect in the pianoforte—the difficulty of sustaining tone— have been made. Possibly, the most interesting is the "Steinertone," in which the inventor, Morris Steinert, sought to apply the principle of the clavichord action. This attempt was not so radical a departure from key-board traditions as the very ingenious and effective mechanism introduced by Paul von Janko in 1882. Six short rows of stubby keys are arranged in tiers and run in pairs. Each row gives a succession of major seconds, and, in combination, the chromatic scale. Chordal successions quite impossible for ordinary hands are made easy—and scales in double thirds lose their terror. Like the radiating key-board—this action has not been adopted to any extent, although the new technique is taught in several European conservatories of music.

1338. SQUARE PIANO. *Circa* 1790 .... England
Oblong case of mahogany, resting on a detached stand. Marquetry decorations. Bi-cord stringing throughout. The stop action, controlling the dampers is missing. Compass of five octaves from E.
Length, 152 cm. Width, 52.7 cm. Depth, 17.2 cm. Height, 66 cm.
Signed—"Longman and Broderip, Musical Instrument makers, No. 20 Cheapside and 13 Haymarket, London."

1339. SQUARE PIANO. *Circa* 1800 .... England
Oblong case of mahogany resting on six legs. Bi-cord stringing. The lowest strings are overspun. Compass, five octaves and a fifth from F. This, and No. 1338, are most significant instruments.
Length, 157 cm. Width, 71 cm. Depth, 23 cm. Height, 70 cm.
Signed—"John Broadwood and Sons, Makers, to his Majesty and the Princesses. Great Poultney Street, Golden Square, London."

1340. SQUARE PIANO .... France
Oblong case of mahogany resting on four spindle legs, ornamented with inlaid brass. Compass, five octaves from F.
Length, 165 cm. Width, 60 cm. Depth, 24 cm. Height, 81 cm.
Signed—"Erard Fréres et Cie, Rue du Mail 37, à Paris, 1808."

---

[17] Weitzmann, "A History of Pianoforte-playing," p. 279.

1341. Portable Piano. Eighteenth century .... Italy

Rectangular body of dark wood. Early form of action. No dampers. Compass of three octaves from f.

Length, 55 cm. Width, 27.5 cm. Depth, 17 cm.

1342. Square Piano.. Nineteenth century............. United States

Rosewood body. Carved legs. The name-board is elaborately decorated with colors and inlaid mother-of-pearl. The naturals are also covered with the same material. Overstrung bass. Compass of seven octaves, from AAA.

Length, 216.6 cm. Width, 120 cm. Depth, 30 cm. Height, 93 cm.

Signed—"F. P. Hale, New York."

(John E. Whitset.)

1343. Upright Piano. Early nineteenth century .... France

Typical form of body. Key-board carried on a projection supported by two legs. This form is also called "Pianino."

Length, 129 cm. Width, 58 cm. Height, 107 cm.

Signed—"No. 22 Rue de Paris, Allovon, Facteur de Pianos au Havre."

This form was first introduced by Joh. Schmidt, of Salzburg, in 1780, who was followed by J. I. Hawkins, of Philadelphia, in 1800, and by Th. Loud, of London, in 1802. (Sachs, p. 297). Largely through the inventions of American makers it has evolved into an instrument of fine musical qualities although the action is too complicated to be really effective. On account of its compact form it has entirely supplanted the square piano to which it is in every way superior.

The Grand Piano (Fr. *Piano à queue;* Ital. *Pianoforte a coda;* Ger. *Flügel*), on account of its longer strings and more responsive action is infinitely superior to any other form. It is manufactured in various sizes and its use in time will become well-nigh universal.

1344. Flügel. Eighteenth century .... Germany

Trapezoidal case resting on four legs. Marquetry decoration. Compass, five octaves. Ebony naturals, ivory-tipped sharps. The dampers are controlled by knee-levers. Bi-cord stringing. The action could be shifted, probably by means of a draw stop, so that the hammers could strike but one string. Maker unknown as the plate on name-board has been removed.

Compass of 5 octaves from FF.

Length, 184 cm. Width, 100 to 18 cm. Depth, 25 cm. Height, 89.

1345. FLÜGEL . . . . Austria

Body of typical form. The peculiarity of this instrument is the introduction of a steel bar, running diagonally under the sounding board, whereby greater resistance was secured. Compass of six octaves and three notes from CC.

Length, 223 cm. Width, 124 to 30 cm. Depth, 31 cm. Height, 86 cm.
Signed—"Frenzel, in Linz, 1837."
(J. E. Ecker.)

1346. KLAVIERHARFE (Eng. *Clavi-harp;* Fr. *Clavi-harpe, Harpe à clavecin*) . . . . Germany

A lyre-shaped body surmounts a typical upright piano body. The action, operated by piano keys, plucks the strings producing the real harp tone. Compass, five octaves from F.

Length, 125 cm. Width, 38.2 cm. Height, 218 cm.
Signed—"Dietz."

Section D. Vibrating Columns of Air inclosed in Organ Pipes, actuated by Mechanically operated Bellows, and an indirectly-acting Key-board Mechanism.

When pipes, placed in a vertical position on a reservoir containing air under pressure, secured by mechanical means, were made to sound by the introduction of this air into the lower end of the pipes; when these pipes were arranged in a pre-determined logical sequence; and, finally, when the speech of the pipes could be controlled through the intervention of some mechanical device, the Organ came into being. These initial steps in the evolution of the instrument were taken long before the Christian Era.

The "slide," a flat strip of wood, in which a hole corresponding to the diameter of the "foot" (lower end) of the pipe was pierced, and running at right angles through a flat chamber above the air reservoir, was the earliest device employed. When the hole in the "slide" came directly under the pipe, the compressed air seeking a vent, rushed into it, causing it to "speak." In the second century B.C. Ctesibius, of Alexandria, devised keys, which, when pressed down by the fingers operated the "slides" by means of levers. This was the beginning of the key-board. When several rows of pipes were used, they were also controlled by means of slides running longitudinally and corresponding in structure to the earliest form. This device was used in the Roman "Hydraulos," or "Water Organ," which frequently had many rows of pipes. In this organ, water had no part in the production of the tone, but, by the application of a law of hydraulics, controlled the wind-pressure.

The logical result of the introduction of added rows of pipes, with contrasting quality and power, was an extension of the possibilities of the instrument by combining several distinct organs, each structurally complete, into one.

PLATE XVI.

CASE XIV. EAST SECTION. NOS. 1343 TO 1345 (LEFT TO RIGHT)

The key-boards were then placed above each other, that they might come under the control of the performer. The "draw-stops," the "outward and visible signs of an inward" mechanism, and which controlled the various rows of pipes, were arranged in rows, later in tiers, at either side, and appropriately grouped. One of these organs was operated by foot-pedals. The key-boards could be connected by devices known as "couplers."

As the mechanism was extended the difficulty of manipulating the keys led to the introduction of various methods of lightening the "touch." First came the pneumatic lever, applied to the "tracker" mechanism, then the "tubular pneumatic" action, to be followed by the more responsive electric action of our day.

In the train of the application of electricity and the consequent elimination of the complications of the old "tracker" system, came many unique extensions of mechanical appliances. Couplers without number; the development of "borrowed stops," by means of which the tonal resources of one manual might be controlled from others, thus extending their range of usefulness; and, finally, the substitution of keys ranged above the upper key-board (manual) for the "draw-knobs" at the side. Possibly one of the most practical innovations is the "Movable Console," which can be placed at any distance or situation desired, while, if necessary, several independent consoles may be installed. All these improvements seemed to be inevitable, but, while useful, involved no real departure from established principles.

The wind-chest invented by John T. Austin in 1895 was a radical innovation, and constitutes the only real revolutionary invention in decades. The wind-chest and bellows are one: the pipes stand on the top of what is practically a chamber, while the simple and effective action running underneath the top is easily accessible at all times.

1347. ORGANO DI LEGNO (Eng. *Positive organ;* Fr. *Positif;* Ger. *Positiv*). Seventeenth century . . . . Italy

Upright wooden case. Eighteen silvered "dummy" pipes in front. Three draw stops. Foot pedals attached to lowest octave of keys. Each register contains forty-five pipes, all of metal, with the exception of the twelve lowest pipes of the Stopped Diapason which are of wood. In addition to this "stop" the organ contains the Flute and Super-octave. The bellows are blown by means of a handle. Its tone is very sweet and soft, as the pipes have a small percentage of tin. By means of rods running through iron rings the instrument could be transported. Compass, from E to c‴.

The upper section, containing pipes, action, and key-board, is 164 cm. high, 82.8 cm. wide, and 74 cm. deep. The lower section, 75 cm. high, 96 cm. wide, and 71 cm. deep, contains the bellows and wind-trunks.

Section E. Vibrating Free Reeds, with Mechanically operated Bellows and Key-board Mechanism.

In the Melodeon, and the more modern Cabinet Organ, the "exhaust" principle—employed in the Chinese *sheng*—supplanted the direct action of the reeds, characteristic of the Harmonium. Very popular in the last century it has been relegated to the background by the ubiquitous pianoforte.

1348. MELODEON .... United States
Oblong case of rosewood and black walnut. Two foot levers, one operating the bellows, the other a swell shutter. One set of free reeds. It has a compass of five octaves, from F.
Length, 94 cm. Width, 58 cm. Depth, 24 cm. Height, 78 cm.
Signed—"Child and Bishop, Cleveland, Ohio."
(Mrs. S. T. Cook.)

1349. MELODEON. Middle nineteenth century .... United States
This instrument has one set of free reeds and a compass of four octaves. Length, 78 cm. Width, 47 cm. Depth, 15 cm. Height, 71 cm.
Signed—"Geo. A. Prince and Co., Buffalo, N. Y."

With the exception of the bowed-zither, it may be asserted with confidence that the instruments listed in Cases XIII and XIV have contributed more to the advancement of musical appreciation than those belonging to any of the preceding types. The stringed instruments legitimately played with a bow have made the orchestra possible. The repertoire of that puissant agency reveals the endless possibilities of creative musical art, while in the realm of chamber-music these instruments have aided in the establishment of some of the most intimate, refined, and satisfying composition-forms known to music. In several of the chamber-music forms, the pianoforte enters as a prominent artistic factor, and through it the key-board type comes into its own. But the last-named instrument fills a more important place in the home; it is, therefore, one of the most beneficent and potent instrumentalities in the development of real musical taste and knowledge. The organ, with its traditional religious associations, fully justifies its title "The King of Instruments," and, in certain respects, may be considered the noblest representative of the key-board class.

While it may be maintained that the improvements already made in key-board instruments predicate future progress in the realization of their possibilities, the same cannot be said of the legitimate bowed types. The earlier types are obsolete, and newer forms, like the *Viola alta* (Eng. *Ritter viola*), invented by Hermann Ritter in 1876, and having a fifth string (g″) have not entered into the equation. The violin type has maintained itself consistently, and may be considered perfect. The same holds with equal force in the case of the bow. Therefore, from the point of view of evolution, this type may claim superiority over all others.

CABINET, East Room (Case XV).

Miscellaneous Instruments and Accessories.

The instruments in this Case come under many classifications. They are all of great interest and in some instances of unusual significance.

1350. Ninfale (Eng. *Portative organ;* Fr. *Orgue portatif;* Ger. *Portativ*). Seventeenth century .... Italy
Three rows of pipes. Compass, one octave and four notes. Bellows blown by handle on left of case.
Height, 86 cm. Width, 30.4 cm. Depth, 30.4 cm.

1351. Barrel Organ .... England
The case contains one row of "stopped" wooden organ pipes. The pallets, governing the entrance of the wind into these pipes, are opened by a barrel on which steel pegs are so arranged as to play a tune when it is turned by a crank, on which a gear wheel engages an endless screw on the end of the barrel. The bellows (at the bottom of the case) are operated by the same crank.
Height, 41.4 cm. Width, 36.6 cm. Depth, 21 cm. (See No. 1395).

1352. Tromba. Brass .... Italy
Length, 75 cm. Diameter of bell, 16 cm.

1353. Tromba in A. Used in the opera "Messalina" .... Italy
Brass, with one semi-circular turn. Painted in bronze.
Length, 147 cm.; of model, 75 cm. Diameter of bell, 15 cm.
Signed—"G. Pelitti, Milano."

1354. Trombone a chiavi. Alto in E flat. Three pistons........ Italy
The body of decorated brass, is bent three times on itself and is of serpentine form. Used in the ballo "Amor."
Length of model, 83.5 cm. Diameter of bell, 20 cm.
Signed—"Pelitti, Milano."

1355. Roman Tibia impares. Metal, painted................ Italy
The *tibia impares* differs from the *tibia pares* (Case VI, No. 599) in that it has two tubes of unequal length, the shorter ending in a bell. Length of right tube (*tibia dextra*), 48 cm.; of left (*tibia sinistra*), 58 cm.
Reproduced by Pelitti, Milano.

1356. TROMBONE A CHIAVI. Bass in F. Three pistons. . . . . Italy
The tube of gaily-painted brass, after bending on itself twice, turns upward, ending in a decorated bell.
Made for use in the ballo "Re Arduino."
Length of model, 106 cm. Diameter of bell, 18 cm.
Signed—"Abbate a figlio."

1357. TROMBA in D. Copper. Of very early date . . . . Italy
The tube, bent on itself twice, ends in a small bell with boss.
Length of model, 79 cm. Diameter of bell, 12 cm.

1358. TROMBA in A. Brass, with copper finish. Incomplete. . . . . Italy

1359. TROMBA in A . . . . Italy
The tube doubles on itself twice, giving an unusually long vibrating length. Length of model, 121.6 cm. Diameter of bell, 14 cm.

1360. TROMBA in D. Brass . . . . Italy
The tube doubles on itself twice near the mouth-piece, and then extends towards the bell in two long crescent-shaped bends.
Length of model, 120 cm. Diameter of bell, 15 cm.
Signed—"Pelitti, Milano."

1361. TROMBA in D. Brass . . . . Italy
The tube has one short bend near mouth-piece, and a long circular bend near bell.
Length of model, 122 cm. Diameter of bell, 14.5 cm.
Signed—"Pelitti."

1362. TROMBA in A. Brass. Unusual form. . . . . Italy
The body, after making two long oval turns, followed by a much longer one of same shape, ends in a large bell, turned outwards.
Length of model, 123 cm. Width, 60 cm. Diameter of bell, 32 cm.

1363. TROMBONE A CLEFS. Bass in F. Six pistons. . . . . France
An incomplete specimen of form shown in Case VIII, No. 886.

1364. TROMBA in F. Brass. Eighteenth century . . . . Italy
The tube makes two long turns. Bell in form of a dragon's head.
Length, 139 cm.; of model, 70 cm. Diameter of bell, 12 cm.

1365. TROMBA in D. Brass . . . . Italy
The tube makes a flat oval turn, ending in a bell with boss.
Length of model, 64 cm. Diameter of bell, 26 cm.

1366. TROMBA. Alto in E flat. Brass . . . . Italy
The tube makes an oval turn and ends in a wide flaring bell.
Made for use in the ballo "Excelsior."
Length of model, 99 cm. Diameter of bell, 25.5 cm.
Signed—"G. Pelitti, Milano."

1366A. HORN (*Corno torto Michiganensis*). Tin. . . . . .United States
This modern representative of a type that might have been responsible for the fall of the walls of Jericho, were it in existence, was invented in 1875 and thrust upon the world under the euphonious designation "Duoterpsichoreanclogpedality." It figured extensively in "hornings" and the academico-sociological functions dear to students. It consists of a conical tube, 197 cm. long, and 20.4 cm. in diameter, bent on itself three times. Formerly it was fitted with a large beating-reed, but without it every demand made on a "noise-maker" can be easily satisfied.
"O salve Universitas Michiganensium."
(Irving K. Pond.)

1367. TROMBA. Alto in B flat. Brass. Unusual form. . . . . .Italy
This *tromba* resembles an instrument mentioned by Praetorius in his *Syntagma Musicum* (1618), shown on Plate XXXII, and called *chorus!* This designation was applied by mediaeval authorities with an apparent lack of discrimination, as it stood for a dulcimer, a bagpipe, a four-stringed cither, a trumpet marine, and the peculiar form of trumpet described by Praetorius.[1]
Length, 147 cm. Width, at middle section, 21 cm.
Signed—"G. Pelitti, Milano."

1368. TROMBA in E . . . . .Italy
The brass tube, painted lead color, with gilt bands, turns on itself closely three times and ends in a conical bell. It was used in the ballo "L'Astro degli Afgani."
Length, 318 cm.; of model, 79 cm. Diameter of bell, 15.8 cm.
Signed—"G. Pelitti, Milano."

1369. TROMBA. Brass . . . . .Italy
Length, 156.1 cm. Diameter of bell, 25.6 cm.

1370. SAXHORN. Contra-bass in E flat . . . . .United States
Brass. Four pump valves, the fourth transposing to BB. flat.
Length of model, 145.5 cm. Diameter of bell, 26.5 cm.
The desk placed in front belongs to No. 1166, Case XI.

1371. TROMBA in C. Brass. Of very early date. . . . . .Italy
The tube makes three turns: two very large and one small. The inside of the bell, which turns upwards, is gilded.
Length, 254 cm.; of model, 117 cm. Diameter of bell, 12 cm.

---

[1] Also shown by Virdung, p. 24.

1372. TRUMPET in D flat. Brass . . . . Italy
The conical tube of brass, painted black, makes three turns—two large, and one small. The bell turns abruptly upward and is gilded in the inside. Length of model, 99 cm.; vibrating length, 478 cm. Diameter of bell, 20 cm.
Signed—"G. Pelitti, Milano."*

1373. FOG-HORN (Fr. *Trompe;* Ital. *Corno da nebbia;* Ger. *Nebelhorn*). Tin . . . . Newfoundland
Length, 156 cm. Diameter of bell, 20 cm.

1373A. MOOSE CALL . . . . New Brunswick
This unsophisticated representative of the speaking-trumpet type was made by a Micmac Indian whose skill in reproducing the call of the cow-moose brought death to many a bull. It was also used by the donor, who was a mighty moose-hunter. It is made of bark and is 38 cm. in length, with a diameter at lower end of 6.7 cm.
(Frederick Talcott.)

1374. MUSICAL WEATHER-VANE . . . . Germany
The wind blowing into the open end sets twenty free reeds in vibration. Length, 45.6 cm. Diameter, 30.5 to 10.2 cm. (at waist).

1375. MELOPHONE. Bass. See Case VII, No. 742. . . . . France
Vertical form. Seventy-eight ivory "touches" control an equal number of free reeds. The bellows are operated by drawing the handle back and forth.

Length, 144 cm.; of body, 108 cm.; width, 36 to 11 cm.; depth, 30 to 10 cm.
Signed—"Jacquard, Paris."

The instruments from 1351 to 1375, inclusive, belong to Class III.

1376. ARPA. Twenty-six wire strings. Sixteenth century . . . . Italy
Height, 168 cm. Width, 97.2 cm.

1377. MACHETE. Circular body of wood. One hundred and six fine wire strings radiate from the center to pegs on rim. Played with a plectrum. Originally it was mounted on a standard which could not be used for lack of room. . . . . Madeira

Diameter, 64 cm. Depth, 23 cm.

1378. BIWA. Identical with No. 1207. Case XII . . . . Japan

---

* This maker must not be judged by his reproductions—mostly admirable—and the instruments of unusual form both in this Case, and those already noted under Nos. 904 to 930 (Case VIII) were made for a special purpose. They are all superior instruments of excellent tone-quality and are in no sense "freaks."

1379. CHENG. Usual size and structure .... China
(B-S.)

1380. MACHETE .... Madeira
Body in form of an aquatic bird. Ten pairs of wire strings. Tuning mechanism. Played with a plectrum.
Length, 121.6 cm.; of body, 62.5 cm.; width, 27.8 cm.; depth, 6.4.

1381. REBECA (Port. for Violin) .... Madeira
Nos. 1380-81 were placed on a large standard representing a tree covered with moss. It is not displayed for obvious reasons. Both are signed. "A. Da Costa, Funchal."
Length, 91.2 cm.; of body, 52.9 cm.; width, 21.6 cm.; depth, 6.4 cm.

1382. ZITHER. Body of wood, inlaid......................... Italy
Of the seven wire strings, four run over a fret-board, and three are free, as are the six gut strings. Two rosette sound-holes.
Called by the maker (possibly Franciolini) *Cetera Napoletana.*
Length, 68 cm. Width, 46 cm. Depth, 10 cm.

1383. LYRE. Metal body. Eight wire strings. Fourteenth century... Italy
Length, 46 cm. Width, 28 cm. Depth, 5 cm.

1384. COUCHED HARP. Pyramidal body of wood. Nine wire strings. The pitches are given on a strip at the base.......... United States
Height, 40 cm. Width, 10 to 7 cm. Depth, 4 cm.

1385. CONDUCTOR'S DESK. Brass. The face bears the following inscription, "To Professor A. A. Stanley, in token of their high esteem, by the University Choral Union, May 30, 1891."
Height, 147 to 165 cm. Surface dimensions of desk, 54 by 34 cm.
(Albert A. Stanley.)

1386. VIOLIN CASE.
Length, 133.7 cm. Width, 25.7 to 12.7 cm. Depth, 13 cm.

1387. DRUM MAJOR'S STAFF.
Length, 133.7 cm. Diameter of silver knob, 8 cm.

1388. "CECILIAN." Piano-forte player .... United States
In this instrument, which is quite representative of its type, we find a most ingenious and novel application of a principle never before so fully exploited. By means of mechanism operated by foot-pedals a cylinder carrying a strip of perforated paper is made to revolve at any speed desired. This strip as it unrolls hugs a box in which is a series of narrow channels corresponding to the perforations in the strip, and leading to "pneumatics," each of which controls a small hammer with which a key may be struck. When the holes in the

strip and in the box correspond, compressed air, furnished by bellows, also operated by the pedals, sets the pneumatic mechanism in operation. The vogue of such instruments is one of the most encouraging developments of the day, for they make possible an extended and intimate acquaintance with the best music.

Length, 112.2 cm. Height, 97.6 cm. Width, 36.8 cm.

Signed—"Farrand and Votey."

(James H. McDonald.)

1389. CHENG. Similar to No. 1379, but in deplorable condition...China

(B-S.)

1390. ORGAN MODEL. (Electric Action) ....United States

This model, with electric action of "Frieze Memorial Organ," when brought to Ann Arbor, was constructed and presented to the University by the makers of the organ, Farrand and Votey of Detroit. The action substituted for this by the Hutchins Co. of Boston, when the instrument (entirely renovated and substantially enlarged) was removed to its present position in 1913, is simpler. The following description may be of interest: The bellows (A), under which are the "feeders," (smaller bellows which force the wind into the larger) are operated by the handle (B). The air in the bellows, compressed by the iron weights (C), is forced through a conductor (D) into the air-chamber (E). Small suction bellows (F) are deflated when, by pressure on the key (G), an electric contact is made and the air rushes into the pipe (H) causing it to speak.

Length, 126 cm. Height, 154.5 cm. Depth, 40.7 cm.

An envelope (I) contains the specifications of the organ and such data referring to it as may be of interest to future generations.

1391. "SONATINA." Self-playing Concertina...............Germany

Hexagonal body. Expanding bellows. False "touches" on both sides. Discs, on which are raised points, are placed inside and operated by means of clockwork. The bellows are operated by the hands. Eleven of these discs are displayed.

Diameter, 29 cm. Length (inflated), 40 cm.; (deflated), 25 cm.

Signed—"Patentirt in allen Staaten, D. R. R., No. 86,324, Made in Saxony."

1392. "PIANO MELODICO" .... Germany

Case of ebonized wood resting on four legs. Under a housing, at the right end, a roller, turned by a crank, carries a strip of perforated cardboard over a set of projections. By a striking mechanism, such of the fifty-four strings, running under the top-board, as are desired, are made to sound.

Length, 86.4 cm. Width, 43.2 cm. Height, 81 cm.

1392A. Similar to No. 1392 but larger . . . . Germany

It rests on four very short turned legs. No name is given it and, like the preceding, it is not signed.

Length, 121 cm. Width, 52 cm. Height, 83 cm.

1393. "TECHNICON" . . . . Canada

An ingenious device for strengthening the fingers, invented in the 80's by J. Brotherhood, a Canadian.

1394. "CONCERT ROLLER ORGAN" . . . . United States

By a mechanism similar to that used in the music-box (Case III, No. 251), twenty free reeds are made to sound. The crank operates both the roller and the bellows.

Height, 30.4 cm. Width, 40 cm. Depth, 24.8 cm.

1395. DREHORGEL (Eng. *Barrel-organ;* Fr. *Orgue de barbarie;* Ital. *Organino a cilindro;* Span. *Organo de mano*) . . . . Germany

Three sets of metal pipes. Usual mechanism. Two extra rolls each for Nos. 1394 and 1395 are hung at the right.

Height, 76.2 cm. Width, 47.5 cm. Depth, 35.1 cm.

The French designation is a play on the name of Giovanni Barberi, of Modena (*c.* 1700), who was one of the first to manufacture the instrument.[2] Incidentally it is interesting to note that the first mechanical instrument was devised by Heron, of Alexandria, two centuries before Christ. After this date none were built until 1740,[3] but since then ample amends have been made for the lost opportunities of the intervening centuries.

1396. "DIGITORIUM." A finger strengthening device . . . . England

Signed—"Metzler and Co., 48 Marlborough St., London."

1397. SERINETTE. Tiny barrel-organ. Eighteenth century . . . . Germany

Compass of nine notes. Usual mechanism. Called "Serinette" because it was used by bird fanciers in teaching the finch (*serin*), and other birds, to sing.

The repertoire is as follows: *Lauterbacher; Suhe Tiroler bua; Man lebt verstohlen in Tag hinein; Ländler; Arie.*

Height, 18.5 cm. Width, 13.4 cm. Depth, 6.8 cm.

1398. "SOBLICK'S PATENT CLAVIATUR" . . . . Germany

This device is placed on the keys of a piano which are moved by striking the "touches," each of which originally bore a letter.

Length, 119 cm. Width, 14 cm. Thickness, 6 to 2.2 cm.

---

[2] Sachs, p. 284.
[3] Sachs, p. 256.

1399. STREET PIANO . . . . England
A piano action is set in operation by the roller-organ mechanism.
Length, 101 cm. Height, 135 cm. Depth, 53 to 43 cm.

1400. PORTMANTEAU, formerly belonging to Franz Liszt. It was taken with him on his last journey to Bayreuth, where he died, July 31, 1886.
(Mrs. M. B. Sheley.)

1401. BIWA. Miniature model . . . . Japan

1402. BANDURRIA. Small model . . . . Spain
Body of gourd with belly of wood. Six fine gut strings.

1403. CONDUCTOR'S BATON. Four varieties of wood from the Sandwich Islands. Two ivory ferules, the larger of which bears the name of the woods. On the gold mounting is inscribed "Presented to Professor A. A. Stanley, December 26, 1890."
(Albert A. Stanley.)

1404-5. BATONS. Ebony (1404), and ash (1405) . . . . United States
Length of 1403, 52 cm.; of 1404, 40 cm.; of 1405, 53 cm.

1406. STAFF RULING PEN . . . . Germany
A five pointed pen used in early days to rule the staff. Used by Ludwig Friederich Rominger (1792-1876). Cantor and Teacher in Waiblingen, Würtemberg, from 1825 to 1859.
(Miss Julia Rominger.)

1407-8-9-10. MODELS, of SAMISEN (Jap.); LIRA-CHITARRA (Ital.); MANDOLINE (Fr.); VIOLIN, a perfumery case (Holland).
These models are very small and measurements are unnecessary.

1411. UPRIGHT PIANO ACTION . . . . United States
By striking the key (A), through a delicately adjusted system of levers and hoppers (B.C.D.) the hammer (E) is brought in contact with the strings (F) with any gradation of power desired. At the same time the damper (G) is raised from the strings by H, returning to its original position on the release of the key.
Length, 55 cm. Height, 57.6 cm. Width, 12 cm.

1412. UPRIGHT PIANO ACTION . . . . United States
Length, 47 cm. Height, 52 cm. Depth, 8.9 cm.
(Nos. 1411 and 1412 were donated by the Ann Arbor Music Co.)

1413. GRAND PIANOFORTE ACTION ....United States
The type of action is more delicately adjusted than the preceding. This is due to the action of the "escapment" (A) which engages the roller (B) on the bottom of hammer lever. It makes possible more frequent repetitions of the blow.
Length, 79 cm. Height, 26.4 cm. Width, 10.4 cm.
(Steinway and Sons.)

1414. STRINGING DEVICE ....United States
This form of stringing, devised by Mason and Hamlin, while theoretically admirable, was found to be undesirable in practice.

1415. METRONOME .... Germany
The Metronome is an instrument consisting of a pendulum, actuated by clock work, and a scale indicating the number of its oscillations per minute. An infallible indication of a given tempo is thus secured. J. N. Maelzel secured a patent for this device in 1816, but, as was demonstrated by the Dutch Academy of Science, the idea originated with one Winkel of Amsterdam, with whom Maelzel was at one time intimately acquainted.

1416. "ARISTON" .... Germany
Through the aid of a circular perforated cardboard disc, and bellows operated by a crank, the twenty-four free reeds enclosed in the body of the instrument may be made to sound.
Width, 37.7 cm. Height, 32.5 cm.

1417. VICTROLA .... United States
No country has brought the so-called "talking-machine" so near perfection as our own. In the "Victrola" (which illustrates the fundamental principles of the type) a delicately adjusted mechanism, controlled by clock work, causes a fine needle to traverse a series of circular lines which represent vibrations produced by the speaking or singing voice, an instrument, (or instruments) or a combination, of these tone-producing media. By the aid of a responsive membrane, and suitably adjusted resonators, the original vibrations are reproduced. There are two forms, the one here represented, in which a horn serves to reinforce the tone; the other, with no horn, the sound coming through the opening under the revolving plate carrying the disc.
Width of body, 22.8 cm. Height, 15.2 cm. Length of horn, 58 cm. Diameter of bell, 32 cm.
Signed—"Victor Talking Machine Co."

1418. "SCHOENHUT'S DOOR-HARP" ....United States
Hung on a door. Through the falling of the suspended balls on the strings it serves to welcome the approaching, and speed the parting guest. Of no musical value. Height, 58 cm. Width, 46 cm.

CASE XVI

Construction Case (including Accessories)

1419. Organ Pipe (dismantled). Wood .... Italy
This pipe, "Bourdon" (c) is simpler in structure than No. 752, Case VII, which is also dismantled to illustrate the process of tone-production. A, B, C, and D show the principal parts.
Length, 93 cm. Vibrating length, 158 cm. Diameter, 8 by 9 cm.

1420. Roller-board. Wood and iron .... United States
This device is now looked upon as a relic of barbarism, but for centuries it did its duty of transferring the action of the keys to the valves under the pipes. In large organs the roller-boards were very complicated and the resulting friction greatly increased the difficulty of performance. The rollers were connected by thin strips of wood called "trackers." In this example, marked G.R.R., No. 379, the rollers are indicated by A, and the trackers by B.
Length, 58 cm.; of rollers, 19 to 50 cm. Height, 46 cm.
(August Möller.)

1421. Organ Pipe.. Metal .... United States
The pitch of this "Open Diapason" pipe is c″.
Length, 50 cm. Vibrating length, 24 cm. Diameter, 8 cm.

1422. Organ Pipe. Metal .... United States
The pitch of this "Open Diapason" is c′.
Length, 84.2 cm.; vibrating length, 63.3 cm. Diameter, 8.6 cm.

1423. Austin Wind Chest .... United States
This illustration of the wind chest of the large organ in City Hall, Portland, Me., shows the interior construction, and enforces the originality and practicability of this invention.

1424. Console of Portland Organ .... United States
It will be seen that the substitution of keys for draw-stops makes a more compact console than the older type. Moreover, through the use of the electric action the location of the console is limited only by the length of the connecting cable.

1425. Elevation of a Complete Organ .... United States
In this illustration, A is the Key-desk; B, the Wind-chest; C, the Exterior of Chest; D, the Door; E, the Action.
(These illustrations are taken from the Catalogue of the Austin Company which is placed in Case XV. for reference.)

1426. THREE DRAW-STOPS ....United States
These specimens are taken from the "Frieze Memorial Organ," before its reconstruction. Their lengths, when compared with those in the present instrument (10 cm.), will prove the superior advantages of the modern system. Frequently in older organs, the rods were *double the length* of the above.
A. "Doppel Floete," 8 ft. pitch, Gr. Length, 84 cm.
B. "Bourdon," 16 ft. pitch, Sw. The split knob was an ingenious device by means of which the lowest octave could serve as a pedal stop. Length, 84 cm.
C. "Aeoline," 8 ft. pitch, Sw. Length, 84 cm.

1427. REED, SOCKET, and FOOT. Metal ....United States
The brass beating-reed is placed inside the "foot" and the combination is placed on the "socket." A wire tuning device pressing against the reed determines its vibrating length.
Length, of foot, 18 cm.; of reed, 3.2 cm. Diameter of foot, 3 cm.; of reed, 7 mm.

1428. STRUCTURAL PARTS OF ORGAN ACTION ....United States
Armature, cable, pneumatic bellows.
(Nos. 1427 and 1428 presented by Earle V. Moore.)

1429. PARTS OF AUSTIN ELECTRIC ACTION ....United States
The delicacy of these parts illustrates a notable characteristic of this action. They are not arranged in sequence.
(Austin Organ Company.)

1430. DISMANTLED VIOLIN. Usual size ....Germany
Of the 57 separate pieces of wood and the 13 movable fittings, the most important are indicated by letters as follows: (A) Belly—(B) Bass-bar—(C) Back—(D) Rim, showing outline—(E, F, G, H) Corner blocks—(I) Sound-post—(J) Bridge—(K) Finger-board, running over neck, which ends in Scroll (L) and Peg-box (M) from which the strings run to Tail-piece (N).

Three sorts of wood are used; maple for back, neck, ribs, and bridge; pine for belly, bass-bar, block, linings, and sound-post; ebony for finger-board, nuts, screws, tail-piece, and button. The strings and loop are the only parts not of wood.

1431. BLOCK, representing a part of the table from which No. 1284, Case XIII, was constructed.

1432. MUTES. RESIN. Etc.
In front, arranged in and about the cover of the case in which No. 714, Case VII, was placed, are tuning-pins and various parts of Oriental and other extra-European instruments.

1433. Bows, of various sizes.

1434. Strings, of various sizes.

1435. Cup Mouth-pieces.
A, *Corno;* B, Cornet; C, Section of B type; D, French Horn; E, F, G, Trumpet; H, Trombone; I, J, Baritone; K, Tuba; L, Contra bass Tuba. Five music-holders, or racks, are placed under this exhibit.
(Carl Fischer, Importer, N. Y.)

1436. Structural Parts of Organ Action.

1437. French Horn Crooks.

1438. Box Valve. 1830. Two pistons .... United States
This valve consists of a tube sliding within another. A hole in the inner tube allows free passage of the air, which, when the piston is pressed down, is directed to a crook which lengthens the vibrating length. Introduced by Graves and Co., of Boston.

1439. Box Valve. 1875. Three pistons............... United States
An application of the same principle displayed in No. 1438 is seen in this mechanism which was introduced by B. F. Quinby, of Boston.

1440. Cornet Mute. Brass, nickel-plated.
Introduced into the bell it modifies the tone.

1441. Cross-section of Piston Valves. Modern .... France
This beautiful model was constructed by Besson, of Paris, to illustrate the action of the piston valve. In this connection it may be stated that the action of valves frequently results in impurity of intonation, a defect remedied by the "Enharmonic Valve," which is a product of the Besson establishment.

1442. Structural Parts of Brass Instruments.
These parts are displayed on the back of the Case.

1443. Rotary Valve. Three valves .... United States
In this form, devised by J. S. Johnson, the defects of the ordinary rotary valve are corrected. When the flat key is pressed down, a connecting arm causes a tube, in which are openings, so to rotate that the air can pass into a crook which is a part of the body of the instrument. A spring brings the key back into its proper position (closed) when the finger is lifted.

1444. Bell-section, and part of the tube formed from such a sheet of brass as is shown in No. 1445.

1445. PLATE. Brass .... United States

This is the first step in construction. The flat sheet is formed into a conical tube, after which the tube is filled with molten lead and gradually bent into its proper form. The lead is then melted out, the mouth-piece section and rim of bell are added, and the instrument is complete, unless valves are necessary.

Length of plate, 130 cm. Width at mouth-piece, 2.6 cm.; at bell, 27.6 cm.; at three equi-distant points from bell, 5.6, 4, 3.4 cm. Thickness, 1 mm.

The complete instrument is the Standard Service Bugle, in B flat, used in the United States Army.

(Nos. 1438-39-43-44 and 45 were presented by "The House of York.")

1446. FRENCH HORN CROOKS.

1447. CLAVICHORD ACTION (Model).

This example of the *gebunden* system shows A, Keys; B, Tangent; C, Strings; D, Damper. C and C sharp are obtained from one pair of strings, D and D sharp from another pair, and E from still another. This is the simplest form of action ever devised, and makes possible an intimate relation between the performer and the tone-producing media denied to other forms.

1448. HARPSICHORD ACTION (Model).

A, is the Key; B, the Jacks; C, the Strings.

This is an indirect type, as a mechanism intervenes between the key and the strings.

(Nos. 1444 and 1445 were constructed and presented by Mr. F. M. Watson.)

1449. GUITAR (dismantled).

The top has been removed to show the construction of the body of the instrument which is of usual size and stringing.

(Grinnell Brothers.)

1450. MANDOLINE (dismantled).

The vaulted form is clearly apparent. Usual size and stringing.

(Grinnell Brothers.)

1451. ORGAN KEY-BOARD.

This is a Solo and Echo Organ Key-board, and is of interest in that it was taken from the old key-desk of the "Frieze Memorial Organ."

The couplers are operated by tablets on name-board, while combinations can be set on the pistons, under the keys. The tablets just over the keys refer to combination pedals above the pedal keyboard. One of these double-acting pedals switches from Solo organ to Echo. Length, 92 cm. Depth, 26 cm. Height, 20 cm.

The Couplers operated by the Tablets are: Great to Pedal, Swell to Pedal, Choir to Pedal, Solo to Pedal, Swell to Great, Choir to Great, Solo to Great, Solo to Swell, Swell to Choir, Choir to Great Sub-Octave, Swell to Great, Super-Octave, Solo to Great, Super-Octave, Solo Super-Octave.

Chart exhibiting interesting details of Japanese instruments:

1452. SHAKU-HACHI (No. 540). Fingerings. Through these a chromatic series from d′ to d″ is obtained.[1]

1453. RYU-TEKI (*Ryu*—dragon, *teki*—flute). Fingerings. To obtain the following tones—d‴, d sharp‴, e‴, f sharp‴, g‴, a‴, b‴, c⁗, c sharp⁗. (No. 533).[2]

1454. HICKI-RIKI. Fingerings through which the diatonic scale from g″ to A″ is obtained. (No. 662).[3]

1455. TUNINGS OF THE JAPANESE KOTO (No. 992).[4]

1. *Hirajöshi;* 2. *Akébono;* 3. *Kumoi;* 4. *Sakura;* 5. *Han-kumoi;* 6. *Iwato;* 7. *Go-sagari Roku-agari.* Special tunings: 8. *Kurama-Jishi;* 9. *Hirajöshi.*

No. 1 has four forms; No. 8 is changed to No. 1 by lowering the 6th and 11th strings a semi-tone. In No. 9 the 4th and 9th strings are raised a semi-tone from No. 1. Nos. 1, 3, and 6 are the tunings most frequently used.

1456. TUNINGS OF THE CHINESE SONO-KOTO (No. 997).[5]

1. *Hyojo;* 2. *Taisiki;* 3. *Banshiki;* 4. Another form; 5. *O'shiki;* 6. *Suijo;* 7. *Ichiotsu;* 8. Another form; 9. *Sojo;* 10. Another form.

1457. TUNINGS OF THE BUGAKU-BIWA (No. 1257).[6]

Four tones of Nos. 1, 3, 5, 6, 7, and 9 of the preceding tunings.

1457A. ORIENTAL SCALES.

1. *Arabian;* 2. *Hindoo;* 3. *Chinese;* 3. *Japanese.*

The following do not strictly come within the most liberal definition of a musical collection, but, as they are of interest and came with the instruments, they will be listed as follows:

In East Room.

1458. EGYPTIAN MUSICIANS.

Taken from a wall-painting on an Egyptian tomb. The instruments in use at the time are graphically represented.

---

[1] Mahillon, *Cat.* II, p. 84.
[2] Mahillon, *Cat.* II, p. 85.
[3] Mahillon, *Cat.* II, p. 85.
[4, 5, 6] Capt. Day, pp. 92, 93.

1459. OLD ITALIAN PRINT. Inscribed—"Compagni a di Borgognoni che Studian Musica. Essiste nel Palazzo della Ju, Sig. Marcha Cassandra Cerretani in Firenze—No. 18, Carravagio-pin. Geo. Batta Cocchi 1784."

1460. "BOHEMIA." A Group of Musical Instruments.
In Foyer.

1461. PORTRAIT OF FREDERICK STEARNS.
Over East Door.

1462. OLD ITALIAN PRINT. Inscribed—"102 grandezza del vero, 3, 4, 5 meta del vero. C. Weidenmuller lit. Fr. Niccoline dir. Lit. Richter and C in Napole." Stamped—"A. Niccolini, Pompeii, Editore."
The following instruments are represented: 1, Roman Cymbals; 2, Reed instrument; 3, Roman Flutes; 4, Egyptian Sistrum.
Over Case I.

1463. MISSAL .... Spain
This beautifully illuminated missal came from a cathedral in Santiago, Spain. Its date cannot be fully determined, but is not earlier than the fifteenth century.

1464. BUST OF FREDERICK STEARNS.
Over middle door, West side of Foyer.

The total number of exhibits—including new accessions which, in order to preserve the sequence in classification have necessitated the addition of letters to certain numbers, and making the deductions noted under No. 54, Case I—is 1487, divided as follows:—Class I, 250; Class II, 152; Class III, 549; Class IV, 386; Class V, 22; Mechanical Instruments, 34; Accessories,

Of the above total, 1358 represent Mr. Stearns' contribution; 35 are from the Beal-Steere Collection, while 94 were donated by the individuals noted in List of Donors, in Appendix.

LATEST ACCESSIONS.

These instruments were received too late to appear under the proper rubrics, but are included in the tabulation.

1344A. GRAND PIANOFORTE. *Circa* 1800 ....England

The body, of unpolished mahogany, is decorated with brass inlay, incised lines in black, ornate fastening devices of bronze, and rests on four spindle legs. The action is the early English type, developed by Americus Backers and the Broadwoods from the Cristofori-Silbermann model. The sound-board has a large F-hole in the widest section. The left pedal, of wood, shifts the key-board: the right is divided into two sections, the left raising the dampers of the lower octaves, the right those of the upper, while pressing both sections affects all the dampers. Bi-cord stringing with the exception of the bass-strings, which are wound, is used. Compass of six octaves and one note from FF. The name-board carries a plate with the following inscription: "Presented by S. Olin Johnson in memory of his wife, Lilla Sturtevant Johnson, 1918." Length, of straight-side, 219 cm.; of curved (including end), 276 cm. Width, 49 to 112 cm. Depth of body, 32 cm. Height, 88 cm.

Signed—"John Broadwood and Sons, Makers to his Majesty and the Princesses, Great Poultney Street, Golden Square, London."

(S. Olin Johnson.)

For the present this will take the place of No. 1342.

251A. MUSIC-BOX .... Switzerland

The case, of walnut, with top and front beautifully inlaid, is 67 cm. long, 39 cm. wide, and 32 cm. high. In addition to the usual mechanism and tone-producing media, 16 reeds and 6 gongs are also operated by the cylinder. The repertoire of 8 pieces includes selections from operas, one folk-song, and a march. Like all such combinations, this instrument is more of a curiosity than a real contribution. It is placed for the present in Case XIV.

(Albert A. Stanley.)

BIBLIOGRAPHY.

In this list of works relating to musical instruments and their uses, to be found in the Library of the University of Michigan, only the most important monographs, and—with the exception of a few distinctly valuable contributions—no reprints, are included. In series, such as the Hakluyt Society's publications, reports of museums, files of the journals of learned societies, etc., it has been found impossible to specify single numbers, as such a procedure would extend the list beyond reasonable limits. For the same reason books of travel have been excluded, although, in many instances they are valuable sources of information.*

Works of special assistance to the general reader are designated by an asterisk.

AALST, J. A. van.
Chinese music, Shanghai, 1884.

ABRAHAM, OTTO, and HORNBOSTEL, ERICH M. von.
Studien uber das tonsystem und die musik der Japaner.
Sammelbände der internationalen musikgesellschaft. Jahrgang IV. Hf. 2, p. 302, ff. Leipzig, 1903.

ADLER, CYRUS.
The shofar, its origin and use.
U. S. National Museum. Proceedings. Washington, 1893.

AGRICOLA, MARTIN.
Musica instrumentalis deudsch. Wittenberg, 1528; 1545.
Reprint, Leipzig, 1896.

AMBROS, AUGUST WILHELM.
Geschichte der musik. 5 vols. Leipzig, 1887.

AMERICAN anthropologist. Washington, 1888-1914.

AMERICAN folk-lore society. Journal.
Boston, 1888-1915.

AMIOT, JOSEPH MARIE.
De la musique des Chinois. Paris, 1780.

***ANDREWS, GEORGE WHITFIELD.**
American history and encyclopedia of music. Vol. III, New York, 1910.
This volume contains an article on the evolution of the orchestra, by Frederick Stock.

ANKERMANN, DR.
Die afrikanischen musikinstrumente. Berlin, 1901.

ANTHROPOLOGICAL society of Great Britain and Ireland. Journal. London, 1872-1913.

---

* A special subject card-catalogue covering publications, reprints, and books of travel, is approaching completion, and will make this important literature available.

ARBEAU, THOINOT.
See Tabouret, Jehan.

ARMSTRONG, ROBERT BURNS.
The Irish and Highland harps. Edinburgh, 1894.

***AUDSLEY, GEORGE ASHDOWN.**
Art of organ building, 2 vols. New York, 1905.
——— Organ of the twentieth century. New York, 1918.

***BAKER, THEODORE.**
Biographical dictionary of musicians. New York, 1900.
——— Ueber die musik der nordamerikanischen wilden. Leipzig, 1882.

BALFOUR, HENRY.
The natural history of the musical bow. Oxford, 1899.

BAUMEISTER, KARL AUGUST.
Denkmäler des classichen alterthums. Leipzig, 1885-1888.

BERICHT über den dritten kongress der internationalen musikgesellschaft, Wien, 25. bis 29, Mai, 1909. Wien, 1909.

BERLIOZ, HECTOR.
A treatise on modern instrumentation. London, 1858.
——— and **STRAUSS, RICHARD.**
Instrumentationslehre von Hector Berlioz, ergänzt und revidiert von Richard Strauss. 2 Theile. Leipzig, 1905.

BERTHOLD, THEODORE J. und **FUERSTENAU, MORITZ, M.**
Die fabrikation musikalischer instrumente. Leipzig, 1876.

BESSONI, JACOBI. (Besson, Jacques.)
Theatrvm instrvmento- || rvm et machi- || narum Iacobi Bessoni || Delphinaris, mathe || matici ingeniosissimi, || cum Francisci Beroaldi || figurarum declaratione demonstratina, || necnon vbique ne- || cessariis ac vitilissimis additionibus nun- || quam hactenus editis auctum atque il- || lustratum; || per Ivlivm Paschalem nobi- || lem Messanensem. || Lvgdvni || apud Barth. Vincent. || Cum priuilegio regis. || 1582.

Fig. XXIX shows a bowed instrument with frets and six wire strings. "Nova organi musici forma, cvivs fides metallicæ digitis et plectro pulsatæ concentvm edvnt varivm, et ivcvmvm, modis temperatvm paribvs, qvibvs lyræ et bvccinæ soni qvodammodo refervntvr."

BIANCHINI, FRANCESCO.
Francisci Blanchini Veronensis.... De tribus generibus instrumentorum veterum organicæ. Roma, 1742.

***BIE, OSCAR.**
History of the pianoforte. London, 1899.

BIERDIMPFLE, K. A.
Die sammlung der musikinstrumente des baireschen nationalmuseums. München, 1883.

BONANNI, FILLIPO.
Gabinetto armonico piano d'instrumenti sonori indicati offerti al Santore David. Roma, 1723.

ROSANQUET, ROBERT HOLFORD MACDOWELL.
Temperament. London, 1876.

BROWN, MRS. JOHN CROSBY.
Catalogues of the Crosby-Brown collection. Nos. I., II., III., IV. New York, 1902-1903.
Introductions and explanatory notes by F. W. Galpin and A. J. Hipkins.
——— and **WILLIAM ADAMS BROWN.**
*Musical instruments and their homes. New York, 1888.

BUCHER, KARL.
Arbeit und rhythmus. Leipzig, 1899.

BUREAU of American ethnology. Publications.
Washington, 1880-1914.

BURNEY, CHARLES.
A general history of music. 4 vols. London, 1776.

CATALOGUE of the loan exhibition of the Worshipful Company of Musicians, Fishmonger's Hall. London, 1904.
Introduction by A. J. Hipkins.

CATALOGUE of Lucknow exhibition (1885). Lucknow, 1885.

***CHAPPELL, WILLIAM**
The history of music. Vol. I. London, 1874.

CHICKERING & SONS.
Catalogue of the historical musical exhibition, Horticultural Hall. Boston, 1902.

CHOQUET, GUSTAVE.
Catalogue raisonné des instruments de cette collection. (2 editions.) Paris, 1875-1884.

CHRISTIANOWITSCH, ALEXANDRE.
Esquisse historique de la musique arabe. Cologne, 1863.

CLARKE, WILLIAM HORATIO.
Structure of the pipe organ. Boston, 1877.

COERNE, LOUIS ADOLPHE.
The evolution of modern orchestration. New York, 1908.

COMETTANT, OSCAR.
La musique, les musiciens et les instruments de musique. Paris, 1869.
——— Musique et musicians. Paris, 1862.

DAREMBERG, CH. ET SAGLIO, EDM.
Dictionnaire des antiquités grecques et romaines. Paris, 1887.

DAVISON, PETER.
The violin. London, 1881.

***DAY, CAPT. C. R.**
Musical instruments in the Royal Military Exhibition. London, 1891.
——— The music and musical instruments of Southern India and the Deccan. London, 1891.

***DENSMORE, FRANCES.**
Chippewa music. 2 vols. Washington, 1910-1913.
American Bureau of Ethnology.

Die **DEUTSCHE** instrumentenbauzeitung. Berlin.

DOMMER, ARRAY von.
Musikalisches lexicon. Heidelberg, 1865.

DUBOURG, GEORGE.
The violin. London, 1878.

EDGE-PARTINGTON, JAMES, and HEAPE.
Ethnological charts of the Pacific islands. Series I, II, and III. Manchester, 1888, 1895.

EICHBORN, HERMANN.
Die trompete in alter und neuer zeit. Leipzig, 1881.
——— Das alte clarinblasen auf trompeten. Leipzig, 1894.
——— Die dämpfung beim horn. Leipzig, 1897.

ELLIS, ALEXANDER JOHN.
Musical scales of various nations.
Jour. Royal Society of Arts, 1884-5. London, 1885.
——— See Helmholtz.

***ELSON, ARTHUR.**
Orchestral instruments and their use. Boston, 1902-1903.

ENGEL, CARL.
Catalogue of the special exhibition of ancient musical instruments, South Kensington Museum, London, 1872.
——— Descriptive catalogue of the musical instruments in the South Kensington Museum. London, 1874.
——— *Musical instruments. London, 1875.
——— *The music of the most ancient nations. London, 1864.
——— *The violin family. London, 1883.
——— Myths and facts. 2 vols. London, 1876.

FACH-KATALOG der musikhistorischen abtheilung von Deutschland und Oesterreich-Ungarn, internationale austellung für musik und theaterwesen. Wien, 1892.

FETIS, FRANCOIS JOSEPH.
Anthony Stradivari. London, 1864.
——— Biographie universelle des musiciens. 8 vols. Paris, 1877.
——— Supplément et complément, Arthur Pougin, Ed. 2 vols. Paris, 1878.
——— Histoire de la musique. 5 vols. Paris, 1869.

FLEISCHER, OSKAR.
Führer durch die königliche sammlung alter musikinstrumente. Berlin, 1898.

FLEMING, JAMES M.
Old violins and their makers. London.

FORKEL, JOHANN NICOLAUS.
Allgemeine geschichte der musik. 2 vols. Leipzig, 1788-1801.

***FORSYTH, CECIL.**
Orchestration. London, 1914.

FREEMAN, JAY C.
Historical sketches of the violin and its master makers. Chicago, 1900.
——— Rare old violins. 4 vols. Chicago, 1890, 1896. 1900, 1901.
——— *The Hawley collection of violins. Chicago, 1904.
Preface by Theodore Thomas.

FUEHRER durch die sammlungen des museums des königreiches Böhmen, in Prag. Prag, 1897.

FUEHRER durch das museum für völkerkunde. Berlin, 1898.

FULLER-MAITLAND, J. A.
——— See Grove.

***GALPIN, REV. FRANCES W.**
Aztec influence on American Indian instruments.
Sammelbände der internationalen musikgesellschaft. Jahrgang IV. Heft 4.
——— Notes on a Roman hydraulos.
Reliquary. London, 1904.
——— Old English instruments of music. London, 1910.
——— The origin of the Clarsech or Irish harp.
Report of the fourth congress of the international musical society.
——— The whistles and reed instruments of the Indians of the N. W. coast of North America.
Musical association. Proceedings. London, 1903.
——— See Brown.

GEVAERT, FRANCOIS AUGUSTE.
Nouveau traité d' instrumentation. Paris-Bruxelles, 1885.

GROSSMANN, MAX.
Verbessert das alter und vieles spielen wirklich den ton und die aussprache der geige? Berlin, 1907.

***GROVE, GEORGE.**
Dictionary of music and musicians. 4 vols. London, 1880-1890.
Second edition, J. A. Fuller-Maitland, Ed. 5 vols. London, 1904-1910.

GUNN, JOHN.
An historical enquiry respecting the Highland harp. Edinburgh, 1807.

HAKLUYT SOCIETY. Publications. London, 1847-1915.

HAMMERICK, ANGUS.
Das musikhistoriche museum zu Kopenhagen. Beschreibender katalog. Kopenhagen, 1911.

***HART, GEORGE.**
The violin, its famous makers and their imitators. London, 1887.
——— The violin and its music. London, 1881.

HAWKINS, JOHN.
History of music. 5 vols. London, 1776.
Edition of 1875, 2 vols.
Its chief value lies in the numerous excerpts (translations) from early works.

HELMHOLTZ, HERMANN.
The sensations of tone as a physiological basis for the theory of music (translation by Alexander J. Ellis). London, 1875.

***HENDERSON, WILLIAM JAMES.**
The orchestra and orchestral music. New York, 1899.

HERON-ALLEN, EDWARD.
De fidiculis bibliographia. 2 vols.

HILL, ARTHUR GEORGE.
The organ cases and organs of the middle ages and the renaissance. London, 1883.

HIPKINS, ALFRED JAMES.
Guide to loan collection of musical instruments. London, 1885.
——— History of the pianoforte. London, 1896.
——— Musical instruments. Edinburgh, 1888.
——— International inventions exhibition, 1885.
——— Pianofortes, John Broadwood and Sons, London, 1885.
——— See Brown.

HOPKINS, EDWARD JOHN, and RIMBAULT, EDWARD FRANCIS.
The organ. London, 1865.

HORNBOSTEL, ERICH M. von.
Phonographierte tunesische melodien.
Sammelbände der internationalen musikgesellschaft. Hft. 1, p. 1, ff. Leipzig, 1906.

HOTCHKISS, JUSTUS S.
Bells. New Haven, 1889.

HOWARD, ALBERT ANDREW.
The aulos, or tibia. Boston, 1893.
——— The mouth-piece of the aulos. Boston, 1899.
Both articles are in the Harvard studies in classical philology.

INTERNATIONAL MUSICAL SOCIETY. (Quarterly and monthly.)
Leipzig, 1899-1914.

JAN. KARL van.
Die griechischen saiteninstrumente. Leipzig, 1882.

JONES, SIR WILLIAM.
On the musical modes of the Hindoos.
Complete works, Vol. I. London, 1799.

KAPPEY, J. A.
Military music. London.

KASTNER, GEORGES.
Les danses des morts. Paris, 1852.
——— Manual général de musique militaire. Paris, 1848.

KIESEWETTER, RAFAEL GEORG.
Die musik der Araber. Leipzig, 1842.

KINKELDY, OTTO.
Orgel und klavier. Leipzig, 1910.

KIRCHER, ANASTHASIUS.
Musurgia universalis, sive Ars magna consoni et dissoni in X libro digesta. Roma, 1650.

KNOSP, GASTON.
Ueber Annamitischemusik.
Sammelbände der internationalen musikgesellschaft. J'h'g VIII.

KOERTE, OSWALD.
Laute und lautenmusik bis zur mitte des 16 jahrhunderts. Leipzig, 1901.

KRAUSE, A.
Catalogue des instruments de musique du musée Kraus à Florence. Florence, 1878.
——— La musique au Japon. Florence, 1880.
——— The one-key-boarded clavicytherium of the Kraus collection in Florence. Florence, 1910.

***KREHBIEL, HENRY EDWARD.**
The pianoforte and its music. New York, 1911.

LA BORDE, JEAN BENJAMIN de.
Essai sur la musique ancienne et moderne. 4 vols. Paris, 1780.

LAHEE, HENRY CHARLES.
The organ and its structure. Boston, 1910.

LANE, EDWARD WILLIAM.
The manners and customs of the modern Egyptians. 2 vols. London, 1871.

LEICHENTRITT, HUGO.
Was lehren uns die bildwerke des 14-17 jahrhunderts über die instrumentalmusik ihrer zeit?
Sammelbände der internationalen musikgesellschaft. Jhg. VII. Hft. 3, p. 315, ff. Leipzig, 1906.

LOCHER, CARL.
Organ stops. London, 1888.

LUTHERIE. L'encyclopédie des arts et metiers. Vero . . ., 1750.

LYND, WILLIAM.
A popular account of ancient musical instruments. (Galpin collection.) London, 1897.

***MACLEAN, CHARLES.**
Bowbells.
Quarterly magazine, international musical society. Year VII.
——— The principle of the hydraulic organ.
Ibid, year VI. Part 2.
——— *The zither (Bavarian Highlands).
Monthly magazine, international musical society. Year I. Part 11-12, p. 341. Leipzig, 1909.

MAHILLON, VICTOR CHARLES.
Catalogue desscriptif et analytique du musée instrumental du conservatoire royal de musique de Bruxelles. 4 tom. Gand, 1893-1896-1900-1912.

MEAD, CHARLES WILLIAM.
The musical instruments of the Incas.
American museum of natural history. Journal. New York, 1903.

MILLER, DAYTON CLARENCE.
The science of musical sounds. New York, 1916.

MORRIS, FRANCES.
Catalogue of the Crosby-Brown Collection, N. S., Vol. II. (Oceanica and America) New York, 1914.

MOULE, A. C.
Chinese music. Journal of the North-China Branch of the Royal Asiatic Society, Shanghai, 1904.
This has been ordered but is not yet in the Library; it has, however, been thoroughly consulted.

MUSICAL association. Proceedings. London, 1874-1917.

MUSICAL quarterly, (O. G. Sonneck, Ed.) New York, 1915-1917.

MUSICAL times. London, 1899-1907.

NAUMANN, EMIL.
The history of music. London.

NEUE zeitschrift für musik. Leipzig, 1888-1915.

OTTO, JACOB AUGUSTUS.
Structure and preservation of the violin. London, 1875.

PANUM, HORTENSE.
Harfe und lyra im alten nord-europa.
Sammelbände der internationalen musikgesellschaft. Jahrgang VII

PARES, G.
Traité d'instrumentation (Musique militaire) 2 vols.

PARRY, C., HUBERT H.
The art of music. New York, 1893.

PELLISOV, C. F., pseud.
See Schafhauetl, Carl Emil von.

PIERRE, CONSTANT.
Les facteurs d'instruments de musique. Paris, 1892.

***PIGGOTT, J. T.**
The music and musical instruments of Japan. London, 1893.

PILLAUT, LEON.
Le musée du Conservatoire National de Musique. Supplément au catalogue de 1884. Paris, 1894.

PHIPSON, T. L.
Celebrated violinists. London, 1887.

PLATT, E A. DU.
Catalogue of first musical exhibition at the Royal Aquarium. London, 1879.

POLAK, A. J.
Die harmonisierung indischer, türkischer und japanischer melodien. Leipzig, 1905.

PORTMAN.
Andamese music. Jour. Asiatic Soc., N. S., XX, 1888.

POUGIN, ARTHUR.
See Fétis.

PRAETORIUS, MICHAEL.
Syntagma musicum. Wolbenbüttel, 1618. Reprint. Berlin, 1884.

***PRATT, WALDO SELDEN.**
The history of music. New York, 1907.

PROUT, EBENEZER.
Instrumentation. London.
———— The orchestra. London, 1897.

PYNNE, J. KENDRICK.
Catalogue of musical instruments (principally the history of the pianoforte). Manchester, England, 1888.

RAGSTER, OLGA.
Chats on violins. Philadelphia, 1905.

RAMBOSSON, JEAN.
Histoire des instruments de musique. Paris.
———— Les harmonies du son et l'histoire des instruments de musique. Paris, 1878.

***RAVEN, J. J.**
The bells of England. New York, 1906.

RAWLINSON, GEORGE.
The five great monarchies of the ancient world. 4 vols. London, 1862.

RECUEIL de planches sur les sciences. Vol. IV.

REPORT of fourth congress of the international musical society. London, 1910.

RIANO, JUAN FACUNDO.
Critical and bibliographical notes on early Spanish music. London, 1887.

***RICE, WILLIAM GORHAM.**
Carillons of Belgium and Holland. New York, 1914.

RIEMANN, CARL WILHELM JULIUS HUGO.
A dictionary of music. London, 1893.

ROWBOTHAM, JOHN FREDERICK.
A history of music. 3 vols. London, 1885.

RUEHLMANN, JULIUS.
Die geschichte der bogeninstrumente. 2 vols. Braunschweig, 1882.

SAALSCHUETZ, JOSEPH LEVIN.
Geschichte und würdigung der music bei den Hebraeern. Berlin, 1829.

***SACHS, CURT.**
Real-lexicon der musikinstrumente. Berlin, 1913.

SAINT-GEORGE, HENRY.
The bow, its history, manufacture and use. London, 1896.

SALVADOR, DANIEL FRANCISCO.
Arab music and musical instruments. New York, 1916.

***SANDERS, W. and FORSTER, S. A.**
History of the violin. London, 1864.

SCHAFHAUETL, CARL EMIL von.
Theorie gedeckter cylindrischer und konischen pfeifen und der qnerflöten. Halle. 1833.

SCHEULER, DANIEL FRANCOIS.
Iconographie des instruments de musique. La Haye, 1914.

***SCHLESINGER, KATHLEEN.**
Instruments of the orchestra and precursors of the violin family. 2 vols. London, 1910.
——— Researches into the origin of the organs of the ancients.
Sammelbände der internationalen musikgesellschaft. Jahrgang II.

SIEVERS, GIACOMO FERD.
Il pianoforte, guida practica per costruttori, accordatori, dilettanti e possessori di pianoforti. 2 Lib. Naples, 1868.

SKINNER, RENEST M.
*The modern organ. New York, 1917.

***SMITH, FANNY MORRIS.**
A noble art. New York, 1892.

SMITH, HERMANN.
The making of sound in the organ and in the orchestra. New York-London, 1911.

SNOECK, C. C.
Catalogue d'instruments de musique anciens ou curieux. Gand, 1894.

SONNECK, OSCAR GEORGE THEODORE.
See musical quarterly.

SOUTHGATE, THOMAS LEA.
English music 1604-1904. London, 1906.
——— The viol da gamba and its music. Manchester, 1914.

SPILLANE, DANIEL.
History of the American pianoforte. New York, 1890.

***STAINER, JOHN.**
The music of the Bible. London, 1882.

***STANFORD, CHARLES VILLIERS, and FORSYTH, CECIL.**
A history of music. New York, 1916.

STEINERT, MORRIS.
The Steinert collection of keyed and string instruments. New York, 1893.

STRAETEN, EDMOND vander.
La musique aux Pay-Bas. III vols. Bruxelles, 1867.

STRAUSS, RICHARD.
See Berlioz.

STRUTT, JOSEPH.
The sports and pastimes of the people of England. London, 1903.

STUMPF, CARL.
Beiträge zur akustic und musikwissenchaft. 2 vols. Leipzig, 1898-1909.
——— Die anfänge der musik. Leipzig, 1911.

TABOURET, JEHAN.
Orchesographie. Paris, 1888.
Reproduction of old edition with plates. Thoinot Arbeau is an anagram for Jehan Tabouret, Canon of Langres.

TAGORE, ZOURINDA MOHUN.
Yantra kosha. Calcutta, 1875.

TOLBEQUE, AUGUSTE.
L'art du luthier. Paris, 1903.

TOURS, BERTHOLD.
The violin. London.

UNITED STATES NATIONAL MUSEUM. Proceedings. Washington, 1885-1917.

VIDAL, ANTOINE.
Les instruments à archet. 3 vols. Paris, 1876.

VIRDUNG, SEBASTIAN.
Musica getuscht. Basel, 1511. Reprint, Leipzig, 1883.

VIERTELJAHRSCHRIFT für musikwissenschaft. Leipzig, 1885-1904.

***WALLASCHECK, RICHARD.**
Primitive music. London, 1893.

WASIELEWSKI, JOS. WILH. von.
Die violine im XVII jahrhundert. Bonn, 1874.
———— Geschichte der instrumental musik. Berlin, 1878.
———— The violoncello. London, 1894.

***WEAD, CHARLES KASSON.**
Contributions to the history of musical scales. Washington, 1902.

WEITZMANN, CARL FRIEDRICH.
Geschichte des clavierspiels u. s. w. Stuttgart, 1879.
———— A history of pianoforte-playing, etc.
Translated by Theodore Baker. New York, 1807.

***WELCH, CHRISTOPHER.**
History of the Boehm flute. London, 1896.
———— *Six lectures on the recorder and other flutes in relation to literature. London, 1911.

***WICKS, MARK.**
Organ building for amateurs. London, 1887.

WILKINSON, JOHN GARDNER.
The ancient Egyptians. London, 1878.

WILLIAMS, CHARLES FRANCIS ABDY.
The story of notation. New York, 1903.
———— *The story of the organ. New York, 1894.

WILLIAMS, SAMUEL WELLS.
The middle kingdom. 2 vols. London, 1871.

***WILSON, THOMAS.**
Prehistoric art. Washington, 1895.
Report United States National Museum.

WIT, PAUL de
Katalog musikhistorischen museum. Leipzig, 1893.
———— Nachtrag zum katalog u. s. w. Leipzig, 1893-1894.
———— Perlen aus der instrumentensammlung von Paul de Wit in Leipzig. Leipzig, 1892.

YOUSSONPOFF, LE PRINCE.
Essai sur l'histoire du violin. Frankfort S/M 1856.

***ZAHM, JOHN AUGUSTUS.**
Sound and music. Chicago, 1892.

ZAMMINER, FREDERICH GEORG KARL.
Die musik und der musikalischen instrumente in ihrer beziehung zu den gesetzen der akustik. Giessen, 1855.

ZARLINO, GIOSEFFO.
Le istitutioni harmonische del Gioseffo Zarlino si Chioggia; nelle quali; oltra la materie appartenenti alla musica; si trouano dichiarati molti luoghi di poeti, d'historici, e di filosofi; si come nel leggerle si potrà chiaramente vedire. Venitia, 1566.

ZEITSCHRIFT für instrumentenbau. Leipzig, 1904-1914.

APPENDIX

I.

LIST OF DONORS

FREDERICK STEARNS

Allmendinger Music Shop
Ann Arbor Music Co.
Austin Organ Co.
Rice A. Beale
(Beale-Steere Expedition)
M. Casman
Chicago Orchestral Association
James E. Church, Jr.
Mrs. S. T. Cook
Theodore De Laguna
J. E. Ecker
John R. Effinger
William R. Farrand
Farrand and Votey
Carl Fischer
Gibson Mandoline and Guitar Co.
Mrs. Lucy Granger
Grinnell Brothers
N. W. House
House of York
Marvin A. Ives
S. Olin Johnson
Francis W. Kelsey
Albert Lockwood
Lyon and Healy
James H. McDonald
August Moeller
Earl V. Moore
Mrs. F. G. Novy
Irving K. Pond
Miss Julia Rominger
Israel G. Russell
G. Schwab
Mrs. M. B. Sheley
Albert A. Stanley
John P. Stanley
Frederick Kimball Stearns
James B. Steere
Steinway and Sons
Frederick Talcott
University of Michigan
University Music House
University Musical Society
J. MacKenzie Watson
John E. Whitset
Norman A. Wood

II.

INSTRUMENT-MAKERS AND INVENTORS REPRESENTED IN THE COLLECTION

THE INSTRUMENTS MAY BE IDENTIFIED THROUGH THE CASE NUMBERS WHICH FOLLOW THE NAMES OF THE MAKERS

Abbate, a figlio, 842, 1356
Abbaye, de la, 884
Adler, J. G., 680
Allen, J. Lathrop, 938
Allovon, 1343
Alta—key . . . gah . . gah, 1075
Altrichter, J., 936
Amatus, Nicolaus, 1277
Amman, C., 642
Andrade, Joas Miguel, 1082
Angelo, Marco da Fumagalli, 541
Austin, C., 740
Austin Organ Co., 756A, 1429
Azevedo, L. A., 1083
Baak, E., 671
Baduel, M., 587
Bainbridge, W. H., 515
Battista, Geo., 1130
Bechonnet et Effiat, 693
Becker, 1164
Bernareggi, 931
Besson and Co., 887, 1441
Besson, F., 857, 891, 940
Brambilla, Domenico, 1049
Broadwood, John and Sons, 1339, 1344A
Brotherhood, J., 1393
Buffet, Crampon, 638
Buffet, Crampon et Cie, 631, 639
Buffet, A. jne., 635
Bullenheimer, John, 1111
Bussetto, Geo. Maria del, 1292
Busson, 737
Cahusac, 560, 665
Carlo, Palanca, 558
Chappel, S. Arthur, 949
Child and Bishop, 1348
Christman, C., 621
Coeffet et Gissen-Enri, 899
Colas, Prosper, 503
Compagnie, Géneral de L'Ocarina, 485
Conn and Dupont, 860
Costa, Augusto M. Da, 1052, 1076, 1085, 1093, 1095, 1112, 1380, 1381
Courtois, Antoine, 869
Courtois, Antoine et Mille, 894.
Courtois, Antoine, Mille-Mille, Jr., 885
Courtois, Frères, 882
Couturier, 850
Cristofori, Bartollemeo, 1336
D'Almain and Co., late Goulding and Almain, 516
David, 932
Dietz, Joh. Ch. sen., 1346
Distin, Henry and Co., 867
Dize, F., 1008
Dubois et Couturier, 902
Durschmidt, 883
Ebblewhite, J. H., 565, 717
Embergher, Luigi, 1058
Erard, Fréres et Cie, 1340
Eschenbach, G., 822
Euw, M. von, 791
Farrand and Votey, 1388, 1390, 1426, 1451
Filano, Luigi, 1108
Fischer, Carl, 1433
Fischer, J. L., 507
Frenzel, 1345
Gautrot, M., 944
Geipel, Ch., 684
Gennaro, 1123
Gibson, Claget G., 1086
Gibson Guitar and Mandolin Co., 1070, 1116
Glasel, Moritz, 1308
Grandjon, J., 1307
Graves and Co., 855, 1438
Grenser, H., 633, 785

III.

MAKERS AND INVENTORS MENTIONED IN TEXT

IV.

OTHER PERSONS MENTIONED IN TEXT

V.

GEOGRAPHICAL DISTRIBUTION

(The numbers refer to pages).

VI.

GEOGRAPHICAL DISTRIBUTION BY WORLD-DIVISIONS AND CLASSES

CLASSES	I.	II.	III.	IV.	V.	VI.	VII.	Un-classified
Africa	57	43	28	59	..	..	..	..
America, North	42	10	62	20	3	4	53	2
America, South	6	..	16	3	..	..	..	..
Asia	63	56	64	95	..	..	9	..
Europe	60	20	362	187	19	30	36	4
Oceanica	20	22	15	18	..	..	..	..
Unknown	2	1	2	4	..	..	..	..
	250	152	549	386	22	34	88	6

The deductions noted under No. 54 are made in Class I.
Class VI. represents Mechanical Instruments.
Class VII. represents Accessories of various kinds.

INDEX

(Names of foreign and primitive instruments are given in italics; "trade," uncertain, and borrowed names in quotation marks)